Praise for *The Garden Awakening*

"Mary Reynolds weaves a wonderful tapestry in which the garden is not only a resilient, productive and healthy space that provides food, it is also a magical place of beauty, peace and inner nurture."

— MADDY HARLAND, EDITOR, PERMACULTURE MAGAZINE

"Mary generously articulates and shares with us her compelling, persuasive twenty years of experience in creative gardening and landscape designs. She opens our world to a natural way of growing food by holistically working in harmony and in balance with nature's bio-diverse ecosystems."

— DUNCAN STEWART, ECO-ARCHITECT AND ENVIRONMENTALIST

"*The Garden Awakening* offers a treasury of insight and advice for anyone who feels that our culture's relationship to land has profoundly lost its way and is seeking new inspiration. Read it, then go plant a paradise."

— ROB HOPKINS: FOUNDER OF THE TRANSITION MOVEMENT AND AUTHOR OF *THE POWER OF JUST DOING STUFF*

"In her hands the wounded earth becomes a living, breathing creature: it sighs and moans and remembers. We really should sit up and take notice she tells us – the earth won't forget"

— BILLY ROCHE, IRISH PLAYWRIGHT

"*The Garden Awakening* performs the miracle of waking up and engaging someone like me with no prior interest in gardens; in fact, showing me an idea of the garden quite unlike anything I had ever imagined."

— GILLIES MacKINNON, DIRECTOR, *THE LAST OF THE BLONDE BOMBSHELLS*

"*The Garden Awakening* is the way forward for gardeners. Beautifully written with a message that will open your eyes to a whole new outside world, you will never see gardens the same way."

— EOIN COLFER, AUTHOR OF *ARTEMIS FOWL*

"Mary Reynolds is really onto something: we must nurture the wildness within us, and see the beauty in the wildness without. She connects back to a deep past, to a timeless growth and regrowth, to the natural, to the voices moving in the land, to a church not made by hands."

— GLEN HANSARD, GRAMMY AND OSCAR WINNING SINGER-SONGWRITER AND ACTOR

"Mary Reynolds, the ambassador for the elemental kingdom and a guide to those of us seeking to come home to ourselves through re-connecting with Mother Earth. Gifted with the Irish heritage of great story-telling, Mary weaves a fine tapestry of stories instilled with ancient druidic wisdom, which she offers helpful practical ways of applying in the modern world. *The Garden Awakening* is a truly wonderful and highly inspiring read."

— MARKETA IRGLOVA, GRAMMY AND OSCAR WINNING SINGER-SONGWRITER AND ACTOR

"*The Gardening Awakening* by Mary Reynolds has put into words what gardeners feel they should be doing and know to be true but society doesn't encourage this way of thinking. Mary has tuned into nature and articulated it better than I have ever read before. Every gardener needs to read this book to empower themselves to do what their heart desires."

— FERGAL SMITH, BIG WAVE SURFER TURNED MODERN FARMER, GREEN PARTY CANDIDATE

THE
GARDEN
AWAKENING

Published by Green Books
An imprint of UIT Cambridge Ltd
www.greenbooks.co.uk

PO Box 145, Cambridge CB4 1GQ, England
+44 (0) 1223 302 041

First published in 2016, in England

ILLUSTRATIONS BY
Ruth Evans
www.thehedgerowgallery.com
WITH CHAPTER 2 GARDEN PLANS BY
Mary Reynolds

COVER ILLUSTRATION
Ruth Evans
www. thehedgerowgallery.com

DESIGNER
Glyn Bridgewater

ISBN: 978 0 85784 313 5 (paperback)
ISBN: 978 0 85784 314 2 (ePub)
ISBN: 978 0 85784 315 9 (pdf)
Also available for Kindle.

3 5 7 9 10 8 6 4

MIX
Paper from
responsible sources
FSC® C016779
FSC
www.fsc.org

FOREWORD BY
LARRY KORN

THE
GARDEN
AWAKENING

DESIGNS TO
NURTURE OUR LAND
& OURSELVES

MARY REYNOLDS

green books

Contents

Acknowledgements 6

Foreword by Larry Korn 8

Introduction 9

Restoring Wellness 10

Sacred Spaces 14

Nature is Stronger than Nurture 17

Finding Your Roots 19

Restoring Health to your Land 22

Garden Design 40

Gardens as expressions of beauty 42

The five elements for designing gardens in partnership with nature 46

Design element 1: The tool of intention. Magic uncloaked 46

Design element 2: Selecting areas to hold specific intentions 61

Design element 3: Designing with the patterns and shapes of nature 71

Design element 4: The power of symbols and imagery 79

Design element 5: Putting your design on paper 93

The Forest Garden 120

Forging an alliance 124

Listen 126

I Never Liked Planting Plans 127

Grow Your Own 128

Forest Gardening 130

Successional Planting 133

Forest Gardening in Steps 134

The Seven Layers of a Forest Garden 160

Bees for Life 204

Joe 208

Alternative Management Practices 210

Mulching 212

Ways to Clear the Land 214

Lawns and Lawn Maintenance 220

Pest Control 225

Natural Remedies 232

Tonics, Fertilizers, Potting Mixtures and Tree Protection 243

The Cultivation and Care of Trees 249

Resources 260

Index 268

This book is dedicated to Ferdia and Ruby Reynolds.
The two most loved, important and magical creatures I have been lucky enough
to plant and grow. How blessed I am to wake up in your world every day.

Thanks to My Tribe

Many, many thanks to my kind, clever, wonderful manager and friend Claire Leadbitter and the wildly talented artist Ruth Evans who illustrated this book so beautifully. The gentle earth energy that radiates from Ruth's work is magical and I am eternally grateful to Claire and Ruth for having these images weave their way through this paper garden. I am honoured to share this journey with these two strong women.

Thank you to my editor and long-time hero Larry Korn from the bottom of my heart. I was more than blessed to have your guidance and wisdom with this work. You nourished and encouraged these pages until they blossomed. What words can I say to express my gratitude Larry? You Rock! What an important warrior you are in natures green army.

Thank you so much to Niall, Lisa, Lindsey and Megan and all involved at Green books for carefully sending this manuscript out into the world. A huge shout out to Glyn Bridgewater for your beautiful and thoughtful book design.

To all of the good people who have been integral to this story. My big brother Paul Reynolds, his wife Susanna and his business partner Declan Owens in Seattle who always opened doors for me as a writer, in and out of my head. A special thank you to my great sisters Mairéad, Áine and her dear husband Joe, my lifelines. My brothers Eoin and Ger Reynolds and their wives Kevina and Martina.

Pat O'Connor from Rathmore in Kerry. Pat, there are no words that can express my gratitude for keeping me alive and well, but thank you is a start. Maria and John Rawlins, thank you both wholeheartedly for your constant guardianship.

My dear friends who occasionally read and encouraged over the years, Marketa Irglova, Karen Allison, Eileen Kelliher, Edel O'Brien, Paula and Tony Hayden, Sheila MacNally, Yvonne McGuinness. Special thanks to Breda Enright, Lauren Williams and Séamus King for giving expert guidance and wisdom. Colm Mac Con Iomaire for your expert Irish and encouragement. Gratitude and love to those who walked with me along the way. Namely Tor Cotton, Áine Berry, Siobán O'Leary, Rachel Ward, Gráinne and Paddy Fenton, Martin Cuthbertson, Bruce Allison, Deirdre Teahan, Eilish McVeigh, Della O'Donoghue, Lesley Devane, Michelle Flannery, Áine and John O'Connor, Joe, Izzy and Ellie Doyle of Claire's tribe, Jenn Halter Prenda, Christy Collard, Libby and Paddy Meegan, James Alexander – Sinclair, Maria Manuel Stocker, Catherine de Courcey, Joyce McGreevy, Joe Mullally, Gaby Smyth, Andrew Smith for the prompting, Vivienne de Courcy, for your courage. Thank you to my Wexford tribe, Linda and Jake Garnett, Janice O'Regan Conroy, Carmel and Patrick Nolan, John Pettit, Claudia O'Brien and all of the dedicated side-line mammies and daddies. Jane Powers, thank you for prodding us towards Green books. Thank you Gillies Mackinnon for our much valued 'wee correspondence' through which I discovered a love of writing. My mother and father, who gave me everything I am, bless you both forever and ever. Amen.

Mostly, thanks to my green family, visible and invisible. You are my heart, my dreams and my reason for being.

Grá agus Ómós.

Love and respect.

Foreword

Mary Reynolds's gardens are not only beautiful to look at, they *feel* different. Walk through one of them and you are transported to a time when people and nature lived together as one family. We still remember that time, but it is lying dormant in our subconscious. In *The Garden Awakening* Mary delightfully guides us along "an old pathway, overgrown and forgotten" to that place. She combines the magic of old Irish ways, sacred patterns and symbols, the power of intention, and sound organic management practices to create spaces in which nature can express itself freely and fulfill its own destiny. In the process the gardener, the land's guardian, experiences a personal transformation in which their painful separation from nature is healed.

This book is at once practical, philosophical, and spiritual. It is a step-by-step guide to restoring health to the land, and in the process discovering the truth of who we are. Although Mary lives in a temperate region and draws inspiration from her Irish ancestors, her approach to garden design is universal and can be applied anywhere, whether on a large property or a small urban yard. It is a matter of listening carefully to the needs and wishes of the land and combining them with your own.

Mary's message is one of vision and hope. It shows the way to a brighter future in which people, nature, and all other forms of life live peacefully together in a world of health and abundance.

Larry Korn, 2016

Introduction

verything becomes simple when you immerse yourself in nature. Life's complications melt away, leaving only the truth of the present moment and the presence of what I call God. In this place we can see ourselves reflected in every living thing, every gust of wind, every splash of rain, and here we can find peace. This is our true home.

Yet we are losing what few wild places we have left; those patches where the spirits of the earth are flowing freely, where harmony and balance still exist, and we feel accepted for the truth of who we are. We have strayed off course and need to find our way again.

An old pathway, overgrown and forgotten, is waiting impatiently to lead us back home.

Nature is willing us on.

Restoring Wellness

Ní féidir an dubh a chur ina gheal, ach seal.

The truth will out.

 have always loved crows. Great families of them would sit in the ash trees outside my parents' farmhouse, gossiping and chatting with big throaty cackles all through the day and into the mellow evenings, when they would eventually fall into a comfortable silence. Not long ago, these creatures began to reappear in my dreams, finally exposing the niggling truth about why I had begun to lose interest in designing gardens.

One memorable dream reminded me of times spent in nature as a child. It made me realize that after years of working as a landscape designer, I couldn't design gardens in the same way anymore. Something was amiss.

I embodied a crow in the dream. Soaring over woods and hills, I could hear my name being called. I swooped and searched to find the source of the voice, through valleys of mossy rocks, ancient woodlands, fields of rushes and reeds, over streams and rivers. As a bird, I had the ability to hear and see every small thing, and the images and sounds were clear and focused. I could hear water bubbling and gurgling in the streams, and the leaves of the trees rattling against one another. The wind was dancing around me and I could see mice scurrying through grassy meadows and life surging through the tree trunks.

The voice calling my name became louder, more insistent. It seemed to be coming from a nearby woodland, so I chased the sound through the trees towards a lone figure sitting on a log waiting for me. As I got close, the noise suddenly ceased and I stopped still in mid-air above the woman's head. I was frozen in time and space, staring down at a human version of myself, but painted blue. Leaning on a large stick, she simply smiled cheekily up at my bird self. She didn't say a word, but somehow it was like a key turning in my head and everything opened up.

Suddenly, the dream went into reverse and I was sucked upwards, out of the picture as if caught in a huge vacuum in the sky.

The moment I woke up, the dilemma I had been struggling with became clear as a bell. I shouldn't be making any more pretty gardens. Gardens had become the emperor's new clothes; something was wrong but no one was saying anything.

Nature and the land were the answers. Gardens were like still-life paintings;

controlled and manipulated spaces. They were poor versions of the real deal – untamed nature, and the delicate yet strong skin of Mother Earth. Somehow, somewhere along our way, gardens had become dead zones.

People are drawn to gardening because it helps them feel connected to nature. The words 'gardens' and 'nature' have become almost synonymous, but in reality they have very little in common any more. You can view this split between gardens and nature as a mighty battle. The frontline on the gardener's side generally involves a lot of hard work and vast quantities of chemicals. Subversive tactics and guerrilla warfare are nature's weapons of choice.

And, of course, time is always on nature's side.

Finally, I understood that despite my efforts to the contrary, I was failing to work in harmony with nature in my garden designs. I made two decisions based on 20 years of designing gardens, which I now realized had failed the ultimate test. They were decisions that forced me to re-examine everything I was doing with regard to my work, and they led to me writing this book.

First, I had missed the most important part of the puzzle. Although my gardens were beautiful spaces that allowed energy to flow freely through them, the land did not want to remain as I had designed it. We had to continue controlling these spaces, to stop things that wanted to grow from growing. The land had its own intentions. Nature had her own ideas about design and I had to learn what they were. Garden maintenance is fighting against the intentions Mother Nature has for herself. I had to understand how to work with this energy rather than against it.

Second, I decided that it was impossible to continue designing gardens for other people without their taking a more active role and assuming responsibility for the land. I could not construct a bond between the land and my client because, at the end of the day, I would walk away as the relationship was not mine to uphold any longer. My clients had to form and maintain their own meaningful connection with their little piece of earth.

I've discovered that gardens can become something very special if we approach them differently. If we invite Nature to express her true self in these spaces and then work to heal the land and bring it back into balance, something magical happens. Nature begins to interact with us on an energetic, emotional and physical level. Your garden becomes your own personal church; a place of safety, abundance and peace. Once recognized, loved, and respected, Nature will embrace you in ways that most people have not experienced for many, many years. A magical doorway opens for us.

This book is steeped in old Irish ways of interacting with the land. It offers a practical step-by-step instruction manual, one that will help you bring the land back to life. The practices I describe are based on those of my own culture, but they are similar to the practices that traditional people have used throughout the world for tens of thousands of years. They constitute a way of life that is deeply ingrained in our DNA.

We need to remember and reset our roots; to acknowledge the pain we feel as a result of our separation from the earth beneath our feet. The earth feels this loss as much as we do. The land we work with on our farms, urban parks and gardens is nearly dead on every level of being, but it is not too late to revive it. Not yet.

Sacred Spaces

All my life I have been chasing a particular atmosphere. It is the same atmosphere I spoke of in the crow dream – the sensation of life bubbling up around you, the energy of creation. I am not sure how to explain it, but I'm certain many of you know what I'm talking about, even if you don't remember right now.

I experience it as a mixed sensation – the energized awareness of a pulsating life force, along with the comfortable and the familiar feeling of coming home. I feel it at least a little whenever I'm in the countryside, but certain places present a more powerful energy than others. Ever since I was a child, I've wondered why this is so. As I grew older, I became curious about why I never experienced this feeling in a designed garden.

This vibrant, energized atmosphere is found in wild natural landscapes; places where nature is no longer interacting with people, and perhaps never did. These are often areas that once were farmed or had otherwise been disturbed, but then were left alone for many years. During that time, nature slowly repaired itself to the point where its primal spirit could return. Healthy woodlands have this energy in abundance; and mountainous areas are often strong, probably because they are not so easy to get to or disturb.

Anywhere wild has a strong atmosphere. Landscapes that have been left undisturbed are simply racing with life. These are places where the life force of the earth flows freely, and you can feel its power and vitality directly. All of us, no matter how insensitive we claim to be, can feel the energy, peace, thrill and, for some, the fear we experience when we step on to an untamed piece of land. Although it can be invigorating and joyful, it can also be laced with feelings of grief, pain, danger, or darkness.

There were other energized places that I didn't understand at first. They were referred to as 'sacred places'; often ancient sites such as stone circles, but they also included old Christian sites, holy wells, some churches, ancient monasteries or their remnants, prayer mounds and so forth. Often they were not even vaguely wild; many were just in open grazed fields. Some of these sites had no special feeling, while others had noticeably charged atmospheres. I wanted to know what it was that created this energy.

The arrival of Christianity in Ireland brought with it the painful disconnection from the earth that still resonates today. Until then, people lived in harmony with nature. The power and importance of the land was understood and respected. For Christians, this life on earth was only a preparation for the next life. They believed it was acceptable to use and abuse the land as much as we liked in order to achieve our goals in the next life.

The pagan religions, however, were deeply ingrained in Ireland, so the clever Christians knew that enforcing their beliefs with brute force wouldn't work there.

In order to facilitate their slow and insidious takeover, they blended the Christian religion with the native earth-based faith, eventually nearly rooting it out, but not completely.

After doing some research, I realized that although they were two distinct cultures, both the Christian and the pagan religions understood how to create energized places. I was eager to understand their reasons and methods, and how to use this knowledge to bring the same magic into my gardens.

Ireland is a great place to seek out and research sacred places because the country is simply littered with them. You can barely walk across a field without tripping over a sacred stone, falling into a holy well, or disappearing into a crack in a bumpy field that turns out to be an underground burial chamber in disguise.

There are many sacred sites where you feel energized – the air is potent, the atmosphere is thick and you move through your environment with complete awareness. In these places, the veil between this world and the world of spirit is very thin. I discovered it was usually where people had 'laid down' an atmosphere, moved things around, built structures and shifted earth, all with a particular intention in mind. In some sacred sites, thousands of years had not diluted the energy. In others, it was gone.

People seek out such sites because we long for the reaffirming connection with nature and with spirit. Some do this by taking day trips and holidays to beautiful places where they have access to wild landscapes. Those who visit our gardens and parks, however, must settle for a critically dumbed-down version of the real thing. These settings bear little resemblance to the radiance of truly natural areas and the healing they provide.

In this book, I hope to impart a very simple system that will allow anyone to connect directly with nature and access the limitless energy available to us. You can conjure up this energy very simply in your own garden.

Nature is Stronger than Nurture

Is treise an dúchas ná an oiliúint

Faery energy, the Gaian presence, the Goddess, Mother Earth. Every culture has had a name for this awareness and understanding of the life force in nature.

Do you remember how Peter Pan insisted that Tinker Bell would die unless the children in the story truly believed in her? According to Peter, fairies only existed as long as children believed in them: "…every time a child says, 'I don't believe in fairies,' there is a fairy somewhere that falls down dead". This is a great illustration of the way things work in the invisible levels of the world.

We only exist if those around us acknowledge we are real; otherwise we would just wither and die.

The 13th-century Holy Roman emperor Frederick II carried out a cruel language-deprivation experiment on a group of orphaned babies. He wanted to discover what language they would speak if they heard no spoken words while they were infants. The experiment was recorded by the Franciscan monk Salimbene de Adam in his *Chronicle*. He wrote that Frederick bade "foster-mothers and nurses to suckle and bathe and wash the children, but in no ways to prattle or speak with them". Eventually the poor creatures died.

The worst thing you can do to another living being is to ignore it. Even hating it is better than ignoring it, as at least then it feels acknowledged and real.

If land is left to its own devices for a long time, it returns to being wild and free. It becomes self-sufficient and independent, just like a feral animal. It develops a strong community of its own, a healthy balanced ecosystem of plants, animals and micro-life. If, however, untamed land is cleared and worked, it becomes dependent on the direction given to it by the people that live or work there. Like a child, it needs love and attention to grow strong, healthy and self-sufficient.

Land creates a bond with people who work with it. If this bond is formed and then the land is ignored, damage is sure to follow – the same as it would for a child. Today, much of the land feels forgotten. It has retreated into itself because we don't believe in it or don't notice it anymore. We only seem to take notice of uncultivated places, which have no bond with us and no need for us. These are what I call lost opportunities. Your land is like a member of your own family. It can form a bond with you but it won't unless you develop the relationship together. The quality of the relationship will determine the strength and quality of the bond.

If we all sit up and take notice, "believe in fairies" and encourage the life energy to emerge in every piece of land we work with, we can infuse our homes, our families and ourselves with the healing, magical energy of the earth.

Our gardens are gifts to us. They can also become our teachers. As guardians of these little patches of the planet, we can learn to work hand in hand with the land to restore each other's health. Every fragment of soil, plant or tree that becomes recognized, respected and loved has a healing effect on the entire planet.

Nature teaches us about the unity of all things. We can create dynamic, balanced and integrated ecosystems that will offer to sustain and nourish us along with all the other creatures that share the land with us. We need a green-fingered revolution to bring nature back into the garden – and this begins with encouraging people to respect and love the land they live on.

Gardens belong to nature, not the other way round.

So do we.

Finding Your Roots

An áit a bhfuil do chroí is ann a thabharfas do chosa thú.
Your feet will bring you to where your heart is.

We are only brief guardians of these portions of land we call our gardens. We do not and cannot truly own them. Our bodies are made of the Earth and return to it eventually, but the land will always remain alive.

Everything we need to survive and all that nourishes us comes from the Earth, its soil, the atmosphere, the sun and the stars beyond. We are simply walking pieces of earth.

We are drawn to certain locations where the land resonates with us and pulls us towards it. People can spend their entire lives looking for the places where they belong, places where they feel at home, where they fit and can comfortably set down roots. We are simply a reflection of the land beneath us, and nature is always waiting for us to return home.

The land connects with us in ways we don't always understand. Each of us is attracted to a different space, reflecting our individual personalities. Every landscape also has its own character that helps shape the culture of the people who live there.

Take Ireland as an example. The Irish are a cantankerous lot – at once charming, impatient, arrogant, passionate, changeable, colourful and always a bit unrestrained. Even if we seem tame at times, the wildness is always there, just beneath the surface. You can feel it, along with the ever-present grief, which is also a hair's breadth away. We Irish have a strong connection with the world of spirit and an inherent belief in magic, prayer and curses. Traditionally, the Irish are also laced with a deeply held sadness. The Irish landscape carries many of these same attributes and reflects them back to us. The land and its people are simply mirrors for each other, reflecting the state of each other's general health and wellbeing. Our ancestors were keenly aware of this. By healing the land, we heal ourselves; and by healing ourselves we can see more clearly what the land needs to return to health.

The land's character is further refined in its counties. Each county has its own distinct landscapes and unique energy, and the people of each county have a strongly defined accent and 'ways' about them. Some areas are flat, open, gentle and 'grounded' like their people; while others are dramatic, ancient and regal, full of stories and myths.

Recently Ireland has seen an influx of people who have come to live here from other countries. It's interesting to observe how even these new arrivals are finding locations that reflect their own personalities. In many cases, the land in those places is in need of the same kinds of support and healing as their new guardians.

The idea that land has its own personality was unmistakably brought home to me one day about 15 years ago. I was rushing around in my spanking new van, working on a garden makeover for a cottage in rural Ireland. It was one of my first attempts at a garden makeover for a TV show and the budget was tiny, so my mandate was to 'beg, borrow or steal' as much of what I needed as possible. I was under a lot of pressure because it was the second-to-last day before the 'finished garden' deadline.

As I drove past a woodland copse behind a dry-stone wall that ran along the edge of the road, I noticed a small grassy knoll rising from the woods. Suddenly, I spotted an interestingly twisted piece of decaying wood at the base of an old oak tree at the top of the knoll and I screeched to a halt. I envisioned a perfect place for the wood in my garden. It would look beautiful as a 'quirky feature' built into a little stone wall I was throwing together at the site. I tucked my van into the grass verge, climbed over the old stone wall and scrambled up the hill to the piece of sculptural wood. As I lifted the wood and slung it on to my shoulder, I remember feeling a bit uneasy, as a child sometimes does when they are about to do something they know they shouldn't, but do it anyway. I shrugged it off.

As I began walking down the hill, everything became quiet. It was a peculiar type of silence that felt heavy with judgement and displeasure. Ignoring it, I clambered back over the wall, placed the wood carefully in the back of my van and jumped into the front seat. I turned the key, but nothing happened! The five-week-old van was completely dead. I'd never had a problem with it until that very moment. Eventually, after much wiggling of knobs and keys, I phoned the local garage for a tow truck, got out of the van and waited.

The atmosphere around me had changed to the strangest feeling. The only way I can describe it is 'smugness'.

Then it dawned on me: I shouldn't have taken the wood without asking first and paying proper respect. At the time it seemed silly to me: it was only a piece of worthless wood, for God's sake! However, once I had allowed the thought into my mind, it couldn't be denied and I came to realize with certainty that it was true. I gingerly took the wood out of the car and carefully returned it to its original position. But forgiveness was not forthcoming. I had a strong sense that I was being shunned for my lack of respect that day; I should've known better.

Eventually the mechanic arrived and examined the van. The problem turned out to be only a loose ground wire. I got the message… This was a piece of land with a powerful sense of territorial pride, a distinct sense of justice and a penchant for mischief. Subtle signs, but subtle and I have yet to meet.

Restoring Health to your Land

In order to understand the method for re-establishing the health of your land, you may have to shift your perspective for a moment. I keep repeating that land is alive. This may be obvious on a physical level, with the myriads of teeming creatures on and beneath its surface (when the land is healthy). But what I mean is alive in the same way that you and I are alive, that is conscious, capable of being damaged, of feeling pain, love, anger, excitement, sadness and grief, of falling sick and becoming well again. This I know to be true at the core of my being. All I can do is share it with you.

The Earth is made up of diverse pieces of land with distinctive physical and emotional characteristics in the same way that individual people have unique personalities. No single piece of land is the same as the next. Each garden will need a unique strategy for healing and only its guardian will know how to create that plan.

The goal is for you to connect with your garden and work with it on a deep level. You cannot do this if you hand over responsibility to someone else. That is why I had to stop designing gardens for people who would not make the effort to form a connection with their land.

The first step in co-creating a garden with nature involves working to heal the land. We are mirrors for the land and it is a mirror for us, so healing the land leads us towards our own restoration, back to our true selves.

This method of healing does not create changes overnight. There are no instant transformations – no miracles to be expected. It is a slow and steady process, but if we are determined, and our intention is to keep reaching for the light, we will get there eventually. If we allow the light to shine on all the dark places in our lives; if we have the courage to face our fears, face adversity with courage and strength, then recovery and growth will take place.

It is the same with land. It takes time, but you will see positive results if you work to acknowledge, release and repair the damage. The blockages will be dissolved and the land's original vibrant and abundant self will emerge.

Healing involves looking at the overall picture. You cannot solve a problem by resolving the physical level alone. You will also need to find and correct the

underlying causes of these physical symptoms, whether conscious or unconscious. If you don't do that, the problem will return as it was or take a different form.

Similarly, if the land you are working with has been damaged by years of misuse or neglect, you cannot just replace the topsoil and expect it to magically become whole again. You must first identify and then correct the underlying issues that caused the problem in the first place.

I consider my garden and the land as a living body. Like any other body, it will have blockages and stresses on different levels. To correct these problems, I focus on three main areas: the energetic or spiritual body, the emotional body and the physical body.

Resetting the energetic land body

We begin by recognizing and delineating the boundaries of the land. This will allow you to focus your own energy as well as that of the land. Unless the energy of the land is flowing freely, any blockages that exist will manifest in the physical realm.

BEATING THE BOUNDARIES

Marking out the boundary of your garden demonstrates your conscious decision to form a relationship with the land you will be working with, whether a small sub-urban garden, a large farm area or an estate.

In Ireland years ago, the ceremony of walking around the edges of the land to make its boundaries clear was performed on a yearly basis. The older generations believed this ritual avoided boundary disputes with their neighbours – so the land knew where your work stopped and where the neighbours' work began.

You need to walk the whole boundary while holding the intention of marking out your garden's limits. This shows the land that you will be working together to reveal each other's true selves.

It is important to tell the land what you are doing as you walk. You should make some noise or sing as you go, or use some other method that springs to mind. Traditional land healers around the world would often beat a drum for this purpose. In Ireland, it was common to beat a bodhrán. Sometimes stones were used that emitted certain sounds when struck together. The sound resonated in the land and helped to unseat stale energies that had become embedded there. The Christian tradition encouraged the practice of sprinkling holy water around the boundaries for the purpose of blessing a piece of land.

Any personal version of this ceremony will hold the energy of the space strongly for you. It will also allow your garden to have a sense of belonging. By belonging, I mean family or guardianship as opposed to ownership. We can never own our land or our children.

This sense of a familial bond can be later strengthened by planting the boundary with a hedgerow or trees that have been set to hold the energy of protection. They guard your space and hold its boundaries secure.

Once you have set the boundaries, you can treat the land as a singular living being. All things have energy fields around them. Blocks within the flow of the human energy field may cause anything from minor illnesses to major maladies, or simply the sense that something is not quite right. Similarly, if the energy in the land body is not flowing freely, blockages will manifest in physical symptoms.

By personifying your land, you may notice that the land you have chosen – though sometimes I think the land chooses us – reflects your own personality. You may also find that your own wounds and dysfunctions and those of the garden coincide. The land often shows you what you need to work on in your own life or in your family dynamic.

Treating the emotional land body

Ní mar a síltear a bítear.
Things are not always as they seem.

Counselling, psychotherapy and supportive parenting know-how all seem to agree on one common method to facilitate healing in people: it is called 'the listening cure'. The main premise of this approach is that the individual in need of assistance must have their past trauma or pain 'heard' in order to move towards a satisfactory resolution. In other words, the pain needs to be listened to and validated by a second party in order for the healing to take place.

I have to use the example of parenting because I am neither a counsellor nor a psychotherapist, but I do have two small children. If a child is traumatized or deeply upset by an experience and no one is available to listen to them, or you ignore their pain by telling them to 'get over it' or 'stop crying', the child will bury their feelings because they haven't been given an outlet to express them. These buried feelings are as much a part of who we are as the pleasurable experiences we encounter. As adults, we spend a lot of time and energy trying to articulate and come to terms with these feelings in an effort to become healthy, happy and well-balanced individuals.

It works the same way for the land. If a piece of land has been abused, disrespected or otherwise brutalized, it holds the damaged within it. You will certainly sense the heaviness and discomfort in a polluted or otherwise ill-treated piece of land because the abuse is fresh. In the same way, it is easy to see the pain in a newly traumatized human being. Over time the pain will likely become buried as the person gets on with their lives. However, the resulting symptoms and reactionary patterns are still within them. You can feel that person is weakened or unhappy, and sometimes dark or violent as a result. As with people, a polluted piece of land does eventually 'get on with its life'. As time passes, it heals on the surface, but the deeper damage remains.

The best example I can think of is the feeling you get in newly felled commercial woodland. The current methods of logging are ruthless and the land shows its immediate trauma for a while afterwards. Eventually, the area grows over enough for it to appear fine on the outside, but the underlying damage and painful feelings linger.

Some areas of land are better able to cope with their pain than others, just as certain people are traumatized by events in their lives, while others are not fazed in the slightest. Some people and places easily let go of uncomfortable experiences, while others nurse them until they fester and they are *forced* to face them.

The 'listening cure' is a very simple way of unloading the trapped feelings and emotions in a piece of land or within a person. To allow this process to take place, first you need to centre yourself and take a break from your internal dialogue. Most of us spend our lives caught up in our thoughts or daydreaming in the clouds, so I realize that this is easier said than done. It helps if you know how to meditate, and for those not practised in meditation, I will describe my favourite way of quieting the mind. But remember, you need to do whatever feels right for you. My way is simply an example – just one of many possible ways.

NATURE-BASED MEDITATION PRACTICE

Find a tree that you feel comfortable with. It should be in a place where you can be quiet and undisturbed for a few minutes. Sit or stand against the tree, barefoot if possible. The energy of a mature tree will support you and smooth the process of making your connection with the earth. Trees spend their whole lives in meditation. They are our greatest teachers; our elders, so to speak.

Before we go on, as quirky as this may sound, consider how to protect yourself from certain negative energies that exist in the world. Humans see only a portion of the light that is reflected within the complete electromagnetic spectrum. Our eyes perceive frequencies within this spectrum and send them as electrical signals to our brain, where they are decoded into three-dimensional images. But as

we see just a tiny fraction of total range, we are in fact surrounded by a multitude of energies that are not immediately detected by our senses.

You may believe in Gaia, God, Buddha, Allah or whomever. It matters little, as long as you are calling on a strong, pure energy source. Simply ask the power you believe in to surround you with protection – it may be the energy of the tree at your back. Provided that you have a sense of being supported and protected, you are set to go.

One thing to bear in mind about a protection prayer is that, although it is a powerful action and does the trick initially, you have to keep doing it regularly. I'm terrible at remembering this, but disciplined people can build it into their daily routine. If you have a piece of jewellery set with a crystal or a stone that has personal significance for you, say your protection prayer directly into it and you will be covered as long as you wear it. You may have to clear and reset the prayer occasionally.

Close your eyes for a moment. Notice your breath and observe it coming in and going out. Imagine you are like the tree behind you, with roots growing out of the base of your feet. With each breath, visualize these roots growing deeper and deeper into the earth. Picture a bright white light entering the crown of your head, passing though your body and down to your roots. When you breathe in, imagine the white light is passing through your entire system. When you breathe out, that light will flush out all the stress through your roots and into the earth. This helps the earth as much as it does you. I truly believe that sending such things as directed thoughts, prayers and visualized light towards a living being has a real and positive effect on them. The world of spirit and magic has always been as real to me as the physical world we can see.

Once you are feeling clear and centred, allow your thoughts to move to any lovely memory you have, preferably from when you were young. Not all of us have pleasant childhood memories, so just find one from any time in your life that fills you with warmth and joy. It can be as simple as having gratitude for the beauty of the blue sky or that moment of snuggling your weary body into a warm comfy bed and drifting to sleep. By filling yourself with comfortable feelings, you are clearing your emotional palette, preparing to feel whatever emerges from the land.

WALK THE LAND

It is important to carry out the practice of listening to the land on an empty stomach, as eating substantially beforehand will inhibit your sensitivity.

Walk slowly and gently around your land, taking in the boundary first, then spiralling towards the centre in an anticlockwise direction – the direction of opening. If possible, do this with bare feet.

Listen to and feel whatever emotions arise in you as you put your energy into the ground with the intention of 'hearing' the feelings of the earth. You have to be committed to hearing it. Be present and patient. Listen to the feelings of the 'child' beneath your feet.

You may feel sad, angry, scared, contented, or sense other feelings from the earth. It is very subtle and you may think you are making it up, but most likely you are not making it up. In order for these messages to pass through you, you need to bypass your egocentric thinking. This may be a memory that reminds you of your own experiences or trauma in the past; it may also be a clear vision of what happened to the land during its lifetime. Trust whatever arises in you.

Don't hold on to the feelings; that helps no one. Just acknowledge and feel them, then let them go. They are not yours to keep. Release them and be done with it. That is your role at this time. If you need to, write down the images or feelings on a piece of paper, then burn it to shake it off.

If you feel nothing but contentment, then the land is content. It doesn't have to have problems, so don't feel you have failed if there is nothing there to clear.

GROUND YOURSELF

When you have finished listening to the land, it is important to ground yourself (as opposed to centring yourself). Grounding yourself involves focusing your energy downwards to anchor yourself into the Earth. It brings you stability and solidity. Centring yourself, on the other hand, is about drawing your energy inward; you connect with your heart energy where everything is quiet, intelligent and sensitive. If you have been working in bare feet, you should be fine. If not, sit for a while with your bare hands and feet resting on the earth. Another easy way of grounding yourself is to eat something substantial, which will bring you down to earth immediately.

Repairing the physical land body

Maireann an chraobh ar an bhfál ach ní mhaireann an lámh do chuir.
The branch lives on the hedge but the hand that planted it is dead.

During my years as a garden designer, I found that most of the land I worked with was in poor physical condition. Perhaps the soil had been overused for many years; or had been used as a dumping ground during new construction. Over time, people disfigured the land in many ways, and we should accept responsibility for repairing it. When rehabilitating damaged land, we need to tackle two layers: below and above the ground.

BELOW THE GROUND

Before chemical agriculture came to Ireland, pastures were full of large white mushrooms every autumn. My dad used to send us out to collect buckets of them; then he would slice them up and fry them in salty butter. It was heaven. These days, there are no more field mushrooms on modern farms. Ploughing, spraying and the application of chemical fertilizers have destroyed the gentle balance that embraced them as part of the natural cycle of life.

By now, most of our soils are nearly dead. You can see this by watching what happens when a modern farm is ploughed or a gardener digs over a bed. Years ago, newly ploughed furrows became a carpet of birds feasting on the earthworms and other small animals that lived in the soil. In gardens, birds would hide in waiting for the gardener to finish and leave so they could dive in and gleefully devour the exposed worms. Nowadays, there are no birds on the freshly ploughed furrows.

In gardens, you may see some birds rooting in freshly dug soil where the land has been treated gently, but invertebrates are barely surviving. We have relentlessly taken and taken. Today, plants growing on our land are completely dependent on the provision of industrially produced forms of nitrogen, potash and phosphates, which we repeatedly supply.

Exposing the earth to sunlight by turning the soil is akin to ripping the skin off the human body. Plants protect the land from erosion and help maintain good soil structure, making it possible for air and water to circulate freely. When you plough, various layers of the soil are mixed together, the communities of microorganisms are sent into chaos, the long strands of fungi that are so crucial to feeding the plants are torn apart, and the organic matter is burned at an accelerated rate. Microorganisms in the soil need small amounts of oxygen to respire, but when you cultivate, many of them die from overexposure to oxygen.

There are up to four billion bacteria in one gram of healthy soil, and in one square foot of undisturbed soil there can be literally thousands of miles of fungal threads holding the soil together. Mushrooms are the fruiting bodies of these mycelia. Trees, shrubs and herbaceous plants form a symbiotic relationship with many of these fungi. Plants produce carbohydrates through photosynthesis and transfer them to the fungi through their roots. In return, the mycelia source nutrients for the plants through their vast underground network and deliver them to the roots. The mycelia not only increase the effective absorption area of the roots many thousands of times, but they also secrete enzymes that dissolve the nutrients, making them available to the plants.

'No-till' methods of gardening and farming have been intensively studied. Results show that there is a period of adjustment at the beginning, but in the long run the practice leads to healthier and more diverse soils, reduces and eventually eliminates the need for pesticides, prevents erosion, and improves the soil's ability to absorb and retain water.

No-till systems also allow the soil to store carbon rather than releasing it into the atmosphere.

When people began ploughing the earth, they turned their backs on nature's gift of perpetual abundance. As a result, we have become responsible for supplying the fertility ourselves. It's not surprising really: children too often think they know better than their parents.

Plants and the litter layer of decomposing plant material form the skin of the Earth's living body. Everything else – bones, lungs, blood, digestive, nervous and circulatory systems – is found inside. Living soil is such a gift! Restoring life to the soil should be the foundation of our efforts to restore health to our gardens. The best way to do this is to build healthy populations of microorganisms.

The branching network of fungal mycelia transports information and nutrients within the soil. They also maintain the structure of the soil and act as a sort of postal service for the Earth by physically connecting everything together. If a plant needs phosphorous, the mycelium will source it and transport it to the plant, often depositing it directly inside the roots themselves. In mainstream horticulture, gardening and agriculture, there is an appalling lack of appreciation for the role fungi play in maintaining healthy plants and soil. Fungi are phenomenally intelligent and mysterious life forms that could hold the key to solving some of our most difficult and pressing environmental problems.

For example, American mycologist Paul Stamets carried out experiments on soil that had been polluted by petroleum. Just eight weeks after being inoculated with spores of the fungus, the soil was cleansed and grew a healthy crop of oyster mushrooms. The mycelia had literally eaten the petrol: plants started germinating, and earthworms returned. Wonderfully fast and simple.

Methods for restoring soil microorganisms

Mycelium restoration

Fungi are the oldest living organisms on the planet. They have evolved by using decaying matter to sustain themselves. If your topsoil is devoid of the white thread-like mycelia, you should help them recolonize the soil using one of the following methods.

Note: It is best to wear a dust mask while following these methods, in case you are sensitive or allergic to spores. Afterwards, wash your hands well.

Method 1

1 Order the spawn of edible mushrooms varieties either locally or online (see Resources). Ask your supplier to recommend the best selection of spawn for your area.
2 Mix the spores with wood ash (or follow specific instructions that came with the spawn) and spread it in the area you wish to inoculate. You can also inoculate bare-root plants as you are planting them by dipping them into a spore mix in a bucket of water. I highly recommend doing this.
3 Cover with a thick layer of mulch, cardboard, leaves, wood chips or any other organic material that will decompose. Anything that creates shade and retains the dampness will do, as fungi need these conditions for optimal growth. Keep the area moist.
4 After a couple of months, check the soil. You should see masses of white thread-like filaments. This is the mycelium network establishing itself.

Method 2

You can also try this do-it-yourself method in the autumn:
1 Find a field guide to mushrooms growing in your area and go hunting for edible ground-fruiting mushrooms yourself. Make sure you cut them at the base, as these parts of the stems are the most potent. If you can acquire some of the

roots, even better. Be gentle in your harvesting. Take only a small percentage of the mushrooms in a given area so that they can regenerate. Make sure the mushrooms are only *approaching* maturity (convex heads) but not completely mature (flat heads), as they produce more spores.

2　Chop the fresh mushrooms, including the stumps and stalks, into tiny pieces.

3　Spread a good layer of wood ash or sawdust around the base of your woody plants. Cover with a layer of mulch. Sprinkle the pieces of your chopped mushrooms, add another layer of wood ash and another layer of bark or leaf mulch. You could also pile on some tree prunings to shade the area and retain moisture.

4　Keep the area moist. In a couple of months the mycelium should be spreading through the top few inches of the soil.

For more detailed information on this topic, I recommend Paul Stamets' books, including *Mycelium Running*. In it, Stamets discusses how to use fungi as a solution to large environmental challenges such as cleaning up pollution and radiation. He also gives practical advice that could be useful to any gardener – such as which fungi species partner well with particular tree species.

Bacteria restoration

A strong and diverse array of soil bacteria is vital for the health of any living ecosystem. The following is a simple and effective method for restoring bacterial communities.

1　Fill a large clean container, such as a new dustbin, with water. If you are lucky enough to have a natural, clean water source – use it. If not, but you are allowed to harvest the rainwater in your area (not always legal, especially in some arid regions), that would be fine too. If you have to use treated water from a reservoir, let it stand for 24 hours to allow the chlorine to evaporate out.

2　Get a handful of soil from a healthy wild place – preferably from the floor of a local woodland. Put the soil into the water along with a pond aeration pump and aerate the mixture.

3 Stir in a spoonful of molasses or sugar. Don't allow the mixture to sit for more than 24 hours, otherwise the spores will begin to degrade. Adding of a pinch of sea salt helps prevent this from taking place.

4 To achieve maximum effect, spray the mixture on to soil and plants within 4 hours after turning off the aerator. The best time to apply the mix is either early morning or early evening to avoid the heat of midday. Apply it as a soil drench and a foliar spray.

I usually add an additional step, which is derived from biodynamic farming practices (see Chapter 2.) Include it after you remove the aeration pump and before you apply the mixture.

First, spend some time in your garden. Centre yourself and quieten your mind. Take out the aeration pump and begin stirring the container of water vigorously with a big stick. Whip the water into a vortex, first in one direction then in the other. Keep in your mind the reason for making this potion as you stir – or, better still, say it out loud. It also helps if you write your objective on the side of the container. The purpose should be to restore the complex layers of soil life and the overall health of the garden, or some version of that.

Using the pond aeration pump is certainly better than having to stir by hand for a couple of hours, which is the standard practice in biodynamics. According to the rituals of biodynamic preparations, you must stir the preparations until a vortex is formed in one direction for an hour and then in the opposite direction for another hour. This is when the intention is set into the water. Most people, including me, have a short attention span, so once you feel your intentions have been set into the mixture, it's fine to rely on the aeration pump to do the rest of the practical work. Besides, if you went on stirring for another hour or more, it might add thoughts of boredom, impatience and muscle pain into the mix!

While you are still holding this intention in your mind, spray or sprinkle the energized water over the land. Focus on your task. If certain music helps you stay relaxed and happy, then play it as you disperse the water.

If you leave the water for a period of time before you spread it, you may be in a bad mood, or at least in a different mood, and that energy will be deposited into the ground, so it is best to do it immediately. You can apply the brew using a backpack sprayer or a watering can. One application in the spring and one in the autumn should be enough to kick-start the soil's vitality. You may want to repeat this for a few years until the diversity above the ground can support the diversity below it.

I learned this simple method from my friend, Breda Enright. She sprayed this tonic on her vegetable garden and the results were phenomenal in terms of yield and vibrancy of plants.

ABOVE THE GROUND

Pulling buachalláns (*Senecio jacobea* or tansy ragwort) was a job most kids with a farming background will remember from their summer holidays in Ireland. Farmers hated this noxious weed and were fined if it was found growing on their land. It was feared that, once it died down, this plant might get mixed up with the hay that was harvested in the autumn. This plant's dried stalks are reputedly so poisonous to livestock that it will kill them if they were to eat it during the winter. Also, in retrospect, I think it was one of those plants that, like meadowsweet and the hard rushes, represented poverty to Irish farmers. They hated the idea that their neighbours would think they were lazy or bad farmers, which would be indicated by the presence of these 'poverty plants'. The worst possible fate was to be considered a bad guardian of the land. It was a matter of pride. Misguided as it may have been, it shaped the face of the land at the time.

When summer was waning each year, our family would be out in the fields, pulling those tall yellow lace-cap flowers before they went to seed. I still remember how horrid this job was. The bruised stem of the ragworts smelled bad, like musty urine, and had to be pulled out of the ground from its roots or it would sprout again. Tomboy that I was, I'd try and pull out as many stems as my brothers, and I'd aim to tackle the larger specimens in order to impress upon the lads that I was as strong as they were. I struggled with the ropey stems of the buachalláns, fighting against their desire to remain right where they were. Finally, my victory over the ragwort typically resulted in a bruised backside, where I'd repeatedly fallen backwards as the ragworts finally relinquished their vice-like grip on the earth.

If you are standing in your garden faced with a mountain of brambles or bracken, or a matted meadow of docks and thistles, the accepted solution these days is to reach for the poison-filled backpack. When I suggest that practical alternatives to herbicides exist, I am met with incredulous looks and a mix of pity and patronizing tolerance. People have come to believe that the only successful management strategy is the use of chemicals to enable their plantings to establish themselves before the weeds can return. This method reminds me of chemotherapy. It also reveals our 'us against them' approach towards nature.

Alternative methods of land management *do* exist! It's just that they don't cost very much so there are no big marketing campaigns to publicize them. Also, they are not considered 'convenient'. Ah, convenience – the root of all evil.

In old Ireland, farmers always left corners and islands of natural land along the margins and in the middle of their fields. These were usually copses of scrubby shrubs and woodland edge plantings, which provided habitat for predators that maintained balance in the fields. Such areas were referred to as 'the hare's corner'. Hares lived in wild places and were therefore generally hidden from view. Modern farmers, in their effort to use every last inch of ground to increase production, have removed most of these hedgerows and ditches, so they have lost their benefit of safe havens for wild animals. Most gardens reflect the same barren conditions as agricultural land: there is no room left for natural predators and often no space for wildlife at all.

Today we have the knowledge and technology to enable us to live comfortable lives in an environmentally sound way, one that considers all of the creatures that we

share this Earth with. We just need to walk towards a more ethical way of working with land. We will need to walk quickly, however, so we get there before it's too late.

In this book, I hope to show how using an integrated living system in your garden will remove the need for the incessant war on nature. I will explain how to design a balanced ecosystem in your garden, including the ancient multi-tiered approach called 'forest gardening' – a system based on observing and mimicking what nature does. This design approach allows ecosystems to be whole and in balance while providing a place for human beings to live happy and productive lives. Although it involves careful planning and hard work at the beginning, a minimal amount of work is required once the forest garden matures.

There are clear steps to the process of developing a new relationship with your land and co-creating a garden with nature as your partner. The first step involves putting a stop to the damaging practices that are causing the problems in the first place. Put the brakes on. We can find our way out of the management nightmare we have created for ourselves by establishing resilient and abundant gardens that can take care of themselves. You can still have a beautiful garden; you just have to approach it differently by designing and planting with intelligence and respect.

Garden Design

An rud a líonas an tsúil, líonann sé an croí.
What fills the eye fills the heart.

T here are countless books explaining how to design the perfect garden in whatever style you choose. The garden design process I am about to share with you, however, is completely different from all of the others. It will help you create a beautiful garden, of course, but it will be beautiful on many levels, not just on the exterior. Most garden designs aim to be superficially attractive, like a woman whose face is so thickly painted you can no longer make out her original features. My designs create a garden that is truthful and beautiful to the core, radiant with life force, bursting with atmosphere and energy, thoroughly magical, and in harmony with the Earth. They are embedded with the intention of creating a living, vibrant space that is connected to the universal flow of energy.

In the Islamic tradition, the word 'garden' carried a different meaning than it did in the West. In India, Persia and the Arab countries, gardens were actually magnificent rugs, each imbued with specific intentions. They were rolled out so that people could sit on them to meditate and journey to heaven, which was understood to be an inward experience. They believed that heaven resided within their own hearts. How wise they were.

I've always liked the idea that a garden is like a magic carpet. My 'alternative' method of garden design weaves that magic carpet and wraps it around your home. It will be beautiful and also serve as a resource for personal growth, a place where you can connect with your own personal heaven and feel safe.

Gardens as Expressions of Beauty

Everyone likes to be surrounded by beauty, although each of us has a different idea of what that is. Gardens are a great place to discover and manifest your own sense of beauty. Even if some of our gardens serve a purely functional purpose, we still want to make them as attractive as possible.

There is no fixed standard for what true beauty is; that changes across centuries and across cultures. Each person's view of what is appealing to them is

determined by a myriad of factors including their genetic make-up, their underlying beliefs and values, and their life experience.

So what is beauty and what does it mean? What does it do for us and why do
we search for it? If you strip away all the smoke, mirrors and cultural trappings,
beauty is truth laid bare. Beauty reminds us of our higher selves, the God within
us, because the original nature of all creatures is divine. The truth in everything is
beauty, its pure essence. That surge of joy that we feel when we experience beauty
somehow elevates us; it connects us to the universal energy source and raises our
consciousness. It gives us a glimpse of who we truly are and who we were when
we arrived on the Earth.

None of the gardens I have visited over the past many years has felt truthful to me.
The underlying spirit of the land was missing, and in its place was the essence of
the garden designer's personality. I could sense the energy of love in those places,
but it was conditional love. The land was loved, as long as it stayed contorted in the
way the garden designer had decided it should look. It was not allowed to be itself.

The gardens were bursting out of their seams because they could not help but
return to their true nature, their original wild selves, and they were consistently

punished for doing so. Within these spaces, nature felt imposed on and suppressed. I felt that these gardens were like children who were originally free at heart, but had been tamed; made to adopt a 'seen but not heard' existence – hidden in the background, kept tidy, encouraged to behave appropriately and obliged to put on a good face when the neighbours paid a visit.

You can force a child to be someone they don't want to be, but only with the predictable consequences of unhappiness and retreat. On the other hand, you could gently discover who this child is, who they want to be, and what they have to offer. What would they like to express and bring into the world?

Every piece of land is the same as this child.

Your garden will have its own core truth and distinctive personality, its own sense of itself. This is referred to as *genus loci*, the spirit of the place. Each garden must be treated as a separate entity. There is no one-size-fits-all solution to garden design.

Unless we allow the land to express its own truth, we are doing it an injustice. By listening carefully and allowing the land to become an extension of ourselves, we can interpret its energy and enable it to emerge through a creative, collaborative process. Its growth becomes a synchronistic dance that pulls you more deeply each day into a healing embrace with the Earth.

Most land that is used for agriculture and gardens has the same core truth: it strives to become a mature woodland – a stable and intelligent ecosystem that has evolved over many thousands or even millions of years. The land longs to experience this harmony. Our job is to understand what the land wants to express and allow it to become what it desires to be. Like good parents, we don't want the land to grow up without boundaries at all. Rather, we need to guide it towards maturity without breaking its spirit through our unreasonable demands. In this garden awakening, we aim to marry the land's true nature with our own personalities and intentions.

Achieving a classic woodland ecosystem is impossible for most people because the individual plots of land are too small. However, it is possible to create a replica of a complete woodland ecosystem in smaller spaces. I describe this process in step-by-step detail in Chapter 3, but for now let's begin by looking at the needs of the land's guardian – your good self, and any loved ones that may share your life with you.

Many people feel lost or intimidated by the thought of designing their own garden, but they needn't feel that way. It's a lot simpler than it seems. Just remember that this garden design process is not in any sense an expression of modern artistic endeavour. You don't need special training to do it and I think you will find it quite enjoyable. Your design can be as simple as you want it to be. It doesn't have to be classic, clever, exciting, futuristic, or follow any 'accepted' style.

My method of garden design is about not designing anything that blocks the flow of energy between you and the living body beneath you.

The underlying intentions are important, as is the eventual creation of a balanced ecosystem, but the most important part of the process is establishing a strong and mutually beneficial relationship with your land. This is a very creative process. You are making this garden for you and your family, and your family now includes the land.

The first step is to form a connection with the Earth. By the time you have got to know your land and have done the land-healing work discussed in Chapter 1, you will have become a uniquely trained expert for the ground you are stewarding. You will be its voice, its chance to express itself.

I use the word 'co-creation' in this book when referring to my unique approach. Co-creation means you are building the garden hand in hand with a partner, and in my approach that partner is nature. It is based on the acknowledgement and understanding that nature is a conscious living entity, real and present, that is willing to join you in this process.

I design gardens without using any particular method other than my own intuition. Intuition is not something that is easily taught, however, so for the purposes of this book I have distilled my design system into five basic elements. In this chapter I will guide you through these elements so you can piece together your own story in the same way I do mine.

The Five Elements for Designing Gardens in Partnership with Nature

1 The tool of intention: magic uncloaked
2 Selecting areas to hold specific intentions
3 Designing with the patterns and shapes of nature
4 The power of symbols and imagery
5 Putting your design on paper

Design element 1:
The tool of intention. Magic uncloaked

Mura gcuireann tú san earrach ní bhainfidh tú san fhómhar.
You reap what you sow.

People often assume that magic is a very complicated and mysterious thing. For centuries its practices were hidden by those who wanted to keep their powers all to themselves, and gradually magic became a vague concept discussed only in children's books and films, or in esoteric treatises belonging to the óccult. Magic is actually quite simple to understand and easy to use. All you need to know is that magic involves a mixture of intention and emotion. Your thoughts, emotions and intentions are a form of energy. Energy moves around and changes, but if you focus your energy in a particular direction you will be propelled there. This is what I refer to as magic. It is also the most important tool you will have for re-energizing the spirit of your land.

The practical value of using intention as a tool for focusing energy and creating your own reality was widely known in ancient times, but today it has been all but forgotten. Using the technique of intention allows you to communicate directly with your land.

I experienced a powerful example of the effect of emotion and intention when I created a garden at the Chelsea Flower Show in an effort to remind people of the importance of wild places. More than a decade ago I decided to design

Chelsea Flower Show, master plan (above) and perspective drawing

gardens based on native plants, but I struggled to find a market for my work. This caused me to sit back and reassess my approach. I realized there was one thing I was really good at – I could hear the land and express its individual story. With that information, I was able to create harmonious spaces that were gentle, beautiful and healing; places that invited nature to shine through as if it were the star of the show.

Eventually I came to the conclusion that I *could* continue to design gardens by using the ancient knowledge about land energy I had learned over the years to create wild and vibrant places. In the process, I also hoped to open people's eyes and hearts to a different way of seeing the world.

Nobody wanted to be my guinea pig client so I had to figure out another way to showcase one of these gardens. In 2002, I decided to reveal my new approach on a grand and very public stage – the Royal Horticultural Society Chelsea Flower Show, the most prestigious garden design competition in the world. As it was the first time I had experimented with my idea, I was taking quite a risk to say the least, but I suppose there's something to be said for naivety.

The Chelsea extravaganza has been held in the grounds of the Royal Hospital Chelsea, London, almost every year since 1913. It is a very exclusive affair that enjoys international renown because it is widely regarded as the birthplace and trendsetter of gardening fashion. What better way to make natural gardens acceptable to the mainstream than creating a compelling garden at this celebrated level of competition? It would send the message to gardeners everywhere that a new era was dawning in the world of landscape design; and those who clung to the old ways would be left behind like the dinosaurs.

I built a simple, magical garden at Chelsea that year and it really did capture people's hearts. My garden won a gold medal, an enormous honour for a young, virtually unknown first-time entrant like me.

Winning the gold medal resulted in substantial worldwide publicity and went a long way towards making wild spaces fashionable. They were no longer relegated to an untamed corner at the bottom of the garden. People started to realize that gardens and nature *can* be one and the same. My team and I had captured the hearts and imaginations of gardeners everywhere and it gave me the confidence I needed to keep going.

While I was designing and building the garden at Chelsea, I had one focused intention in my mind and heart. I wanted to remind people of how beautiful wild places are before they were all gone. It was extraordinary to observe the result of this intention as it played out during the exhibition. People queued for a long time just to look into the garden, and viewing it had a strong effect on them.

Irish people thought it was charming – "just like a little piece of Ireland". That's because Ireland is still a vibrant place, full of magic and wildness. English people, however, were brought to tears. They all wanted to tell me about the garden's impact and how it reminded them of places in nature that were special to them when they were young – places that didn't exist any more. These were pockets of land where the energy and life force of nature had been real for them. They may have been just a copse of trees on the other side of their granny's garden, a rocky outcrop near their house, or perhaps a wild meadow beside a holiday cottage where they spent time when they were children. My garden at Chelsea contained that same tangible life force. It reminded people that our separation from nature, the source, caused deep distress and grief to our psyches.

The outpouring of grief I encountered in that small space in the middle of London, which had begun as a blank slate just three weeks earlier, made it clear to me that I was on to something; that my beliefs about nature were real, and that by holding an intention in a garden you could create a strong, living relationship with the Earth.

THE POWER OF 'THE WORD'

In the beginning was the Word, and the
Word was with God, and the Word was God.

John 1: 1 (NKJV)

I have always been fascinated with ancient Irish history and learned a lot about magic and intention from studying old Irish ways. In Ireland, there is a long and well-documented tradition of magic, rituals and prayers. These traditions have been recorded in ancient monastic texts and mythological lore. By examining the patterns in these traditions and the reasoning behind them, we can see how simply the world works on the level of magical energy and learn out how to utilize this energy in a positive way. Curses were the opposite of prayers in old Ireland. They carried a lot of power because people believed so strongly in their results, just as people did in other parts of the world.

Having never been conquered by Rome, Ireland kept its culture intact for a long time, allowing it to develop and flourish as an advanced and refined society. The Druids (the bards) were the learned class in pre-Christian society. They carried all the knowledge and wisdom of their culture in their minds, often in the form of songs and verses. They did have a system of writing based on symbols, called *ogham*, but the most sacred teachings were not written down lest they fell into the wrong hands.

Modern writing came to Ireland with Christianity. The written records that survive from that time were substantially biased towards supporting the Christian religion, which was aiming to infiltrate and prevail over other faiths. The early Irish monks recorded few accounts of the Druids' good deeds and blessings. Instead they mostly speak of "backward blessings", or curses, so the most reliable accounts from that time regarding the use of focused intention are of a malevolent nature.

In recent Irish history (the past few hundred years), cursing has always been used vengefully. This is largely the result of disempowerment and the injustices the native Irish people suffered at the hands of landlords from foreign shores. The Irish not only cursed the person responsible for these dark deeds, but they also cursed the victim's offspring, resulting in sorrowful lives and a painful death for generations to come. People don't really believe in curses anymore, so they have lost their power. However, we can still use the recorded curses to learn how to put magic to good use today.

Land curses

A curse placed on a piece of land was referred to as a *piseóg*. The person carrying out the curse only had to utter the words to the land, and perhaps perform a few simple rituals, and the work was done. The earth absorbed the intentions and carried out its instructions, even though they were often destructive. The land was only affected as far as its boundaries, so the tradition of beating the boundaries helped to hold the curse inside. Sometimes the piseóg would result in milk turning sour or the stock getting sick. Heavy curses resulted in starvation as crops failed or the fertility of the land became depleted. People who lived on cursed land often ended up in workhouses because they couldn't produce enough food to support their family.

Every country area and every town had its own unique curses and ways of inadvertently acquiring them, such as accidentally roaming into a cursed ráth, or fairy fort (an ancient earthen mound associated with the fairy people), or standing on a famine grave. Anyone from my generation and earlier who grew up in Ireland knew of local places that were cursed, and we were certain to keep away from them. Piseógs are carried out to this day in Ireland. They are so feared that it is difficult to get older people even to talk about them. Understanding piseógs was a eureka moment for me, in terms of relating to the land in a positive way, although I learned about how to use the power of intention from the negative side of it.

EYE OF NEWT AND WING OF BAT

At one point in my life a number of years ago, I was feeling quite low. After unsuccessfully trying nutrition and other such remedies, I went to see an Irish healer named Maria Rawlins. During our session together, she informed me that the reason for my lack of strength was that I'd had a curse placed on me from having unknowingly wandered on to a cursed piece of land. Maria did some energy work on me and then told me that in order to remove the curse, I had to find a pink rose and throw its petals into a river just where it flowed into the sea. She said the salt water would wash the curse away.

At first I was sceptical, as I hadn't thought of the concept of curses in years and when I did I found it filed away in my imagination with fairy tales such as Cinderella and Snow White. Maria's instructions didn't enter my mind again until a few days later. After dropping my kids off at school, I decided to go for a walk on the cliffs. I bought a pink rose at the local supermarket and took it with me in case I found myself by a suitable river. There couldn't be any harm in it, I thought. It was just to be sure to be sure, as the saying goes.

When I came to a powerful-looking river that flowed dramatically over a high cliff into the sea below, I performed the rose petal ceremony just as Maria had suggested.

I thought no more about it until that night when I was putting my kids to bed. I usually went to sleep at the same time as they did, as I was always exhausted by then. As I took off my T-shirt and vest, my young daughter Ruby let out a cry of surprise, claiming there was something on my back. I immediately checked in the mirror and saw a large black symbol on my back, drawn in what seemed akin to the ashes smudged on foreheads on Ash Wednesday. It was also large, extending from below my shoulder blades to the base of my spine. I scrambled around in fright, grabbed cleanser and a washing-up brush from the kitchen, and scrubbed it off as quickly as possible. Then I checked my T-shirt and vest thinking I must have leaned against something, but there was only an imprint of the symbol on the inside of my vest – nothing on the outside or on any of the other layers I'd worn.

The next morning I rang Maria in a flustered state. She was very matter of fact about the whole thing and told me to relax. Apparently she saw that sort of thing all the time and said at least I knew the curse had now been removed. From then on I felt much better. The cloud had lifted and everything became brighter again. I began to seriously protect myself after that. Wouldn't you?

Other, direct curses were often cast from person to person. When the victim was cursed by a jealous or wronged neighbour, it often resulted in poverty or even death for the family. To successfully curse a person, the victim had to be directly informed of the deed for the curse to take effect. It was usually said to their faces, and if it was absorbed, the victim caused the curse to inflict harm by holding the belief within them.

Biodynamic agriculture

Modern biodynamic agricultural practices are a living example of how incorporating the power of intention in rituals and traditions can lead to very positive outcomes. Biodynamics is a pagan-based farming method that grew from a series of lectures given in 1921 by Rudolph Steiner, an Austrian philosopher and spiritualist. It uses many standard organic practices but also adds its own techniques, such as aligning farm activities with the movement of heavenly bodies and applying specially made 'preparations' to the soil. It is as close to witchcraft you will ever find and the results are truly miraculous.

Biodynamics is all about theatre and ceremony, and some people might be put off by the methods used for making its slightly peculiar preparations. For example, one method for increasing soil fertility involves stuffing a stag's liver with yarrow flowers. This is hung in the sun for half a year and buried for the next half-year. A small amount of this preparation is then stirred into a large quantity of water for several hours, creating a vortex as it is stirred alternately in opposite directions. This water is finally sprayed on the land a specific number of times during a particular phase of the moon.

It seems like the only thing missing is the black cat, right? But it is astonishing to witness the effects it has on crop production. Perhaps it's because I'm Irish, but I have a natural affinity with bending rules, so I looked into the reasons behind the pomp and rituals to see if they were really necessary. After much research and practical trials, I came to the conclusion that they were just a way to get people to add specific intentions to the water and then use this water to give instructions to the earth. Soil holds a lot of water and the water is where the intentions and instructions are absorbed, held and communicated.

Water magic

Dr Masaru Emoto, a Japanese scientist and researcher, carried out fascinating experiments on the effects of our words and thoughts on water, and wrote about them in his ground-breaking book *Messages from Water*. His experiments revealed physical proof of how water holds memory and intention. He froze water taken from lakes, rivers and even tap water, then photographed the water crystals under a microscope in a cryogenic chamber in order to capture the instantaneous effect that different words, thoughts, music and frequencies had on water as reflected in the changing shapes of the crystals. Water that had been instilled with positive words such as 'love' or 'gratitude' had a beautiful crystalline structure. Water that had been subjected to negative words or thoughts had aesthetically displeasing and disconnected shapes in its crystalline form. The effect was the same when positive or negative words were written on pieces of paper and taped to the bottles of water.

It's simple. Water is life. It has the unique ability to rearrange itself according to our thoughts and intentions so can be a direct channel for communicating with your land. A strongly held positive intention will transform water molecules and instil in them a positive structure. This structure will automatically change the other water molecules in the container – the container being your garden within the energetic boundary you created when you walked around your land and defined it (see Chapter 1).

In similar experiments, water molecules were shown to shift and restructure when positive prayers (from any religion) were said over them. Prayers, like symbols, have countless years of intention present in the arrangement of the words. Saying the prayer's words automatically transfers intent and restructures the water accordingly. This so-called 'holy' water has particularly beautifully shaped crystals when it is frozen and photographed. When a small quantity of holy water was put into a container of ordinary water, the ordinary water restructured itself until all the molecules took on the higher energy and exquisite shapes of the holy water. By higher energy, I am basically referring to good and evil. In my understanding of this, good thoughts are higher and brighter than bad thoughts; they are thoughts that have chosen light over darkness.

Water is an optimist, it seems, always willing to take on the more powerful positive structure of thoughts and intentions. It wants to be healthy, strong and beautiful. Therefore, even a small quantity of positively charged water has the potential to communicate with and transform a large area or a large body of water.

MAGIC BEANS

The land is like a sponge. It is waiting for us to tell it what to do, to co-create with us. It will soak up our intentions and bring them into existence if we ask. The land has intentions of its own, of course; it will manifest the human guardians it wishes to manifest, learning the lessons it wishes to learn. Everything is connected in this way.

All forms of ritual ceremony are simply tricks, for want of a better word. They are devices that allow us to bypass our minds and connect our intentions directly with the universal energy, where we are infinitely powerful. This is useful because our minds often get in the way by blocking this flow of energy. All we need to do is believe in the trick. If we have complete faith in that ceremony, ritual or prayer, we can join directly with *An Abhainn*, the river of life in old Irish, where we can make anything we imagine come to pass.

This is the simple power of faith healers, medical placebos, biodynamic agriculture, magic potions, spells, curses and prayers. By using rituals, the magician or healer comes to believe that once they carry out a specific set of instructions, they can dip directly into the river of life and achieve their desired outcome.

Our mind is our greatest obstacle. That is why spending time in nature or practising meditation is so important. Meditation trains us to quieten our minds, to observe our busy thoughts and allow them to fall into the background, enabling us to hear more subtle voices. Sitting quietly in nature has the same effect. People who spend a lot of time in nature are strikingly different from those who don't. A lovely, gentle energy emanates from them and they are usually more heart-centred than ego- or mind-centred. Historically, all our great spiritual leaders acquired enlightenment by spending time alone in nature.

For an intention to have its desired effect, the presence of strong emotion is vital. You need an emotional source powerful enough to carry your positive intentions deep into the fabric of reality.

The way to do that is to tune into your heart centre, and amplify it by generating strong visceral feelings that lie deep within it. Gaining access to this universal energy source is not a complicated process. We are already there; we are always there. That is the simple reality of life. We are always filled and surrounded by the river of universal energy, filled and surrounded by the energy of nature, filled and surrounded by God.

We simply have to let go and tune in.

Everybody knows what is meant by 'put your heart and soul into something'. Have your heartbeat match the heartbeat of nature, allow yourself to resonate with the energy of life. Use the nature-based meditation I described in Chapter 1, or some other method you prefer. Focus on warm, lovely memories and expand your heart energy. Close your eyes and visualize, turn the memories into a strong warm light expanding from your heart outwards. It is more powerful than you can imagine. This practice of bypassing your thoughts and sitting in silence is a direct route to your innate supply of power and strength.

Once the energy of the land is flowing freely and in partnership with you, supporting you to find your truth because you are doing the same for it, you can access the magic fairy dust. The land is willing and available to act as a conduit to send your wishes and intentions into the world and bring your true heart's desires home to you.

My method of creating a powerfully conscious garden simply suggests using some form of ceremony to focus your feelings and intentions into a particular form and direction. You can make up your own ritual, as long as you believe it works. *Belief is the key*.

I have always believed that the earth and plants communicate in the same way animals do – through feelings. I suppose we could call it telepathy, but it isn't from the head, it's from the heart. People who have pets or work with animals in some other capacity are well aware that animals are tuned in to subtle feelings. Dogs get up and walk to the door as soon as their owner leaves their place of work to return home, and almost all animals start moving towards safety before any sign of an impending earthquake or tsunami is evident. They are responding to feelings. In order to communicate our intentions and requests to the land, we have to some- how transfer our feelings into the earth. The spoken and written word is our most effective tool, as words are laced with intention and power.

When you are drawing your garden design on a piece of paper, always write your intentions on the page somewhere. This helps keep them in your heart and mind as you work, and directs your energy in constructive ways. It will inform your design and the symbols you choose to include.

BASIC INTENTIONS

You may have many different intentions for your land, and of course you can have more than one. You may want to create a garden that is specifically a healing place, or a sparkly, nurturing atmosphere for children that is dripping with enchantment and giggles. We each have varying needs and relationships to nurture with our land. However, there are a few simple intentions I recommend you begin with. You can use the methods I describe to implement them or find others that resonate more comfortably with your personality.

Protection

Set a protection prayer of your choice into a stone or crystal (the method is described on page 63), requesting a web of protection to surround your house and land. Ask for this protective net be forever held by the land you are working with. I usually ask a strong, pure energy to protect me and my family, but it is up to you how you chose to do this. There are protection prayers in all existing religions or you can make up your own.

Nourishment

Insert a request into the soil asking that the food that you grow there will be bursting with all the nourishment and healing properties you and your family require to thrive. If you, or anyone in your family has any ailments, point this out and ask the land to provide you with the specific nutritional support you need to heal your body, mind and spirit. Nature is the great provider, if we choose to ask. If your bare skin makes contact with the earth as you walk or work, the land will have a better chance to know what you need through the intimacy of skin on skin. We really have very little understanding of the intelligent being beneath us, except for the fact that it is the place from where we emerged and where we will ultimately return.

Love

The final initial intention should be to co-create a garden that is alive with the energy and exuberance of nature. This is a place where magic will pour out of every leaf as a result of Nature's recognition of your unconditional love for her true self. With this loving and mutually respectful relationship, you will feel forever supported, grounded and safe.

Now that the fundamental intentions are established, the only limits you apply are the ones that you set yourself. Enjoy!

WARNING: BE CAREFUL WHAT YOU WISH FOR

A few months after I fell in love for the first time, the object of my affections went off to work at a land rehabilitation site in Ethiopia. I felt that I couldn't bear to live without him. Certain that the distance would put an end to his feelings for me, I decided to take the situation in hand. In other words, I tried to control the outcome.

I found a passport-sized photo of the two of us that we had taken in a booth on a ferry to England once. From my cottage in the Wicklow Hills, I made my way across the fields to a ring of ancient standing stones called the Pipers Stones, which had a twisted old hawthorn tree at the entrance. I had always felt there was a strong portal available there to tap into subtle realms of existence. I was highly emotional at the time. My energy was fuelled by the adrenalin of fresh, young love and fortified by the fear of losing my beloved. The energy was so strong I felt like I was floating as I walked across the fields.

I climbed the hawthorn tree and found a hollow in one of the branches. I insisted, politely but firmly, that the tree energy hold my lover's heart together with my own in an energetic bond that would never be broken or destroyed, unless I wanted out. Then I got on a plane and travelled to Ethiopia. Once I had won his heart, however, I left him for another man. He was distraught and remained heartbroken for some time.

After I returned I suddenly remembered my hawthorn ritual, grabbed my coat and a torch, and set off for the Pipers Stones. In the dead of night I stumbled across the fields in a fit of guilt, found the hawthorn tree and climbed up its twisted branches. After much searching I found the photograph still stuck in the hole where I left it and asked the tree to release my friend from the bonds I had set in place that fateful day. I went home and burned the photograph – to be sure to be sure. He recovered soon afterwards. Thank God I had the wherewithal to add that opt-out clause in my ritual!

I told this short tale about my first love to illustrate something you must understand before you begin to use intention methods to fulfil your desires. I believe everyone arrives on earth with a series of things they need to learn and do. This is our destiny. Most of us never even set foot on the path of our destiny, let alone walk it our entire lives in peace and acceptance.

For example, if you are meant to be alone in life, learning how to step into your power without the support or love of a partner is part of your destiny. If, however, you insist that you want a partner in your life, no matter what, and you send that request out to the universe, there may be serious consequences. You may, for example, lose years to a relationship, dealing with your lover's baggage without having the time or energy to address the things you were meant to address in your own life. If you are lucky, one day you will finally realize you are lost and must walk away from the relationship so you can find your own path again.

Words are very powerful, so you must be careful what you wish for. That's why I recommend that after every request, you always add a proviso along the lines of 'if it is part of my destiny' or 'if it is meant to be' or 'if it is for my higher good'. If you do not consciously add a stipulation of this kind, then unexpected, negative consequences may appear along with your wish.

In order to manifest something, you need to imagine that your wish has already come to fruition, otherwise you are holding the vision for it in the future. The present is where and when the gift should arrive. Saying thank you for your desired outcome, rather than wishing for it, is the best way around this.

Also, your wish needs to be a true heart's desire. If you are unsure, don't worry. As long as you accept that your request may not be right for you and clarify that you don't want it to manifest if it isn't meant to be, then all will be well.

I have noticed that people who are in tune with nature seem at peace with themselves and their destiny, and have no need to make wishes anymore. They simply trust in life and assume that everything they require will show up, as long as they keep walking their path and following their heart. They realize that the only thing that really exists is this moment. Everything else is illusion. Happiness and peace are available to us at any time.

Design element 2:
Selecting areas to hold specific intentions

- Night-time place
- Wishing place
- Praying place
- Releasing place
- Other practical places

NIGHT-TIME PLACE

Dá fhad é an lá tagann an oíche.
However long the day, night comes.

The most magical time in your garden is during and after dusk. If you have the space, design a separate area as far away as possible from your house and your neighbours' houses. It doesn't have to be a large area – it could just be a comfortable seat. But it is somewhere you can go to experience your garden at night-time.

Find your way through the garden to this place as often as you think of it. Leave your phone behind, and avoid outdoor lighting, except perhaps a torch to get you there safely if the moon isn't out. Lights pollute the darkness of night, preventing us from seeing the enchanting show of stars in the sky, which we all too often take for granted. The darker the better.

Settle yourself somewhere comfortable and spend as long as possible in silence. An hour is food for the soul but even 10 minutes is a fine start. Magic is particularly noticeable outside in the dark. You'll be perfectly safe. There's always enough light once your eyes adjust. Sit still and reconnect with the stars, observe the wild creatures that might appear, the fresh night scents, the familiar and unfamiliar, curious sounds.

For most people, being alone in nature in the dark is way outside their comfort zone, but it is important to push yourself out of your comfort zone once in a while. It is an ideal time to experience that peaceful feeling of being at one with nature. If you are quiet, you will hear the earth breathing and sense the life force all around you. During these times, when you are not doing anything but being present, your connection with your plants is heightened. They will lean towards you, overjoyed to be near you, thrilled to have a chance to spend 'quality time' with you. Children react to our freely given and undivided attention in the same way. Their personalities are intensified at night and our senses are more finely tuned to noticing them.

Go on, try it. I promise, you will survive *and* you will be greatly energized. Face your fears and take back the night.

WISHING PLACE

Having a specific place in your garden to make wishes or requests is always a good idea. It doubles the intention. The land will know the reason for the space, so all the actions you carry out there will be supported.

I like to use stones and crystals to transfer my intentions to the world. Somehow they hold feelings and memories quite strongly for me. Once they have been activated through ceremony and strong emotion, they hold the intention and pass it on to the soil long enough for the information to be transferred to the entire piece of land and beyond. I prefer to use smooth water stones, perhaps ones you find on the land itself. You may feel drawn towards a stone on the beach or beside a stream during your rambles, or you may be drawn to a particular crystal. Use something that resonates with you, something that just feels right.

HOW TO CLEAN AND PREPARE A CRYSTAL

Wash the stone in spring water, sea water, or bury it overnight in the earth (marking its position of course). Leave it in the moonlight overnight so that it will be cleansed of old energies. Then leave it out all day in the sunshine. After that your crystal will be prepared to absorb fresh intentions.

Using a stone or crystal is simply a conscious way of placing your words and intentions into the land and into the river of life, where everything is available once you are no longer attached to the outcome.

Write your intention on to a piece of paper. Remember to add 'if it is for my higher good' or 'if it is part of my destiny' or some other get-out clause. Wrap the paper around the stone and put it in your pocket or hold it in your hand until you feel the intention has been absorbed. The stone then is ready to go into the ground. Regardless of what language the note is written in, the land will understand and carry out your instructions.

Select a day when you are feeling good and grounded. Spend as much time as you need in the garden to establish your connection with the land, perhaps mulching or planting. Then sit with your back against a tree. You will be surrounded by the support and love offered to you by the land.

Play some music or sing or hum a song with the intention of it being a gift to nature. Even if you think you cannot play or sing well, it doesn't matter. Nature will listen and love the attention. If you're sensitive and can listen well, you will find yourself singing the songs with sounds of the earth. These sounds will resonate deeply and facilitate healing for both of you.

After the music or song stops, you will hear a particular type of silence, like that of an audience just before the applause. Then you'll feel a wave of energy. It's such a powerful blast that it is practically impossible not to feel it. Use this gust of energy to help expand your heart until all the cells in your body are humming like a tuning fork. Quieten your mind, and step into the true beauty of who you are. The more you practise this, the easier it is to hold that feeling.

When you are ready, place your stone in a special place designed for wishing or praying in your garden. You can bury it in the ground or put it in a crook of a tree branch, wherever feels right. As you place it, speak the intention out loud, drawing your voice directly from the earth and the stillness of your heart. Be sure to say thank you. Gratitude is imperative for this to work as it makes the request a done deal, rather than holding it away from you at some future destination,

You will find many wishing trees in Ireland and other places throughout the world. They are trees that grow over a holy well, out of a fairy mound, or have been considered sacred for some other reason.

In old Irish lore, fairy mounds were hills that had been designated as special because of the presence of nature spirits. They were known as portals to the underworld by the ancient pre-Celtic race known as the Tuatha Dé Dannan, the Tribe of the Gods. The belief was that the spirit of the fairy mound tree would grant your wish if you asked in the correct way. These trees were often hawthorn trees but it doesn't really matter which species you choose. Hawthorn is known as the heart tree (the flesh of the haw berries providing heart medicine), but it is also a practical choice, as it is generally a low-growing species so the branches can be easily reached.

A torn piece of cloth was tied around a twig or a branch of the tree while a prayer was said or the wish was requested. The rag was left behind to rot, holding the energy of the prayer's intention for as long as it survived. People also used other tools to transfer their intention. Ribbons, coins, crystals buried at the roots, or wishing 'altars' built in the crook of a branch all served the same purpose.

Wishing wells have a similar effect, since water is so effective at transporting intentions into the land. If you have a source of spring water you can make it into a wishing well – just be sure it is safe for kids to be around because every child loves the wishing place. A stream or natural pond is another great place to toss stones or crystals that have been infused with an intention.

You could have a personally meaningful symbol carved into a paving stone and set this down at the point of wishing. It will become a powerful place to stand while grounding yourself before casting your wish into the water. Despite their reputation to the contrary, coins are not very good conveyors of intentions, as they have passed through so many different energies that they become overloaded and are difficult to clean properly.

Alternatively, plant a tree in your garden with the specific intention of creating a wishing place. As you plant it, stow the stone or crystal infused with your intention in the roots. Your wishing tree will become a focal point, the place you send your dreams out into the world. You can also use an existing tree for this purpose once you set it with the instruction.

Different trees have different energies. Birch represents change and fresh energy. Willow has a very feminine energy. You are the expert here, so choose a tree that means something special to you, or a tree that feels appropriate for your particular desires. There are no rules, other than 'do no harm' and 'be careful what you wish for'. Believe it has already happened, and it will.

PRAYING PLACE

In ancient Ireland, certain trees were used to channel prayers. Prayer trees aren't quite the same as wishing trees, which acted like a personal postal box. Creating a prayer space requires an alternative approach, with a slightly different set of instructions. It is softer and more compassionate – a spiritual place with the purpose of directing light into our lives, the lives of other people, or into any chosen situation. The evocation, direction and power of the prayer can be intensified by creating a meaningful symbol in the form of a sculpture or a path around the tree's base.

Sometimes when someone we love is ill or in trouble, we want to do something to help them. By focusing good energy on to that person or situation, we can. To do this, however, we need to believe strongly in our ability to affect the course of events with our directed and energized thoughts. Prayers from any culture are simply a collection of words that carry a very powerful and positive intention. You can make up your own prayer or use one that you have encountered in your own life experience.

To send a prayer, expand your heart energy by using the method I explained on page 29, or use your own preferred method. Call upon any or all of your icons to help carry the prayer to bring light and healing to the situation. Again, you can use the prayer tree energy itself, the Earth, Jesus, Buddha,

Muhammed, Archangel Raphael, your benign ancestors, or anything at all, as long as it is a strong, pure force. Ask them to hand-deliver these prayers for you. The underlying intention of this prayer tree will strengthen the prayer and increase its potency. You can light a candle, put your prayer into a stone or crystal, or tie ribbons or photographs on to the branches. Whatever you choose, just do no harm and say thank you.

LABYRINTHS FOR PRAYER GARDENS

A labyrinth is a distinct symbolic pattern often used for a meandering yet purposeful path. It is similar to a maze but the labyrinth has only one path, which leads to the centre, while a maze has more than one possible route and offers choices. The 'classical' labyrinth is based on the ancient seven-circuit geometric symbol, which is found on prehistoric boulder carvings and laid out in stone in Ireland, Iceland, Russia and many other places. The labyrinth at the palace of Knossos on the island of Crete contained at its centre the lair of the Minotaur, a mythical beast that was half-man, half-bull. In Ireland, a boulder incised with a labyrinth motif was found along an old monastic pilgrimage walk in the Wicklow Mountains, close to where I lived for many years. In medieval times, the design was adapted and laid as a floor decoration in Chartres Cathedral in France and in many other sites in Europe.

The labyrinth has a strong intention behind it, one that draws you deeper and deeper into your own centre as you walk towards the destination. Different cultures used labyrinths for a number of purposes, including fertility, initiation and protection from evil spirits, but its primary purpose was always a spirit journey. It was a moving meditation that eventually brought you to a place of peace and power.

Walking the path of a labyrinth is a mind-calming, heart-focusing exercise. If you walk the path before you get to your wishing or prayer place, you will expand the power of your wish or prayer by evoking the additional power of this ancient symbol and using it to direct your energy in a more focused way. If the classical labyrinth shape does not resonate with you, find another one that does. Even a simple spiral path with the tree at its centre will work perfectly well.

RELEASING PLACE

If you have the space and a safe climate for it, consider having a fire pit. No garden should be without one! It's wonderful to spend an evening sitting wrapped in a blanket around the fire within your magical garden. You can use pruned branches or the wood from fuel-specific coppice trees in your forest garden to maintain the fire. Each time you get a chance to huddle around a fire in the open air, it gives you the opportunity to ground yourself and reflect on the simple pleasures in life. It's better than any film or TV programme and it's a great place to bond with family and friends, although I sometimes prefer to be alone. Fires help transport you into the magical world of memories and fairy tales, as well as providing a general sense of well-being.

If you live in an area with restrictions on open-air fires, find a safe alternative that will satisfy the regulations, such as a chimnea or ready-made outdoor stove. Or you could build your own fireplace that will double as a pizza oven.

I like fire pits that are sunken, cosy spots protected from the wind, or else sheltered by trees and shrubs. It's nice to have comfortable seats too – perhaps a wrap-around bench with a place to store wood underneath. If you don't feel comfortable in the fire area, you won't be drawn to it.

You can also use the fire area as a place of ritual. If we are angry, or if we lose a dream, friend or lover, it is best to process and let go of our feelings as soon as we are able, otherwise they become heavier and heavier until they weigh us down altogether. Write your feelings on a piece of paper so you can experience them one last time. When you are ready, throw the paper into the fire. The garden will help you release anything that is blocking the flow of your energy in the same way you helped the land release blockages that existed before you arrived.

OTHER PRACTICAL SPACES

Within your garden you will need to designate certain areas for storage and for accomplishing practical tasks. Here are some of them:

Kids

If you have young children, their needs will likely take precedence over your other plans for the garden until they get older. For example, you might require a large open area where your kids can run around and burn off some energy. This shouldn't stop you from gardening in the boundaries and other available spaces, and at a later stage you can reclaim some of that lawn for other purposes.

Start by creating shelter belts, covering boundary walls in climbers, and perhaps creating a strip that is protected from the children around the edges for planting your first and maybe second layers of trees. You have set an intention for the land, so begin building your relationship with it. Do the healing work, plant as much as you can to establish the soil and create diversity. If you tell the land your plan, it will understand it. A few years to us may seem like a long time, but to the land it is a moment in time that passes easily with the comfort of knowing it is loved and respected.

Composting area

If you have the space, build a compost area that allows the compost to sit on the earth. If you are in an urban area where that is not allowed, there are many great container composters and wormeries available from your local council or garden centre.

Duck, goose, hen, pig or dog run

If you have or want any of these creatures, they need space to run around and protection from the weather and predators. Ducks and geese need a pond or pool in their enclosure. Pigs also enjoy a shallow wallowing pond to roll around in.

Clothes line

Try to design in a clothes line somewhere. It's better than relying on an energy-guzzling tumble dryer.

Garden shed

You will almost certainly need a place to store tools and machinery, process food crops, hang herbs, fruit and vegetables to dry, so why not think about designing something yourself? It would be a perfect opportunity to create a wonderful structure, especially if it's small enough to avoid the need for planning approval, and would be a chance to learn about and experiment with ecologically sound materials and practices. You could design a structure of cob (a straw/clay mixture), straw bales, wood or reclaimed materials.

The roof can be designed to harvest rainwater, or it can become a green roof, making it another place to plant. Sun-loving annuals can find a home on a shed roof that is designed to hold soil – just be sure it is structurally sound. There are so many possibilities and all the information you need is readily available online.

Design element 3:
Designing with the patterns
and shapes of nature

Tús maith leath na hoibre.
A good start is half the work.

The key to my simple method of design is harmony. The aim is to create spaces that feel right; spaces that appeal to the heart rather than just the intellect.

Nature is a living entity consisting of an interdependent collection of systems. Inside each system are specific components. And each component contains patterns that repeat themselves through the system all the way down to subatomic level.

Since every living organism is made up of precise, repetitive numerical patterns, it makes sense that we should try to follow the same patterns in our garden designs. This allows us and our gardens to become linked with the universal flow of energy.

Prior to the Industrial Revolution, artists and architects from all cultures and walks of life studied nature's patterns. Each work of art and architectural structure was an expression of nature's patterns and the artist's own creativity. This collaboration was considered necessary in order to create harmony and beauty.

The arrival of the Industrial Revolution removed this type of design from the mainstream. We decided to separate ourselves from nature and assume dominance over the land. For the most part, design became an intellectual activity, a way to express the pain we felt as a result of our estrangement from the source. As a reflection of this, many designers and other artists began creating works that were confusing expressions of disharmony. Discord became fashionable. Friction, unease and conflict became the vernacular.

'Sacred geometry' is the modern term for the study of the universal patterns in nature. These patterns are revealed on every scale. Each pattern of growth or movement adheres to one or more of the same repetitive geometric shapes and relationships.

Circles, triangles, rectangles, hexagons, spirals, squares, and the patterns that form between the various arrangements of these shapes, are all used as nature's way of unfolding and interconnecting. If you explore the world of sacred geometry, I guarantee you will be amazed at the beauty and harmony that exists in the shapes and patterns of all things.

Each shape has specific characteristics and emits a specific frequency. Any one of them, or combinations of several shapes, can be integrated into your garden in different ways and for different reasons.

The 'golden mean' or 'golden ratio', is the name given to the repeating relationship of the various shapes and patterns in nature. It is like a key that opens the door to the frequency that connects everything in the universe. By inviting this universal frequency into our gardens, we are creating a sacred space in the same way that places of worship have been created for centuries. Pagan religions, and later the more structured 'higher' religions, understood the power of sacred geometry and its role in inviting 'God' energy into places of worship.

THE GOLDEN MEAN AND
THE FIBONACCI SERIES OF NUMBERS

Here's a brief background explaining how the various natural patterns in sacred geometry were derived mathematically. It will help you to understand them, and soon you will begin noticing them everywhere you look. I will then explain how to incorporate their flow of energy into your own garden.

If you examine the flowers of any member of the *Asteraceae* family, including asters, cone flowers, chrysanthemums, daisies, marigolds and sunflowers, you will see that the seeds swirl from the centre of the flower in a very specific pattern.

The lines of the seeds move in two directions. The number of seeds moving in one direction is proportionally related to the number of seeds going in the other direction. That ratio is known as the golden mean or the golden ratio. This ratio manifests in the physical world as a spiral pattern. The Fibonacci series of numbers describes this proportional relationship.

Overlap two equal circles from their centre points and you get an almond shape in the centre called a vesica piscis ('fish's bladder' in Latin). If you draw a line across the centre of this shape and then draw two more lines down to meet at the base, you create an equilateral triangle. This shape leads to the construction of a square. By placing the equilateral triangle on top of the square, you create a rectangle known as the 'golden rectangle'.

The reason this rectangle is important is because the ratio between the lengths of the two sides is 1:1.618. This ratio has been used by artists and architects for centuries to incorporate the patterns of nature into their work.

The Fibonacci sequence of numbers, which was introduced by the mathematician Leonardo Fibonacci during the Middle Ages, follows this sequence: 1, 1, 2, 3, 5, 8, 13, 21, 34, 55, and so on. You simply add the two preceding numbers to form the next one in the series. If you divide any of these numbers by the preceding one, you will get 1.618 or thereabouts. This becomes more exact the larger the numbers become.

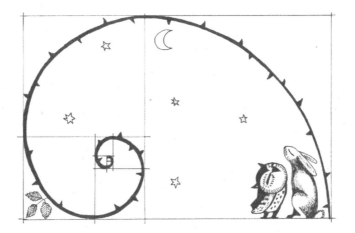

The golden mean spiral derived from the Fibonacci series of numbers

The arrangements of shapes and ratios I am describing replicate themselves in everything, from the way things grow to the shapes of flowers, trees, snails, shells, snowflakes, and the human body. The flow of water and air, the structure of DNA... Everything adheres to the spiral shape described by the golden ratio. It also describes your thought patterns and the way they connect to everything else. Even the relationship between subatomic particles displays these ratios.

In this way, each small thing contains within it the whole of nature; and within the whole all things are included.

There is an energy surrounding and pervading all things that falls within these universal patterns of structure and flow. We intuitively recognize beauty in these patterns because they express the true nature of the world. By designing your garden with these rules and patterns in mind, you will strengthen the flow of energy through your land. You will be working within the flow of the universe instead of against it. Your garden will become a magical and grounding place that feels right, the way all things in nature feel right and beautiful.

EXAMPLES OF NATURE'S PATTERNS

The patterns in nature form a language we can feel rather than understand. As far back as Plato and Euclid, about 2,500 years ago, these patterns were studied and explored. Even then, the only tools you needed to transfer this sacred geometry to paper was a compass and a straight edge.

All geometric patterns begin with the point of a compass on a page and a circle drawn from it. The circle is the easiest and most important shape. It is said to contain all the properties of the universe. It represents the cycle of life, the nature of all things.

A circle overlapped with another circle of the same radius, crossing at the centre point, will form the vesica piscis shape in the centre. If you continue to overlap circles, you will get the 'Seed of Life' (7 overlapping circles). Keep going and you will end up drawing the 'Flower of Life' (19 overlapping circles).

The Flower of Life

There are five perfect three-dimensional forms that emerge from the Flower of Life: the tetrahedron, hexahedron, octahedron, dodecahedron and icosahedron.

Collectively these are known as the 'platonic solids' and are the foundation of everything in the physical world, as demonstrated by Professor Robert Moon at the University of Chicago. He proved that the entire periodic table of the chemical elements – the building blocks for literally everything in the physical world – is based on these same five shapes.

This explanation is meant to give you the basic theory of these shapes and how they appear in nature. It isn't meant to overwhelm you. As you design, you will know when you have the proper relationships because it will feel right; it will have resonance. Resonance is the simply the manifestation of nature's life energy expressed in a physical form. Practice makes it easier to recognize this resonant feeling, just as developing your creativity will take practice. Like any other skill, it takes time and effort.

Experiment with some of the shapes and patterns I have listed below to design the structure of your garden. Which ones are you drawn to? Which ones do you feel you and your garden need? You can mix and match or get more ambitious with them, if you like. Just try to stay within the flow of natural patterns.

All these patterns emit a frequency, and natural energies flow freely within these frequencies. There are no blockages and nowhere for energy to get caught. Using these shapes to facilitate the flow of energy through the land will open channels for the free flow of energy everywhere. It's akin to tuning the land to the music of nature.

Circle

In nature, the circle and sphere are used as the primal con-
tainer for energy and consciousness. The circle and sphere are
formed around a central point, the point of creation. Universally
the circle means unity, wholeness and completion. It represents
sacred feminine energy, so if you build a circle with this intention in mind, you are automatically creating a sacred space. You can't go wrong with
this simple shape and any garden can be based around it, no matter how small.

Two equal circles crossing at the centre, creating the vesica piscis shape

The intersecting circles represent the overlapping of the natural and the spiritual
worlds. The resulting vesica piscis symbolizes the union of your energy with the
energy of nature, the garden being the result. Some cultures see it as a representation of the Christ energy, as he was seen as the embodiment of spirit in the form of
a human being. Many lovely mergers can be created and celebrated using this pattern: the sun and moon, heaven and earth, and other marriages. I love the feeling of
this shape. It is a powerful and simple space in which to create.

Spiral

Nature uses the spiral to circulate and transmit energy and
consciousness from one place to another. It emits a powerful
frequency that evokes movement, energy and growth. Spirals
make a great path design for smaller gardens, a paving pattern
within a circle, or a layout for a prayer walk. A spiral can also
be used as a special symbol engraved on stones to celebrate and embrace change, or
at least to practise accepting its inevitability.

Anti-clockwise spirals are for opening things up. Clockwise spirals are for closings or endings. In this way spirals can be used as an entrance or an exit to specific areas. The double spiral represents balance.

The triple spiral, or *triskel* in Irish, can be interpreted in many ways. For me it represents the threefold nature of the world – the world of spirit, the world of our ancestors, and the creative world in which we live. It can also represent the past, present and future, or whatever your personal or cultural interpretation might be.

Concentric circles

Three concentric circles can signify whatever you feel fits, really. The intention you place with the symbol will give it its meaning – the past, present and future, for example, or the awareness of how all things are affected by each other. Concentric circles can also be a good shape for the primary  path layout within a large forest garden, providing access to all parts of the land.

Cross

The cross symbol originally stood for balance, until Christian religions turned it into a crucifixion image. The cross represents the point at which heaven and earth meet, and the promise of harmony found through the balance between the two. The vertical line stands for the spiritual, masculine principle,  and the horizontal line for the earthly, feminine principle. The intersection is the point at which heaven and earth come together, and the result of their union is life on earth. In a garden I find that a circle surmounting a cross, or an ankh, is a highly usable space in which to create.

Square

In sacred buildings such as temples and churches, the square represents the union of the four elements – earth, air, fire and water – and the attainment of unity. The square also symbolizes the soul in some cultures.

It is an easy enough shape to work with, but for some reason it never resonated with me. I find it heavy. However, you can certainly use it if you are drawn to it. The square is a particularly handy design solution for a small space.

Square framing a circle or circle framing a square

The union of the square and the circle represents the union of heaven and earth. It also symbolizes the perfectly balanced human being.

Yin yang

This well-known Chinese symbol also represents balance. I love the intention behind the character, its central message reminding us of the duality of all things. There can be no light without darkness, no good without bad, and no life without death. I find the symbol very reassuring. It gives me great strength.

Equilateral triangle

The equilateral triangle represents the threefold nature of the universe: heaven/earth/humanity, father/mother/child, body/mind/spirit. It is the strongest of all of the shapes. The

equilateral triangle symbolizes completion and is an excellent grounding symbol for your home garden.

Six-pointed star (Star of David)

As above, so below. The six-pointed star reminds us of the union of opposites: male and female, spirit and matter, heaven and earth, and so forth. Creativity comes from the friction created between two opposites. This is my favourite symbol for creativity.

Design element 4: The power of symbols and imagery

In the design phase, symbols are used to bring a particular atmosphere or intention into the garden. Symbols are images. They can also take the form of a poem, story, sound or colour. Some symbols hold thousands of years of focused intention within them, and together they form a universal language. Symbols were used to convey a certain concept, emotion or specific intention. For example, a star shape represents transformation, a lion means courage, and the colour blue is associated with spirit.

By purposefully using symbols within your design, you automatically draw a specific intention to your space. You may have already chosen a symbol in the form of a pattern for the overall design of your garden, but other symbols can also be used within it to strengthen its atmosphere and sense of purpose.

Holding an image in the mind's eye is how we create the world around us; we get an image of what we want to do and then we proceed to make it happen. Imagery can inform the physical design of the garden by creating the symbol shapes in a tangible form. In that way it also influences the design on an energetic level.

Symbols may arise from the conscious or subconscious level, especially when they involve specific healing needs. They may also come to you as dreams or memories. Selecting symbols is an intuitive and very personal process.

ASK THE LAND TO REVEAL A SYMBOL TO YOU

An rud nach fiú a lorg, ní fiú a fháil.
What is not worth seeking is not worth finding.

If we ask for an image when we are working on our gardens, one will come to mind. If it lingers and resonates within you, you must trust that this is a direct message from the land. The image will contain something that both you and the land require. The image revealed is the one you need to hold dear as you design the garden.

There is no sense in latching on to a symbol just because you like the idea of it, or you like its outward form. It must mean something to you — truly, deeply mean something, even if you cannot quite put your finger on it. This resonance is how you recognize that the symbol is the right one. You may not understand why you are attracted to an image or a symbol until long after the fact. At the time, you simply *sense* they hold a message for you.

You will recognize them as being part of your journey, a signpost along your life's path. There are a few symbols and images that have resonated with me all my life, while others have been important only at certain times. Sometimes it was a particular poem, sound or colour. At other times I was drawn to certain trees or plants. The spiral has always been with me. I doodled it in my first copybooks in school. Later I moved on to the Celtic triskele, or triple spiral, and then labyrinths.

The spiral gave me my first insights into how a symbol could help create peace in my mind. It was a kind of meditation. I drew spirals over and over again when I was stressed or distracted. I created shapes around them that flowed outwards and became stories in themselves. Those doodles eventually became my garden designs.

The flow of water, air, energy, thoughts and the growth of every living thing — all these occur in a spiral pattern. For me it brings a surge of energy into any space. The Irish triskele is a lovely symbol that represents the threefold nature of all things.

You will probably doodle different images such as flowers or triangles. Some of them are just absent-minded scribbles, but certain symbols will arise because they carry a special meaning for you. You'll know which is which by their unmistakable resonance, or lack of it.

Symbols help you hold an image in your mind or body. They make the work easy. By including them in your design, their meaning will be automatically instilled in the garden. This is why they must have special significance for you; if they don't, the symbol will not hold any special healing power.

Once you have found your symbol, draw it on a piece of paper and keep referring to it as you make your design.

INTEGRATING THE SYMBOL OR IMAGE INTO YOUR GARDEN DESIGN

The American mythologist Joseph Campbell defined a symbol as "an energy evoking and directing agent". He hit the nail squarely on the head, at least as far as I am concerned. Symbols evoke a particular energy and send it in a focused direction. Hold the symbol or the image you want to use in your mind, then allow your imagination to direct it. The root of the word 'imagination' is *image*. Focus on the image, carry it with you, keep it under your pillow at night, and draw it on top of your design sketches. Eventually your subconscious will find a way to work it into the garden. Drawing the symbol on a stone and placing it in the garden is also a good idea, but you must draw it purposefully and place the stone with intention.

If you hold an image in your mind for a sustained period of time while producing the design, it will be sensed and experienced by everyone who enters the garden. Objects of artistic expression, including gardens, allow the viewer to participate in the original artistic vision.

If you meditate on an image, it opens for you. When I visualize a specific colour, image or word, I experience peace and serenity almost immediately. Focusing on a single symbol allows me to sidestep my busy everyday mind. I can calmly float out of space and time because I have an image that holds me safely. The energy of the image expands and then reveals itself in unexpected ways. When my awareness returns to the piece of land or design I am working on, the image finds ways of expressing itself. It may not be obvious, but it is there if you believe it is.

How do you integrate your chosen symbol into your garden design? You could paint or carve a pattern on a bench, place an evocative poem somewhere, or lay paving stones in the pattern of a specific symbol. The entire garden could be in the shape of the symbol. You might install canvas panels of a particular colour, use a sculpture with the imagery of a poem or a myth, or create a labyrinth. The possibilities are endless.

HOW I HAVE APPLIED IMAGERY AND SYMBOLS TO INFORM MY DESIGNS

Using imagery from a poem to create an atmosphere

A garden for Royal Botanic Gardens, Kew

Six months after the Chelsea Flower Show in 2002, I received a call from the British government's Department for Environment, Food and Rural Affairs (Defra). They asked me to design a garden promoting biodiversity for a summer festival of biodiversity at Kew Gardens in London. I have never had such support and plant choices available to create an ecosystem planting scheme as I did while working on this garden. Kew was one of the few times I was completely free to design a garden of this type, and I did it with the help of the wonderful people at the Future Forests nursery in Bantry, West Cork.

Designing a planting scheme for the garden was not as simple as ordering a selection of plants from various nurseries in Ireland and beyond. I wanted to re-create a selection of plants that would naturally grow together in the same soil type, microclimate and general situation in hand.

In other words, for all you gardening enthusiasts, I was going to use a selection of compatible 'weeds' – plants that almost everyone else is at great pains to remove from their gardens.

Changing people's perception of weeds from 'bad' to 'good' is no easy task. I always felt disheartened when I walked with my mum in her traditional and much-loved garden, carrying out my duty by making appropriately admiring remarks. Standing beside her flowering herbaceous borders, she would reach down to some beautiful plant she didn't recognize as one of her garden-centre-sanctioned

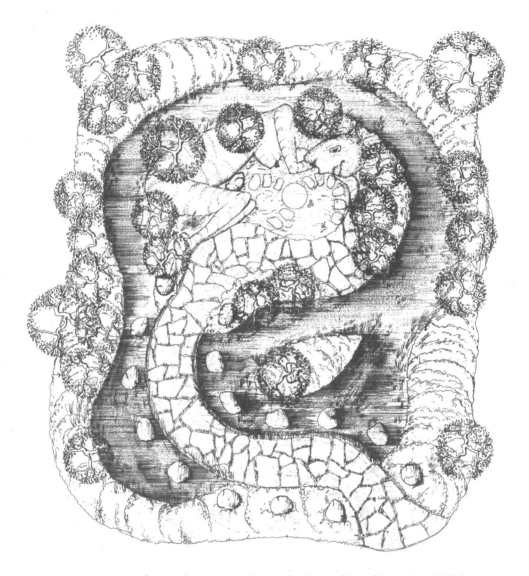

Master plan for Kew biodiversity garden, inspired by Yeats' poem 'The Stolen Child'

purchases and grab the poor thing threateningly by the neck. She was fully prepared to yank it out, depending on my reply to her question, "Is this a weed?" At
those moments my heart would plummet and I was clearly fighting a losing battle.
Change can be hard.

Since Defra gave me no design brief apart from 'biodiversity' for the garden at Kew, I found inspiration in a poem by WB Yeats while searching for an atmosphere to put into my garden. Yeats wrote many beautiful poems, but my favourite is 'The Stolen Child'. When I was a teenager, I pasted a copy of it on the wall above the desk in my bedroom. Instead of concentrating on my homework, my eyes would often drift to the poem and I would disappear into its ambiance; that mysterious, otherworldly realm where ghosts and fairies were as real as we were, and the veil between our world and theirs was just a thin, misty film, waiting to draw us in if only we would allow it.

Weaving atmospheres into a piece of land is like telling a story and placing the listener under a spell. An effective way to begin weaving that story is to build the design around a poem or a story that is already brimming with suggestive imagery. By holding the atmosphere of the poem or story in your mind when you are dreaming up the design, you can recreate the same feeling in the land.

Yeats' 'The Stolen Child' evokes mystery and sadness. For me, it underlies the separation we have from nature as adults. It reminds us that the secret to finding our way back to a true connection with the land involves slipping back into that light, open-hearted energy we naturally dwelt in as children. Its verses conjure up an atmosphere reminiscent of wild, haze-shrouded lakesides, river banks that are teeming with life, and the haunting fragrances of sweet grass, meadowsweet and damp, decaying leaf mould.

The garden is designed as a memory map, a way for us to find ourselves if we get lost. By recalling our true selves – the way we were as young children – and by holding that memory, we can find our way back to nature, back to the place that nourishes us and supports us to follow our destiny.

THE STOLEN CHILD BY WB YEATS

Where dips the rocky highland
Of Sleuth Wood in the lake,
There lies a leafy island
Where flapping herons wake
The drowsy water rats;
There we've hid our faery vats,
Full of berrys
And of reddest stolen cherries.
Come away, O human child!
To the waters and the wild
With a faery, hand in hand,
For the world's more full of weeping than you can understand.

Where the wave of moonlight glosses
The dim gray sands with light,
Far off by furthest Rosses
We foot it all the night,
Weaving olden dances
Mingling hands and mingling glances
Till the moon has taken flight;
To and fro we leap
And chase the frothy bubbles,
While the world is full of troubles
And anxious in its sleep.
Come away, O human child!
To the waters and the wild
With a faery, hand in hand,
For the world's more full of weeping than you can understand.

Where the wandering water gushes

From the hills above Glen-Car,

In pools among the rushes

That scarce could bathe a star,

We seek for slumbering trout

And whispering in their ears

Give them unquiet dreams;

Leaning softly out

From ferns that drop their tears

Over the young streams.

Come away, O human child!

To the waters and the wild

With a faery, hand in hand,

For the world's more full of weeping than you can understand.

Away with us he's going,

The solemn-eyed:

He'll hear no more the lowing

Of the calves on the warm hillside

Or the kettle on the hob

Sing peace into his breast,

Or see the brown mice bob

Round and round the oatmeal chest.

For he comes, the human child,

To the waters and the wild

With a faery, hand in hand,

For the world's more full of weeping than he can understand.

This design was an effort to recreate the timeless, serene lake atmosphere of the poem. I drew a picture of this image in my mind – a lake surrounded by untamed shoreline, a native ecosystem planting, and a path meandering through the lake. Very simple. The path was intended as a portal that allowed the visitor to find their way through the veil that separates our world from the world of magic and spirit, so I lined the path with large stones to strengthen the feeling of its being a gateway. The path led to a mossy island with lots of trees and shrubby plants.

If you look more closely, you'll see that part of the island was actually a sleeping woman sculpted out of the earth and covered with 'years' of growth – mosses, liverworts, ferns, mossy pearlwort and their allies. Rough stepping stones led the visitor to a clear space by the woman's head where they could sit and rest on some upended tree stumps. Here they were invited to whisper their wishes into her ear. The invitation to whisper their innermost wishes was intended to open a channel and trick that child-like energy out of the visitor's heart.

Even the most hard-hearted adult couldn't help but say a wish, even if only quietly, or to themselves if they didn't have the courage to lean over and whisper into the ear of the earth itself. It was a simple ploy but it really affected people. They got pulled through the veil and into another dimension, if only for a few moments.

Using ancient symbols

A garden using the symbol of the tree of life

This particular symbol chased me around for a while, often turning up in unexpected places. Eventually I had a vivid dream that helped me understand it.

It was dark in this dream and the land had been destroyed, as if there had been a nuclear holocaust. I could taste fear and pollution in the air, and rubbish was being violently blown about by the wind. There was no life anywhere. I stood at a crossroads in a grey, run-down, industrial cityscape. Several paths of various textures diverged from where I was standing. I chose to walk down a twisted old wooden path because it felt familiar. The path itself was an object of peculiar beauty.

It had been formed over a long period of time, as if many yew trees had woven their roots into spirals and waves to knit the path. (The yew is a symbol in itself. It is said to be the tree of our ancestors, containing all the knowledge and wisdom of those who have gone before us.)

I followed this path down a hill and under a motorway flyover to where a river with a dangerous-looking channel of dark, deep water rushed silently past. On the other side of the river the land was pristine, the sun illuminating a beautiful countryside scene. It was a quintessential Irish landscape with old and twisted fairy woods of hawthorn, oak and hazel, stone walls heavy with moss, and lush, hilly green fields. The field directly opposite me in this magical world of light and life was bounded on three sides by stone walls, and on the closest side by the river. I knew immediately that I was looking across at the grave of my ancestors.

As I watched the field from my grey riverside, large vulva-shaped plant shoots started growing out of the ground. From these shoots numerous ethereal screaming women emerged like smoke coming out of a chimney. There were warrior types, fairy types, crones and witches, all roaring a war cry. The sound of the army got louder and louder until it became overwhelming. The women swirled around me like a thick fog, screaming angrily at me, until I couldn't see or hear anything but blurs and noise. Then it stopped abruptly.

I opened my eyes in the dream and realized I was now standing on the other side of the river, alone in the sunny, lush and ancient field that housed my ancestors, looking back at the desolate landscape where I had been. A colourful band of warrior women were stoically standing across the river looking back at me. They had taken my place. They had come from the earth and given me their strength to carry on and fight for my life.

At that time in my life, I interpreted it as a personal rescue dream. It inserted a much-needed rod of strength in my spine to help me carry on. But it also led to me to design one of my favourite gardens based on the tree of life, an ancient universal symbol that describes the world as existing on three levels simultaneously: the world of our ancestors (the roots), the world of spirit (the crown of the tree), and the world we live in (the earth level where the tree emerges from the ground).

Concept for the tree of life garden

This tree of life garden is a moving meditation. It is a simple way for people to access the knowledge and guidance that is always there for us. The Native Americans referred to this otherworldly support as 'father sky' and 'mother earth'. The world of spirit is found in the sky above, in the world of our ancestors, and in the powerful, intelligent and nurturing energy of the earth.

Our ancestors believed that we existed in three different realms of being at the same time. Their concept of time was hazy and to explain their belief they used the image of a tree divided into three: the roots, the trunk and the crown.

The roots: the realm of our ancestors in the earth beneath us. This includes all the generations who have come before us. The belief was that our ancestors are still with us, although they cannot be seen in our realm any more. Their knowledge and experience helps to ground us and give us the strength and wisdom to fulfil our path in life.

The trunk: the earth realm where we live and breathe. This realm was believed to be like a blank canvas, full of potential.

The crown: the realm of spirit. Here we can draw on the higher powers of the spirit world for guidance and inspiration. If we listen to this guidance, we will walk an enchanted path throughout our lives – safe, secure, healthy and happy.

The tree of life garden is an interactive garden that acts like a meditative journey. Wild places in nature allow us to connect with the earth and feel that quiet place within us that is safe from the fears that keep us from moving forward. From this place we have unlimited potential. We can draw inspiration from above and bring those dreams into reality.

Tree of Life Garden, master plan

Tree of Life Garden, perspective drawings, with/without trees

THE JOURNEY

You enter the garden through the realm of the ancestors. The path slopes down into a dark, mossy area filled with ferns and mushrooms. This 'subterranean' garden is strongly atmospheric, as if one were in the realm of roots and soil. It is shaded by a thick canopy of hazel trees and bordered by a high hedge of yews. These trees are associated with the knowledge of our ancestors and the cycle of life and death. Along this path you are invited to take a smooth black pebble from a bowl and hold it with you. This stone represents the strength and support offered to us by our ancestors to help us achieve our potential. You now pass through a gateway into the earth realm, a clear and simple space.

However, you do not linger there. You are then guided to move through another gate to the crown of the tree, into the realm of spirit, a dreaming place.

This garden is protected by a high stone wall, old and draped with ferns and wild flowers. Within the stone walls, the earth is sculpted into hills and mounds and carpeted in sea thrift, thyme and chamomile, all clifftop and mountaintop plants native to Ireland. You are invited to climb some stone steps to the sky garden at the top of the highest mound. Here you are asked to take a smooth white pebble from a bowl, then to lie on the earth, which is covered thickly with chamomile (a plant associated with dreaming), and infuse the pebble with your innermost dreams as you rest there inspired by the world of spirit above you.

Afterwards you climb on a slide to come down from this dreaming place, emulating the way one wakes up from a sleeping dream, only to be cast back into the earthly realm. This space consists of a clear circle of grass protected by a grassy mound planted with birch trees. Birch trees carry the energy of rebirth and support for embracing change. You are in an open space of unlimited potential. Then you are asked to leave your two stones in the sculpted bowl in the centre of the area. As the bowl becomes filled with people's dreams, it becomes a more and more powerful place. Leaving your dreams here to manifest, supported by the strength of your ancestors and the energy of nature, you leave the garden and end the journey.

Design element 5: Putting your design on paper

Is fearr réchonn ná iarchonn.
Foresight is better than hindsight.

The first step in creating the actual design is to put your ideas on a sheet of paper. This helps you place all the elements in the right place and work out how large each area should be.

ESSENTIAL TOOLS

- Pencil and eraser
- A4 or A3 pad of paper for taking survey measurements
- Large sheet of paper for transferring the survey information. Depending on the size of your garden space, this sheet may be A4 or A0.
- Long measuring tape. If your garden is large, a 30-50m (100-165ft) tape is helpful, otherwise a smaller tape will suffice.
- Scale ruler. You can buy one of these from an educational supplies or stationery shop. A scale of 1:50 (¼"=1'-0") or 1:100 (⅛"=1'-0") is ideal if your garden is small. If your garden is bigger, then 1:100 up to a maximum scale of 1:200 (¹⁄₁₆"=1'-0") should be used. A scale ruler allows you to draw a small representation of your garden to a fixed scale. A drawing using a scale of 1:50 means that 1 metre on the ground is 50 times smaller on the paper; a drawing with a scale of 1:100 is 100 times smaller on paper than it is on the ground. You don't have to use a scale ruler, but it helps me a lot. I know the exact sizes and shapes of the spaces I am working with, so I can avoid the mistake of designing too much into a given area. It also allows you to hold the integrity of your design on paper and bring it faithfully into reality when it is installed.

THE SURVEY

Carrying out a survey allows you to get to know your garden intimately. It is best to do it yourself if you can manage it, but if your garden is large and you have enough money for a proper survey, then have it done by a professional (your local architect or engineer will know who to recommend). It is difficult to survey a large space or a small, strangely shaped space with lots of existing features, but if your garden is relatively simple and you are up for a challenge, just follow the steps below.

1 Roughly draw the boundaries of the garden and the position and outline of your house and other buildings. Do this on three sheets of paper – it will save your brain from melting later. The sketch can quickly get messy with scribbles and numbers, so it can be difficult to deduce what the numbers refer to when you try drawing it up afterwards.

2 On the first sketch, mark the position of your doors and windows. Sketch in the position of all the other existing features, such as paths, sheds, ponds, rivers, as well as any underground services, such as percolation units, manhole covers, tanks, wires, water pipes and so forth.

3 On the second sketch, mark the approximate positions of the existing trees and shrubs that you will keep. If you are unsure whether or not these plants will be part of the final design, just mark them all in for now. If you are *sure* the plants will go, leave them out.

4 On the third sketch, mark changes in elevation by drawing contour lines. This can be approximate enough. If you are going to dig water retention ditches along the slopes, however, the contour lines will have to be marked out phys- ically on the land before you actually dig them. We'll talk more about these ditches, or 'swales', in the next chapter.

5 The next task is to take all the measurements. This is tedious work so try to choose a comfortable day so you'll be encouraged to keep at it. It's easy to get bored or tired and decide you have taken enough measurements when you have actually barely begun. Using your tape, measure the lines of your boundary,

the opening and position of the entrance to your property, the distance of your house from each boundary, the dimensions of the outside walls of your house, and the position of the windows and doors along the walls. Note all of this on your preliminary sketch.

6 Use triangulation to mark the positions of the various elements on your preliminary and secondary sketch. This means taking a measurement from three different places to the same point. This allows you to find an exact position of a lone tree, for example.

7 Note the distances from the boundary to all outbuildings, walls, paths, ponds, streams and other permanent features. Also locate the existing trees and the spread of their crowns (how far the shade of their branches currently extends, indicated by a circle with an approximate diameter).

You will need a drawing of your existing land so you can visualize a realistic and practical redesign for the space. This is called a base plan, or a base map. Here's how to create one from the sketches you have already made:

1 Take a large sheet of paper and a pencil. If possible, set yourself up outside in the garden. If it's wet – which is more likely than not where I live – find somewhere inside where you can sit at a table by a window that overlooks the garden.

2 Using the measurements you have already taken, draw the land's boundaries to scale. Then draw your house and the other permanent features, including the plants and trees you plan to incorporate into the final design. If there are changes in elevation, mark them using contour lines. Once this drawing is adequately prepared, draw over the pencil lines in ink. This is your base plan.

INTEGRATING YOUR CHOICES INTO A DESIGN

Now that you have a survey drawing in ink, you can lightly sketch over it in pencil to your heart's desire, erasing early unsuccessful efforts until you are happy with the plan for your future garden. You may want overlay the base drawing with tracing paper or greaseproof paper (also known as baking or parchment paper) for this step to avoid rubbing holes into it. Write your intentions for the land clearly at the top of this plan and make a note of any images, symbols or feelings you want to blend into the land through your design.

Draw as if you were a child. When you shift your intentions and interactions into a youthful headspace, you will be able to remember your dreams more clearly along with the things that excite your soul today.

Place your chosen patterns, symbols and intentional spaces into your survey drawing. Keep them as small as possible for now. You may find that you don't have enough space for everything.

Using a bag of flour or colourful thread, mark the paths temporarily on the land to see if they are too large or too small. The paths should be wider than you think, as the plants will encroach on them over time.

Try not to take up more than half the garden for yourself. Remember, you are sharing the space with other creatures. This isn't easily done in a small yard, but in larger plots the planting should serve nature's needs as much as your own. All you need is a few glades and intentional spaces with access paths allowing you to work with the plants and harvest the produce. The design of your garden will work, once it flows with the energy of nature. It doesn't matter what design you choose, but generally the simpler the better.

DESIGNS FOR GARDENS OF VARIOUS SIZES

Gardens of different sizes pose different possibilities and challenges, and lend themselves to different designs and layouts. In this section, I give examples of designs for gardens of all sizes in the hope that this will help you to learn how to integrate harmonious shapes and symbols into the intentional spaces you will create yourself. Your garden may not be shaped even remotely like these examples, but they should give you an idea of how to pull all the information together.

Small gardens (20-80m² / 215-860ft²)

If you have a small garden, you may have room for only one central space. If that is the case, choose a simple shape for your design and work around that. The rest of the garden should be encouraged to follow its own intention of becoming a balanced ecosystem. The space you use should be modest so you can allocate as much space as possible to nature's own expression.

Medium gardens (suburban-sized gardens, 80-200m² / 860-2,150ft²)

Although a space this size still seems restricted, a good design can work wonders. If you plan properly, it's incredible how much food you can produce.

Large gardens (200-1,000m² / 2,153-10,765ft² and upwards)

With this much land, you may be able to combine several shapes to create more than one intentional space within the garden. Anything larger than this allows you to go altogether wild! For very large plots of land, you can allow at least an acre or two of land to be planted as a forest garden which I describe later in the book. Any excess should be returned to woodland by restoring a multi-layered native planting scheme for a rich and diverse habitat. This is the land's ultimate desire.

Examples of integrated designs

The overall basic intentions for each of the garden designs outlined below are as follows:

- This will be a garden that is alive with the energy of nature; a place where magic is pouring out of every leaf as a result of Nature feeling loved for the beauty of her true self; a place where everything is in balance, and you and the land will feel safe and supported.
- All the food you grow here will be filled with the specific healing and nourishment that you, the land's guardian, and your family require.
- A net of protective energy will surround this land.

Small garden example 1

Intention behind this design
This design is intended to strengthen the bond between the guardian and the land. It is a place to reconnect with nature.

Intentional spaces within the design
- Quiet space for reconnecting.
- Night-time space

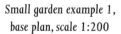

Small garden example 1, base plan, scale 1:200

Symbols and shapes incorporated into this design
- The Vesica Piscis is marked at the entrance to the garden. This can be done using any material of your choice. The shape will be built from wooden flooring, carefully cut to size and shape and laid at different angles, leaving a subtle pattern at your feet. It could also be built using mosaic tiles, colourful pebbles or some other material.

This vesica piscis symbol represents the crossover between the spiritual and the natural worlds, used here to strengthen the intention to co-create this garden with nature. It is a symbol of respect, a recognition that the guardian is aware of the consciousness of the land and the other creatures that flourish there.

- **Moon and sun.** The central mound is in the shape of the moon, which is nestled around the circle depicting the sun. These symbols and shapes represent the male (sun) and female (moon) energies, and the understanding that balance is required for life to exist harmoniously on the land. Having them here is a declaration of intent to create that balance.

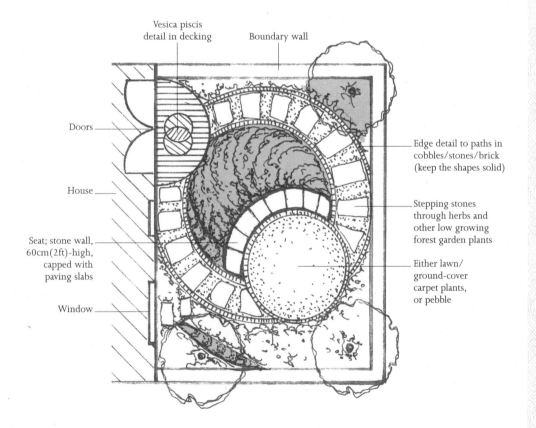

Vesica piscis detail in decking

Boundary wall

Doors

House

Seat; stone wall, 60cm(2ft)-high, capped with paving slabs

Window

Edge detail to paths in cobbles/stones/brick (keep the shapes solid)

Stepping stones through herbs and other low growing forest garden plants

Either lawn/ ground-cover carpet plants, or pebble

Small garden example 1, masterplan, scale 1:100
Key: ■ *= Swales* ■ *= Hügelkultur mounds*

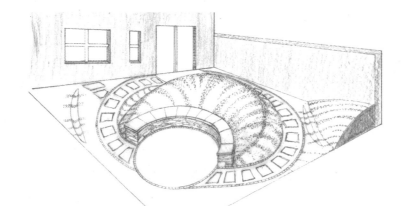

Small garden example 1, landscaped

Small garden example 1, planted

Small garden example 2

Intention behind this design

This design is meant to create a protected space where you and the land can feel safe enough to heal and grow.

Intentional spaces within the design

- Quiet space / meditation / prayer space
- Wishing tree
- Space to draw strength from the earth

Symbols and shapes incorporated into this design

- **Equilateral triangle.** This is the strongest and most stable of all shapes. It is meant to bring strength and support to this garden. Its position underfoot as you enter the garden is a reminder of the threefold, interconnected nature of the universe. Sometimes this triad is expressed as heaven, earth and humankind, or body, mind and spirit. This is intended to remind you that we are never alone. We are always loved and supported.
- **Spiral.** The spiral-shaped path leads you in a clockwise direction to a space in the shape of a circle. The clockwise direction is the direction used for closing energy. Here it is meant to quieten things down, to bring you inwards and into a place of safety. It is a place where you can feel supported enough to begin to heal and grow.
- **Circle.** This shape represents sacred feminine energy. The intent is to create a safe, womb-like presence in the garden.
- **Double spiral.** This stands for balance and harmony and is used here to create the intention of co-creating this garden with nature's energy.

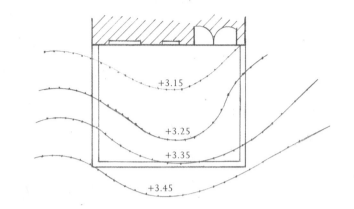

Small garden example 2, base plan, scale 1:200

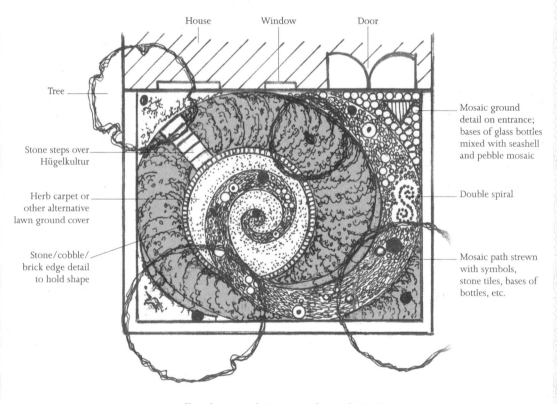

House   Window   Door

Tree

Stone steps over
Hügelkultur

Herb carpet or
other alternative
lawn ground cover

Stone/cobble/
brick edge detail
to hold shape

Mosaic ground
detail on entrance;
bases of glass bottles
mixed with seashell
and pebble mosaic

Double spiral

Mosaic path strewn
with symbols,
stone tiles, bases of
bottles, etc.

Small garden example 2, master plan, scale 1:100
Key: 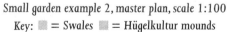 = Swales   = Hügelkultur mounds

Small garden example 2, landscaped

Small garden example 2, planted

Medium garden example 1

Intention behind this design
This design creates a space for meditation. The intention is to bring healing, harmony and balance to the guardian and the garden, and for that healing energy to radiate outwards.

Intentional spaces within the design
- Quiet space / meditation / prayer space
- Wishing tree
- Night-time space

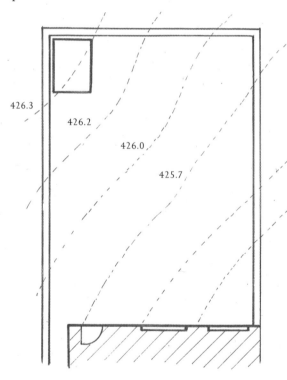

426.3
426.2
426.0
425.7

Above: Medium garden example 1, base plan, scale 1:200
Opposite page: Medium garden example 1, master plan, scale 1:100
Key: ▩ = Swales ▩ = Hügelkultur mounds

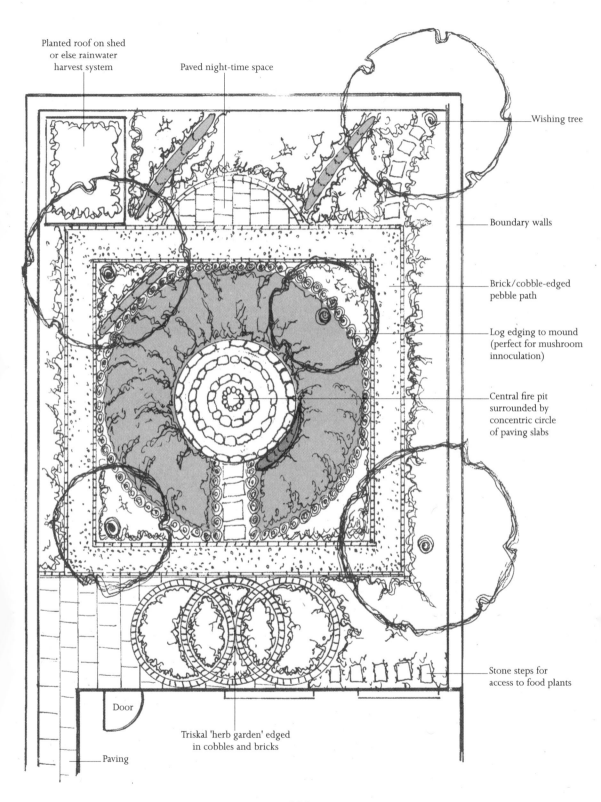

Planted roof on shed
or else rainwater
harvest system

Paved night-time space

Wishing tree

Boundary walls

Brick/cobble-edged
pebble path

Log edging to mound
(perfect for mushroom
innoculation)

Central fire pit
surrounded by
concentric circle
of paving slabs

Stone steps for
access to food plants

Door

Triskal 'herb garden' edged
in cobbles and bricks

Paving

Symbols and shapes incorporated into this design

- **Square.** In sacred buildings the square symbolized the mystical union of the four elements and the attainment of unity. In this example, I used the square with the same intention.
- **Circle within square.** This represents balance.
- **Concentric circles.** The concentric paving slab design evokes a ripple effect. At the centre is a fireplace, a place to reignite our connection with the earth. Circles are formed around a central point, the point of creation. This design is meant to form a sacred space. The fire burns away all the energetic blocks that keep us from healing. The concentric circles acknowledge that all things are affected by everything else. Meditation within the protection of the circle and the square brings healing energy. The concentric circles show that this energy radiates outwards.
- **Three interlocking circles.** The double use of the vesica piscis shape strengthens the bond between the natural and spiritual worlds in this piece of land. The three circles can be interpreted in the same way as the tree of life and the triskel symbols, underscoring the interconnected nature of all things.

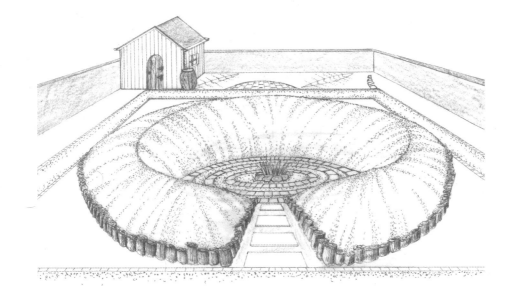

Medium garden example 1, landscaped

Medium garden example 1, planted

Medium garden example 2

Intention behind this design

This design aims to create a magical space filled with child-like energy and fun. The garden will be filled with the energy of creation. Connecting with universal energy will be easy here, and immersing yourself in nature will seem effortless. It is only through our childlike energy that we can truly remember and allow our own truth to emerge.

Intentional spaces within the design

- Quiet space / meditation / prayer space
- Wishing tree
- Night-time space

Symbols and shapes incorporated into this design

- **Spiral.** The spiral symbol that moves in an anticlockwise direction in the lawn will open the flow of energy to this garden.
- **Circle.** The circle, which is repeated throughout the garden, demonstrates that the sacred feminine energy will be encouraged, nourished and embraced here.
- **Three interlocking circles** or triple spiral (another version of the triskele). The triskele, like the tree of life, reminds us that we are supported by the world of spirit and the world of our ancestors. The Native Americans phrased this beautifully: "Father sky and mother earth co-create and support us, the children, to dream up our own worlds."

Night-time space; wooden
seat, paved circles with
cobble or brick edge detail

Stepping stones for access
to food forest and leading
to wishing tree

Spiral of flat field stones
through an alternative
lawn/ground cover/moss

Door

House

Shed with
planted roof

Stone steps over
mound for access
to roof

Pebble/mulch path

Edging of stone keeps the
shapes solid and flowing

Medium garden example 2, master plan, scale 1:100
Key: ▨ = Swales ▨ = Hügelkultur mounds

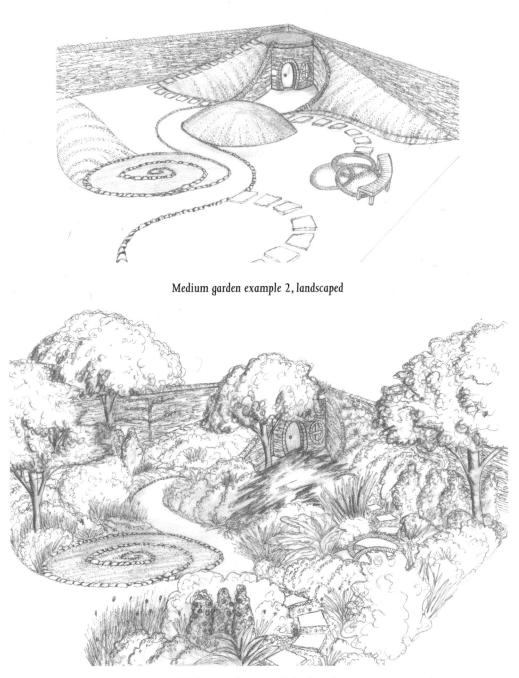

Medium garden example 2, landscaped

Medium garden example 2, planted

Large garden example 1

Intention behind this design

This garden space intends to create a strong flow of creative energy. It will support the flow of abundance and the manifestation of ideas, wishes and dreams.

Intentional spaces within the design

- Quiet space / meditation / prayer space
- Releasing place
- Wishing tree
- Night-time space

Symbols and shapes incorporated into this design

- **Spiral.** The main path leads you in a spiral to a magical circle with a wishing tree at the centre. The anticlockwise (opening) direction indicates that the doorway to the universal flow of energy is open to you when you post your wishes or otherwise explain what you want to manifest.

- **Star.** A star shape is enclosed in a double circle with another circle at the centre, indicating that this is meant to be a protected space. Creativity comes from the friction created between two opposites. Since ancient times, the six-pointed star has represented the union of opposites. This space acknowledges that we are already the result of creativity and that every intentional thought we have is supported from above (spirit) and below (the ancestors). This space, which has a fire pit at the centre, is designed as a place to contemplate what we want to manifest. It also provides us with a space for letting go. It offers us a chance to write down our worries and fears, then release them by burning the notes. When we set free emotions, it allows room for our wishes to grow and take up residence within us.

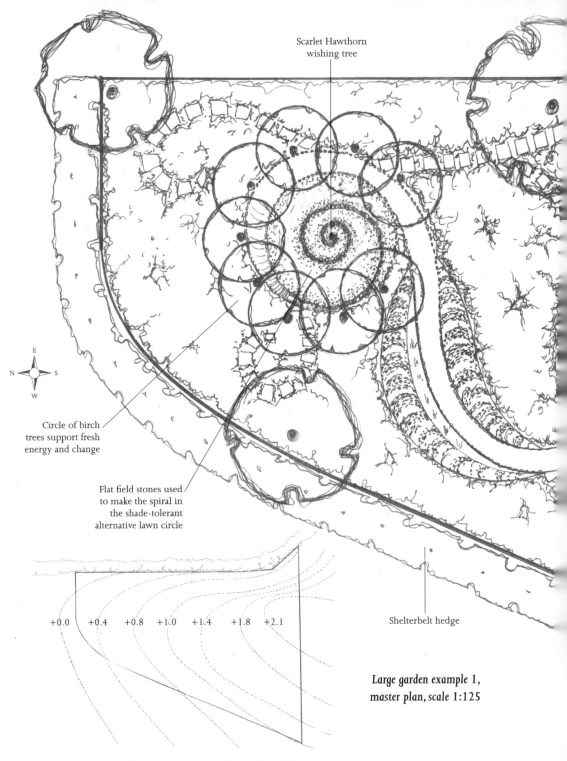

Scarlet Hawthorn
wishing tree

Circle of birch
trees support fresh
energy and change

Flat field stones used
to make the spiral in
the shade-tolerant
alternative lawn circle

+0.0   +0.4   +0.8   +1.0   +1.4   +1.8   +2.1

Shelterbelt hedge

*Large garden example 1,
master plan, scale 1:125*

Large garden example 1, base plan, scale 1:500

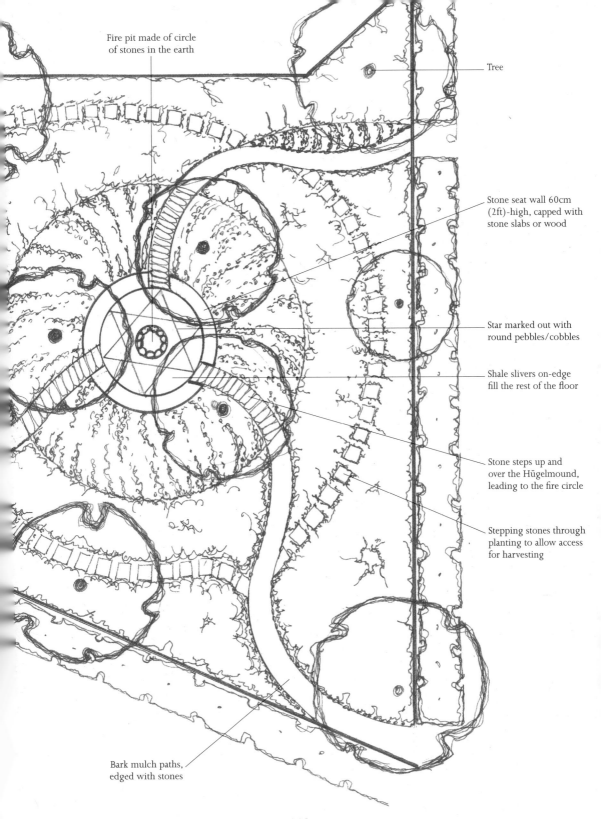

Fire pit made of circle
of stones in the earth

Tree

Stone seat wall 60cm
(2ft)-high, capped with
stone slabs or wood

Star marked out with
round pebbles/cobbles

Shale slivers on-edge
fill the rest of the floor

Stone steps up and
over the Hügelmound,
leading to the fire circle

Stepping stones through
planting to allow access
for harvesting

Bark mulch paths,
edged with stones

113

- **Triskele.** The three paths leading away from the fire area represent the triple spiral symbol. It strengthens the star shape to support the energy of manifestation. The triskele, like the tree of life, reminds us that we are supported by the world of spirit and the world of our ancestors. This is my own interpretation of that symbol. You can interpret in it any way you wish. Some symbols have more than one application.

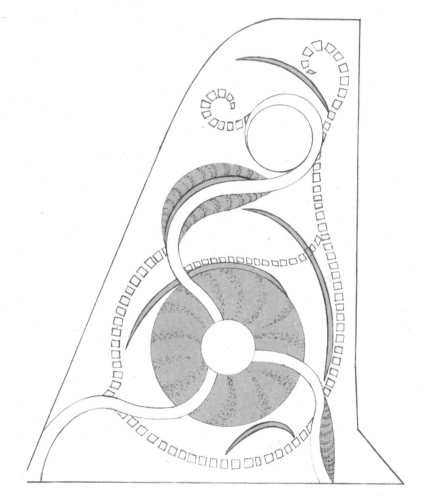

Large garden example 1
Key: ▓ = Swales   ▓ = Hügelkultur mounds

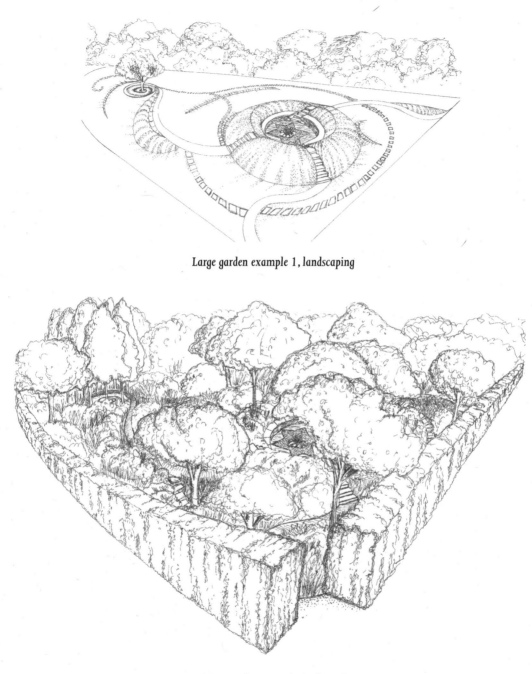

Large garden example 1, landscaping

Large garden example 1, planted

Large garden example 2

Intention behind this design

This garden is intended to be a space to reconnect with yourself and with nature. I designed a number of hills and mounds in this layout, believing that the height would add a feeling of protection.

Intentional spaces within the design

- Quiet space / meditation / prayer space
- Wishing tree
- Night-time space

Symbols and shapes incorporated into this design

- Cross This symbol represents the intersection of heaven and earth and the promise of harmony through the balance between the two. The vertical line represents the spiritual, masculine principle, while the horizontal line stands for the earthly, feminine principle.
- Circle The fireplace is within a circle that is built on a true line with the vertical line of the cross. The circle represents unity and wholeness. In this design, lighting a fire is intended to reignite our connection to the source. The centre of the garden is a circular shape within another circle. It is meant to open a channel of communication with the universal energy and offer access to the wishing tree. With those channels open, it becomes possible to manifest your wishes in this world.

Remember, the design of your garden must resonate with you and you alone. You have to feel that it's right because you are the land's guardian, the collaborative spokesperson for your needs and the needs of the garden. Therefore, there is no need to copy any of my designs, although you can of course, if it suits you. I encourage you to see my designs as examples of simple shapes and patterns that have the capacity of healing both human beings and the earth.

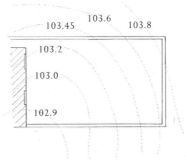

Large garden example 2, base plan, scale 1:500

Large garden example 2, perspective detail

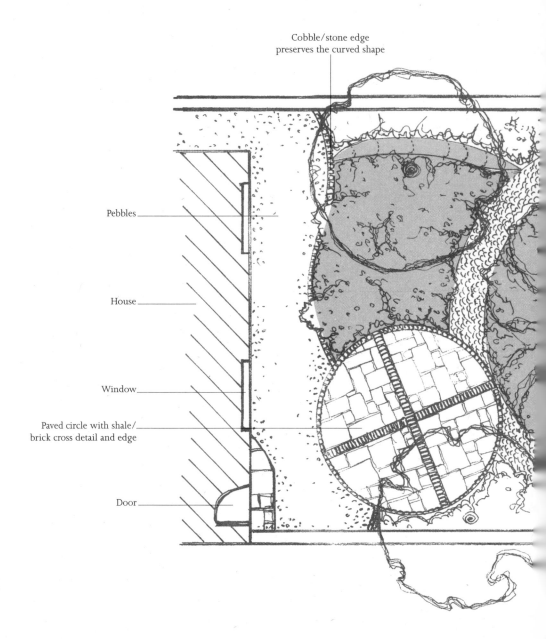

Cobble/stone edge
preserves the curved shape

Pebbles

House

Window

Paved circle with shale/
brick cross detail and edge

Door

Large garden example 2, master plan, scale 1:100
Key: 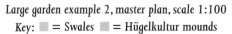 = Swales ▨ = Hügelkultur mounds

Stone shed with
planted roof

Wishing tree

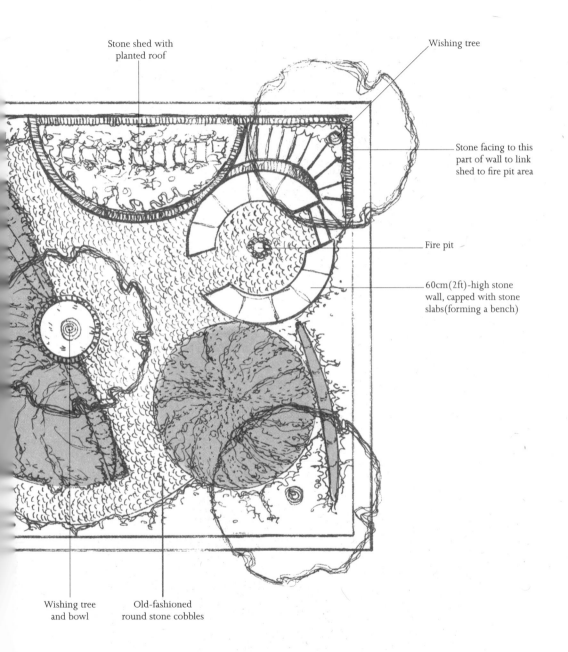

Stone facing to this
part of wall to link
shed to fire pit area

Fire pit

60cm(2ft)-high stone
wall, capped with stone
slabs(forming a bench)

Wishing tree
and bowl

Old-fashioned
round stone cobbles

The Forest Garden

Anáil na beatha an t-athrú.
Change is the breath of life.

he land was very different when I was young. The methods of farming were gentler then, as industrial farming hadn't yet been completely embraced and the earth was still teeming with life.

One fine afternoon in May, I went wandering from my parents' farm and made my way to a favoured little field some distance from the house. This particular field was bordered and enclosed on all sides by spiky gorse bushes, thorny brambles, foxgloves, fuchsias, crab apples, blackthorn and sweet-scented hawthorn trees.

While walking on my short, plump legs towards the centre of the field, I remember turning round to look behind me, because I had the feeling I was being watched and saw that the gap through which I had entered had completely disappeared. It was as if the trees and shrubs had moved tightly together and the entrance had been swallowed up. There was no way out of the field any more and I felt frightened and confused.

At first I spent what seemed like a long time shouting for my mum and dad, and searching for a way to get out. Eventually, though, I became distracted by the sunshine, the happy chatter of the hedgerow birds and the familiar, intoxicating perfume of the hawthorn blossom. The forest of grass beneath my feet was busy with creatures of all kinds – creepy-crawlies and tiny dancing butterflies. The trees and plants were bursting with life. I could feel their individual presence, their unique personalities. They all seemed animated and slightly exaggerated, as if they were vying for my attention. Certain bushes were shimmering and preening. Some of them seemed soft and benevolent, while others appeared curious, if not slightly formidable.

Eventually, I forgot about being scared and sat down in the grass to soak up the sun and the magic. There was a feeling of comfort around me that seemed playful, almost childlike, and very familiar. The emotion I experienced there was somewhere between tickles and giggles. It had the sense of pure joy simmering beneath it.

Nothing else special happened that day, as far as I can remember. Time passed and I became familiar with my ancestor's land and its inhabitants. Eventually, a neighbouring farmer's daughter shouted a greeting to me from the other side of the hedge and the spell was broken. I looked around and noticed that the gap in the field had been restored, so I left and wandered home.

Years later, I recounted this story to my dad. He said the same thing had happened to his grandfather in that same field. Years before, it had been known locally as a fairy field. The experience I had that day changed me, and it has informed everything I have done in my life since, including my garden designs and my understanding of nature. I spent most of my years as a garden designer trying to recreate the atmosphere I had met that day. However, it turned out that there were three ingredients to that particular magic potion: up until recently I had only been working with two of them – intention and design.

However, I finally understood that the third magic component is a familial bond with the land I belong to. What I met in the field that day when I was young, was love. The love and curiosity of a supportive family. I felt a longing for the land and the plants to spend time with me.

Forging an Alliance

Mol an óige agus tiocfaidh sí.
Praise the young and they will blossom.

Once you have completed the healing and design work on your land (see Chapters 1 and 2), the foundations are in place and your intentions are deeply held by the land. The next step is to address the land's needs alongside your own.

Each individual patch of land longs to evolve into a healthy, self-sufficient grown-up, the same as any child. Even without your presence as guardian, the piece of earth you are working with has a strong intention of its own – a fierce need for stability and growth. It has the core intention of working towards harmony, balance and health.

It's just plain silly to work against the intention the land has for itself. Most of our gardening energy is spent trying to stop our gardens from becoming what they want to become. We call it 'maintenance', and a 'low-maintenance' garden is one that brutally smothers life out of the land. If we work to facilitate the land's needs, managing it just enough to allow our own expression and requirements to be part of the process, we are working within the flow of life.

Maturity is reached when nature is allowed to move through all the various stages of succession until it has settled into a balanced ecosystem. Most land that has been inhabited by people (apart from landscapes such as savannahs, wetlands and flood plains) would naturally revert to woodland over time, if allowed to do so. Forests have evolved over millions of years to become the most efficient and balanced growing system possible.

Land *can* bond with the people who work with it, but that doesn't mean it always does. The special relationship between you and your land is the same as the bond that develops between a parent and a child. The parent can choose to love, cherish and support the child, or treat the child harshly and without respect. The quality of their bond will be forever shaped by the quality of love, care and attention the parent puts into it.

Cleared land is like a mirror: it reflects the love and attention it receives from us. Children, in large part, develop their self-image through their interactions with their parents. In the same way, if land receives the message that it is valued only as long as it looks pretty, it will try to contort itself to wear those ill-fitting garments you may insist on as the standard for beauty. But I guarantee, it will not want to stay clothed in an enforced planting scheme of colourful annuals, lavenders and roses (for example) forever. It will inevitably burst out of the seams you have imposed – sometimes gently, sometimes not – and its true character will emerge.

The land simply cannot help itself; that is its nature.

When walking through woodland, have you ever felt uncomfortable, as if someone was watching you? You might also have noticed an unsettling undercurrent of distrust and anger. It can feel unnerving, even dangerous. These are the dark woods from which frightening fairy tales are made. They are wild woods, with no good memories of healthy relationships with humans. You are not trusted here; not welcome.

Alternatively, in a happy, healthy forest where land has been treated with respect and has been allowed to pursue its destiny, you will experience the opposite sensation. There is a special energy about such forests that has both light and magic. It feels similar to the exhilaration children feel at Christmas time – less intense perhaps, more of a stable joyful undercurrent. People have been a positive factor in the growth of these woods; here you will find sanctuary.

Wild places that have regained their natural form (or were never cultivated to begin with) can be likened to mature adults: they are independent, solid beings that have a strong character and life force. However, when land is stripped of its natural covering and its soil is mechanically disturbed, it becomes vulnerable, as if it were an infant again. Its established, complicated structures and relationships are removed, and it is left alone and naked, without the ground networks that support and nourish each other. When that happens, the land must depend upon you, the person who is in control of its immediate destiny.

If left alone in that condition, the land would eventually find its way back to maturity, but you can and should aid the process. By encouraging that 'child' to become what it wants to become, a strong bond between you will naturally emerge … *and this is where the magic lies.*

Over time, like any living being, the land will recover, even if that means limping along in a weakened and damaged state for a long period of time. It will re-establish the community of plants and microorganisms that support and nourish each other until it becomes self-sustaining again – an intuitive, diverse, unified and powerful piece of land. But like the dark woods that feel so uncomfortable, it will not trust people as easily any more.

For me, this is a missed opportunity.

Listen

Is gaire cabhair Dé ná an doras.
God's help is nearer than the door.

Co-creating a garden with nature involves lots of listening. Careful observation and understanding about which plants the land is willing to support, and which ones it isn't. This is key. The aim is to achieve harmony and balance. Working with rather than *against* your land is vital, your overall goal being to restore health to the land.

If you live in a harbour town or city, the true nature of the land may well be a floodplain or wetland system. In these situations, I encourage you to work with the land as if it were once a woodland site. The garden will still develop a strong sense of self-worth as it moves towards becoming a stable and healthy system, but you will have to support it by providing some of the ecological services it cannot provide for itself.

Each garden must be treated as an individual – there is no one-size-fits-all recipe for success. Every piece of land has its own tribal associations, with plants that are native to that particular environment as well as 'blow-in' plants that will comfortably fit in. Of course, natural factors, such as the availability of water, microclimate, soil type and topography, will determine the community of plants your garden will support. The existence and general health of pollinators, inverte-brates and wildlife are also important factors.

It is very difficult to imitate nature. It takes time, patience, and a deep understanding of the land that can only come from familiarity. But surely this is better than suffocating the land with concrete and herbaceous borders? That method tends to be fast and convenient, and may be more accepted by our culture and the gardening industry, but it doesn't encourage an intimate relationship between you and the land – or any connection at all, for that matter.

If nature is left to its own devices, and without imbalances in the ecosystem such as the overpopulation of hungry deer or an infestation of rabbits, it will reclaim its territory and become woodlands once more. Eventually, I realized that recreating a woodland wasn't feasible for most smaller gardens, so I wondered how best to allow the land to become what it wanted to be while still serving the guardian's needs.

I Never Liked Planting Plans

Designing the planting layout for a garden always felt wrong to me, even alien. I longed to recreate the lushness and complexity of wild places in my gardens, but the typical planting designs just didn't allow me to do that. I was irritated by the bland, sweet-shop selection of plants that was available, and distressed by my clients' requests for unnatural combinations of colours, textures and form.

All I ever wanted to achieve was the sensual simplicity found in a mossy woodland or a dancing grassy meadow. In the end, I began trying natural planting schemes to create truthful atmospheres in my gardens. It helped a little, but it still didn't quite do the trick.

Creating what I call 'ecosystem-planting schemes' is not an easy task. You cannot produce a fully detailed planting design on paper for this of type of garden. In one square metre of earth, there might be 50 or more different types of plants all layered atop one another. It's a constantly changing and mutually supportive community.

Gardening like this involves having an intimate relationship with nature. No college degree is necessary; in fact, for this type of garden it is probably a waste of time, as formal schooling may actually block your ability to hear the subtle voices of the land.

My way is a learn-as-you-go approach that teaches you first-hand about natural patterns and the complexity of life. You will begin to learn about local plant associations and get to know your land's microclimate. As helpful as these lessons are, nothing is more important than what you learn intuitively by listening directly to the land.

When I met new clients as a garden designer, I had to accept that few of them had the time, energy, or even interest, in learning to garden this way. Still, creating planting designs that were in harmony with nature was clearly the way forward for me. I decided the most ecologically beneficial garden just *had* to be one that mimicked a woodland glade, but there was still one more piece of the puzzle that was missing: growing our own food.

Grow Your Own

Nil aon tinteán mar do thinteán féin.
There is no fireside like your own fireside.

The environmentally sound future of planting design involves producing our own food within a balanced, self-sustaining ecosystem. We can do this by restoring land that is currently given over to unproductive landscapes. In the United States alone, more than 40 million private acres are planted with grass lawns. This is horrifying, to be sure, but it also reveals the opportunities that exist by restoring that one habitat alone.

Eventually, we will all return to local, sustainable living. I don't believe we will have a choice.

Mostly, people stopped growing food themselves less than a hundred years ago. Vegetable gardens were replaced with lawns, which gradually became symbols of status. It was a way of saying to neighbours, "Hey, look at how wealthy we are! We don't even have to use our land to grow our own food!"

People have become way too separated from the production of their food and have come to depend on processed food and food produced on industrial farms. Over the years, this has led to a general decline in physical and emotional well-being. Our food is filled with hormones, agricultural chemicals, genetically modified organisms, and various concoctions that were created in a laboratory. It is not real food but a combination of 'food-like' substances. Our current system of food production is poisoning us, our farmed animals, the land, the water and the air. That human beings are getting sicker and sicker is a reflection of the earth's ill health. It is slowly dying from those self-same chemicals we are ingesting ourselves.

As above, so below. We are simply a mirror image of each other, the land and us. That connection is deep and mysterious, and only becomes apparent upon close observation and contemplation. We have objectified most of our land; used and abused it. Land is the embodiment of feminine energy, and our treatment of it reflects the way women have become objectified, used and abused throughout the world. Balance needs to be restored.

Our modern landscapes are gradually becoming depleted of diversity and character, forced into simplistic, unsustainable systems, such as farmlands deadened with monoculture crop systems, restrained urban parks and disciplined gardens. (Similarly, I've noticed, many of the people who populate such landscapes are becoming suppressed and unvaried.)

Most of our native edible plants have been forgotten. In Ireland alone, there are approximately three hundred plants growing in the wild that used to be eaten for food. These days people don't even bother to pick the fat, juicy blackberries that grow by the sides of the road. Ecosystems with a diversity of native plants, which were once so varied and widespread, have now dwindled to isolated, threatened islands – and even those small pockets are under pressure.

There are 80,000 species of edible plants in the world, yet fewer than 20 species provide 90 per cent of our food. Large expanses of land devoted to single crops increase the dependence on chemicals and intensive methods of cultivation, bringing the added threat of chemical-resistant insects and new diseases.

At first, combining ecosystem design with the idea that we needed to grow our own food presented an enigma for me, because the two types of gardens traditionally required two separate areas. It just never felt right to mix them. Then I had my personal 'eureka' moment. I came across a simple template that encompassed both these qualities. It involved developing natural woodlands that also produced an abundance of food in a diverse, chemical-free environment. Maybe there *was* hope after all!

Forest Gardening

Forest gardening is a method of producing food by replicating a woodland system. You are not exactly gardening in a natural forest, but developing a multi-tiered woodland of your own making. Initially it sounded unrealistic to me, especially for someone who has a small garden, but after I looked into it and did some research, I realized it was a simple, gentle and productive system of pure genius for gardens large and small.

Forest gardening is by no means a new idea; it is simply a new name to describe what ancient cultures practised for thousands of years throughout the world. The three-part 2011 British TV documentary series *Unnatural Histories*, produced by the BBC, investigated some of the world's most iconic 'wild' places and showed that they were not pristine after all, because they had been moulded by the activity of human beings. One episode, which investigated the Amazonian rainforests, maintained that large areas had been shaped by humans for more than 11,000 years through practices such as forest gardening. The inhabitants had identified plant species that bore food, or had medicinal or other practical uses, and encouraged these species to grow. Those that responded well to human intervention thrived in even greater numbers, while others died out. The overall effect was that the landscape became even more diverse and abundant than it had been before.

In the process of tending the forest in this way, they created 'black earth' soils, which are among the most fertile in the world. These soils are only present in the inhabited areas of the Amazon rainforest, where forest gardens were created. Those areas supported large populations before the Europeans arrived.

These ancient woodland management systems still exist in isolated pockets of the world. For example, in northern Tanzania the Chagga people still survive by cultivating versions of the natural woodland ecosystems, and the Indian state of Kerala has over three million forest gardens, which they refer to as 'home gardens'.

Creating a forest garden is a responsibility, a dedicated effort to support the land to develop strength, maturity and independence. By emulating natural woodlands, we can grow a diversity of plants such as fruit and nut trees, interplanted with smaller trees, shrubs, berries, herbaceous plants, ground covers and vines. This is a method of planting that weaves plants into a sustainable network of beneficial relationships. The system emphasizes perennial plants, self-seeding annuals and plants that fix nitrogen. Forest gardening makes it possible to produce enough fruits, nuts, seeds, leaves, roots, vegetables and sometimes even fuel to last the entire year. You don't have to use native plants exclusively, but they should be included to support the re-establishment and integrity of the local ecosystem. You can mix in exotic plants, if you like – just try not to include plants that might grow so strongly they will become difficult to control.

While you *can* grow a forest garden nearly anywhere in the world, it is easiest to do so in areas where the natural vegetation is deciduous forest. The thick vegetation smothers weeds, renews the soil, and keeps it vibrant through self-mulching and perhaps a little mulching help from you. This system also ends the need to till the soil or provide irrigation.

Careful thought is applied during the design phase to ensure the forest garden will be self-sustaining – that is, it will produce everything it needs by itself and require a minimum of human maintenance. It takes a lot of work to install the garden and shepherd it until the garden is mature enough to manage on its own, but no more than a conventional garden. And, unlike a conventional garden, there is light at the end of the forest-garden-maintenance tunnel.

Approach the design phase with an awareness of your own abilities and limitations, and don't be afraid to ask for help! To use a comparable learning curve, I, for one, would have been lost when it came to knowing how to bring up my children without the benefit of practical advice I received along the way. Some people already have the support, knowledge and inner confidence they need to parent successfully on their own. For me, it was more like sink or swim without a lifeboat.

In the same way, some of you will be able to take on this land guardianship responsibility with full confidence right from the start, without the need for practical support or further explanation. Others will need step-by-step instructions and guidance. You are the only one who knows your inner resources, so make your decisions accordingly.

There are no set rules for a forest-garden planting scheme. Each one will, and should, be different, depending on a person's needs, desires, and the unique environments with which you will be working. I encourage you to explore the native plants in your area and their natural associations, and use as many of these plants as you can. This will help maintain their numbers and diversity in the general landscape and so foster their resilience. Also, notice the plants you are particularly attracted to, and bring some of these into the garden as well.

You don't need a lot of knowledge about forest gardens to successfully create one, but a sincere effort to get to know your own land is required. I consider myself a life-long student. I will *always* be learning because every piece of land I work on is different and each of my clients has unique needs that the garden must supply. The variations are endless.

This book is designed to give you a gentle nudge in the right direction. It's a guide to help you parent your garden through the early years, then on to the 'teens' and early adulthood. My goal is to explain the basic principles, and then push you out of the nest, so to speak, so you and your land can learn to fly on your own.

There is a whole world of information available about forest gardening. There are many 'experts' who have years of experience and have written detailed books about what they did and what they learned. Some of my favourite authors are Patrick Whitefield, Josef 'Sepp' Holzer, Geoff Lawton and Martin Crawford. I also learned a great deal from the natural farming philosophy and practices of the Japanese farmer Masanobu Fukuoka. His first English-language book, *The One-Straw Revolution*, opened my eyes to an entirely new way of seeing the world, and for that I will be forever grateful.

I've also included lists of plants for various uses, and other resources to help get you off to a good start. My plant lists are modest, in the hope that you will not feel overwhelmed, and my methods are often intuitive. My experience is based on a temperate climate, but the approach can be applied anywhere – just select species that are appropriate to the conditions where you live. Have fun, and happy gardening!

Successional Planting

Is fearr réchonn ná iarchonn.
Foresight is better than hindsight.

The development that ecosystems go through from youth to maturity is never simple or predictable. Disturbances such as fires, floods, insect attacks, gales and human activity are a natural part of this dynamic and complex process. With guidance and support, it is possible to develop stable and abundant systems faster than they would have occurred otherwise. In fact, the whole point of designing and installing a food forest is to *fast-track* the process.

The final outcome won't be the dense, tree-shaded canopy of a late-successional forest, but rather a lush mixture of trees, shrubs, perennials, vines and groundcover plants that more closely resembles a mid-succession forest. Installing the planting scheme can happen over a short or long period of time. There are benefits and drawbacks to both approaches.

Short time period: For those with plentiful cash

Placing all your plants at one time is possible if you are in a hurry and money is no object. The composition of plants will change over the years as the tree canopies spread. In the beginning, you will need to plant shrubs and perennials that will grow happily in the sun – this is ideal for annuals, including vegetables. As the trees grow and their canopies spread, the garden will become shadier and perennials will start to dominate.

Installing plants from all stages of succession at one time is great for achieving maximum productivity in the shortest period, but the development and fertility of the soil will lag behind. As the soil-building ground cover and mulching begin to take hold, the plants will respond by growing more vigorously. For most people planting everything at once is only practical for small gardens because it requires so much energy and expense.

Long time period: The road less travelled

Planting your garden over an extended length of time will give you the best long-term results, because you can wait until the land is ready for each succeeding stage. Yes, it may take several years for the garden to achieve its full potential, but production will gradually increase each year. In the meantime, you can use your raised beds to grow lots of conventional vegetables that will provide you with a stable source of home-grown food. You can also establish meadows of wild flowers and clover, which will help build the soil for later on.

Forest Gardening in Steps

Bíonn gach tosach lag.
Every beginning is weak.

Timeline

The following timeline is meant to give you an overview of the stages needed to establish and maintain a forest garden. It is intended for a large garden. For smaller gardens that use smaller plants, the timeline will be shorter.

Year 1

1 Accept that this is not an overnight process.

2 Get to know your soil and amend it as necessary.

3 Build swales (ditches dug out on contour) to drought-proof your land (see page 139).

4 Plan and plant your lines and areas of planting where the aim is to provide shelter (shelterbelts) (see page 147). You may have enough shelter on your land already, or it may take one to three years for your trees and shrubs to grow large enough to provide protection.

5 Build Hügelkultur raised beds to grow sun-loving vegetable crops so you will have enough food to eat right from the beginning. Hügelkultur beds are an alternative raised-bed system (see page 150). An ancient German practice of building dense woodpiles, covering them with soil and sowing with seeds and plants. The wood acts as a slow release system for water and food.

6 Cover the ground with fast-growing nurse crops (see page 156) and green manures.

Years 2-3

As soon as the shelterbelt and nurse crops are providing enough shelter, plant your upper canopy trees, mid-level trees, and the trees you will use for coppicing.

Years 3-10

As the trees grow out and cast more shade, the nurse crops will start dying back. Replace them with shrubs, berries, perennials and vines that are adapted to the shadier environment.

Year 1 onwards

Continue cutting back the plants and mulching to increase soil fertility and sustain the entire system. If the tree canopy becomes too thick and casts too much shade, you may need to thin branches or remove some of the trees to keep the forest garden at the mid-succession stage.

Year 1, step 1: Nurture patience and understanding

Forest gardening is not a quick solution, but rather a long-term commitment. For this type of design to be successful, you need to be willing to put in the energy at the start, then exercise an abundance of patience, acceptance and restraint.

You cannot expect children to develop into adults overnight, and raising your garden is no different. It compels you to get to know your land and form a bond with it, so make that commitment and hold true to it.

Year 1, step 2: Understand your soil

The soil type will largely determine your most appropriate course of action and the type of plants that will thrive there, so it is important that you become acquainted with it as quickly as possible. You might not know how to determine your soil type, but it is easy enough to find someone living nearby – perhaps an avid gardener or a farmer – who will point out its characteristics. The existing cover of native plants will indicate whether you have acid or alkaline soil, but if you don't have the experience to tell simply by looking, ask a local farmer or gardener who does. They could also advise you whether or not the soil needs help in that regard. You could buy an inexpensive soil-testing kit from your local hardware shop or garden centre, I suppose, but those kits are notoriously inaccurate. If you're really stuck, send a sample of your soil to a soil-testing laboratory. A final possibility is to go online, find your local soil survey, and then find your land on the map. A soil survey will reveal everything you need to know about your soil … and more!

Sandy soil, for example, is often seen as problematic because it doesn't hold water or nutrients very well. Unless you initially choose plants that do well in sandy soil, you may end up with weak plants that struggle with insects and diseases. Heavier soils have different benefits and challenges. They are easily compacted, plant roots find them difficult to penetrate, and the circulation of air and water is restricted. However, they do hold lots of water and nutrients. They also have a lower overall temperature, which makes it easier for the plants to survive during the cold winter months.

Almost all of the shortcomings in soils are solved over time by increasing the amount of organic matter in the soil. This is accomplished by not ploughing, growing a ground cover of soil-building plants, and continuous mulching.

Acid or alkaline

In order to achieve a wide variety of plant diversity, you may need to adjust the pH of the soil, as different plants thrive in different soils. The pH is a measure of how acid or alkaline the soil is. pH is simple to measure and usually listed numerically on a scale of 1 to 14. A pH of 7.0 is considered neutral. Acid soils have a pH value below 7.0, and alkaline is above 7.0. Most plants prefer a pH of 6.5-7.0 – where nutrients are most easily available. High acidity or alkalinity inhibits the activity of earthworms and microorganisms in the soil and makes it difficult for certain nutrients to be released to the plants. You can adjust the soil pH in the beginning, but over time the mulch, organic matter and diversity of plants will buffer the pH and bring it back in to balance without further intervention on your part. The ideal soil has a neutral pH, although certain plants prefer more acid soil and others prefer more alkaline conditions.

Of course, you can always ignore the pH issue altogether and continue with your planting scheme. If you build up a substantial litter layer and increase the amount of humus in the soil, over the years the pH will naturally move towards the neutral range, so sidestepping the pH issue may only mean that your garden will take a little longer to establish.

To reduce soil acidity, add lime; to reduce alkalinity, add gardener's sulphur (see table below). However, as the garden develops and the soil becomes rich and complex, these measures will no longer be necessary.

Adjusting soil pH

Existing soil pH	Solution
Lower than 5 (acidic soil)	On a day that is neither too hot nor too cold, mark out 100m² (1,076ft²) sections of ground and spread 9-11kg (20-25lb) of lime on that area. Use the higher amount if the soil is very acidic. Repeat this process a month later.
Higher than 7.5 (alkaline soil)	On a day that is neither too hot nor too cold, mark out 100m² (1,076ft²) sections of ground and spread 4.5-9kg (10-20lb) of gardener's sulphur on that area. Use the higher amount if the soil is very alkaline. Repeat this process a month later.

As I mentioned earlier, some plants, such as blueberries, like acidic soil. You can accommodate this preference by using companion plants, such as conifers, that keep the soil slightly acid or by using lots of acidic plant material, such as pine needles, as mulch.

Heavy clay or wet soil

The amount of drainage in your soil will affect what type of plants you can grow there. If you have a high proportion of clay, or if the area is waterlogged or compacted, you should plant your trees on the side of a berm. Berms are the extracted soil from digging out your ditches on contour. Usually they are simply piled in a long mound at the lower edge of a swale. However, I think these should become hügelkultur beds which will support the plants in a much more dependable way (see page 150). Fruit trees in particular will not grow cheerfully in heavy or wet soil. If you have this type of soil, increase the number and size of the raised beds in your design.

Freely draining or sandy soil

If you have the opposite situation with sandy, excessively well-drained soil, using swales and Hügelkultur beds (see page 150) is also a good solution. Plant the food-bearing trees at the base of the swales and on the lower side of the berms or raised beds, where they will have the most abundant supply of water. Once the forest garden is established, the earth will respond with increased moisture and fertility so your planting options will gradually expand.

Year 1, step 3: Capturing and using water

Permaculturists Geoff Lawton and Bill Mollison, among others, have shown that arid regions and dry, temperate hillsides can be turned into fertile, productive agroforestry farms by sculpting the earth to capture rainwater and storing it in the soil. This avoids the expense and environmental impact of summer irrigation. It also stores water in the subsoil during periods of abundant rainfall so it is available to plants during droughts.

The main method of achieving this is to install swales on sloped land. Most land, even in small gardens will have a gentle slope to them, even if it is not visible to the eye. Contours are lines along slopes with a constant elevation, in other words, they are connected points in your garden that are all at the same level. A *swale* is a ditch that has been dug along these contours in order to catch and store rainwater and preserve the soils from being washed away.

You can't really depend on your eye to dig out the swales on contour. The path of the swale that you create must be dug out along the same level (the same elevation curve of a slope). If you don't accurately pinpoint the contour lines before you dig, then with the help of gravity, the swales will fill up in one part only, the lowest part, making the swale destructive rather than passive. It would cause water to flow out of one point quickly, rather than sit passively along a long stretch of ditch which allows it to be absorbed slowly. To find the swales, you can be very posh and use a laser level, or you can build a simple A-frame level with a plumb line.

Its easy to build your A-frame level with just three pieces of 3'–5' (90-150cm) long cut timber, a level, a few wood screws and bolts and a 5' (150cm) piece of strong string with a stone tied to one end (see Resources).

How to find the level contour lines for your swales

1 Start at one end of your land.

2 Put one leg of the A-frame level down and mark it with a peg.

3 Swing the other leg around, putting it down until you find a place that allows the plumb line to hang over the 'level' mark.

4 Mark this point with a peg again.

5 Lift the first leg and swing it over, keeping the second leg in position, until you find the third level point.

6 Keep walking the A-frame around like this until you have marked out the length of swale you require in this position.

7 Get your spade out and start digging.

Swales slow down the movement of rainwater, allowing it to percolate deep into the soil rather than running off the surface. Swales can be about 30-90cm (1-3') deep and 30-120cm (1-4') wide, depending on the steepness of the slope and the texture of the soil. They are dug either by hand, using pickaxes and shovels, or by using an excavator. Even a small and shallow swale will be beneficial to the health of the general ecosystem.

Swales should be sized and spaced so they can hold all the run-off without overflowing. So on steep slopes and in areas of heavy rainfall, swales need to be spaced closer together. Swales should be wide and shallow in sandy soil, narrower and deeper in clay soil, and their sides sloped to avoid collapse. The excavated earth is piled on the downhill side of the ditches to form berms. Trees, shrubs, perennials and groundcover plants are then installed on and below these raised areas to stabilize them and take advantage of the water that collects in the ground.

The very best place to store water on your land is in the soil, ground water (held in crevices in the upper layer of bedrock) and aquifers (permeable rocks that store and transmit ground water to wells and springs). Unlike conventional irrigation systems, swales require little maintenance once they are built.

Swales are pure magic in arid regions, but they are also an important tool in temperate regions. This may sound like madness to people who have to deal with increasingly damaging annual flooding, but remember that floods are largely the result of deforestation and the removal of wetland ecosystems. By encouraging more vegetation of all kinds, swales help to counteract the devastating effects of flooding and erosion while allowing the ground water to recharge and flow freely again.

I believe that soil loss is the most pressing challenge we face today: greater even than climate change. In 2014, the Food and Agriculture Organization (FAO) of the United Nations calculated that we have only 60 years of plentiful harvests left if we continue to farm using intensive methods. We currently lose millions of hectares of soil each year due to deforestation, ploughing, overgrazing and other careless agricultural practices, which cause fertile topsoil to be swept away by wind and sea.

Planting woodland systems effectively solves the problem of accelerated erosion. The land is always covered with several layers of vegetation, so the rainwater can seep down rather than rushing across the surface and carrying the soil with it. Swales can reduce water run-off by more than 85 per cent compared with bare fields. Using swales in conjunction with the permanent cover provided by a woodland ecosystem is an excellent way to drought-proof your land, prevent its erosion *and* increase its productivity.

If you have enough space, ponds are wonderful additions to any farm or garden, adding to its beauty and benefiting wildlife. Ponds also make it possible to grow speciality crops such as fish and edible water plants, plus they provide a place to swim on a hot summer day.

Even smaller gardens can benefit from water-collection structures. You can harvest the rainwater from paths or rooftops and channel it into mini-swales that are dug on contour through the garden. Contours are not always apparent in a seemingly flat area of land, but there is usually a gradient. Swales planted with rushes and reeds filter the water as they absorb it, so run-off from gutters, grey-water systems, roads and parking areas can be directed to them. Grey water is water from sinks, baths and and showers and it is a resource you should aim to keep in your land as long as you have been using eco-friendly cleaning products. Densely planted swales and reed based overflow ponds clean grey water as it passes through their roots. You can also direct grey water into your swales. If the source of grey water is uphill from your garden, it can be channelled down entirely by gravity. If not, use a solar pump to move it to a storage tank at a higher elevation. If you run the overflow water through a reed bed that has been planted with rushes and reeds over layers of sand and gravel, it will be effectively filtered and cleaned. Again, you'll find plentiful information about how to build one of these clean-flow reed bed systems.

For swales to work properly, they should, in my opinion, always be planted with vegetation. This will stabilize the structures, clean the water and keep the surface cool. I have included a list of good deep rooters below, but you can infill around these initially with a wild-flower meadow mix, or cover them with clover. Just to make sure all of the soil is covered in quickly.

In a larger-scale garden, a nitrogen-fixing ground cover should be planted on the uphill sides of the swales, with trees and shrubs planted below. Over time they will spread shade over the area, reducing evaporation. Eventually, the land around the swales will become oases of greenery.

Plants for swales

The following list gives some of the many examples of swale-friendly plants.

Swale-friendly plants

Botanical name	Common name	Height	Spread	Notes
Butomus umbellatus	Flowering rush	1m (3')	0.5m (1'6")	• Hardy perennial that needs sun.
Carex pendula	Pendulous sedge	1m (3')	0.8m (2'6")	• Hardy perennial that tolerates semi-shade. • The grains are easy to harvest and can be ground into a flour.
Iris pseudacorus	Yellow iris Yellow flag	1.5m (5')	2m (6'6")	• Hardy perennial needing sun or partial shade.
Juncus effusus	Common rush Soft rush	1.5m (5')	0.5m (1'6")	• Perennial that grows in water and is deep-rooting. • Stems are used for weaving, basketry and thatching. In Ireland, the stems were traditionally peeled (except for one green strip left for structure), soaked in oil and used as candles. The fibre inside stems can be used to make paper.
Mentha longifolia	Horse mint	1.5m (5')	Spreads into a thick carpet.	• Deciduous perennial. Happy in wet soils.
Mentha spicata	Spearmint	0.8-1m (2'6"-3')	Spreads into a carpet.	• Deciduous perennial. Happy in wet soils. • The leaves can be used to make herbal tea or as flavouring in many dishes. Mint oils sprayed around window edges will keep spiders and ants out of your house. • Aromatic pest confuser (see page 185)
Phragmites australis	Common reed	3m (10')	3m (10')	• Hardy perennial that enjoys sun or partial shade. • The roots are a good potato substitute, cooked in similar ways. Young shoots, harvested before the leaves form, are delicious when cooked (like bamboo shoots).

Botanical name	Common name	Height	Spread	Notes
Sparganium emersum	Simple bur reed	1m (3')	0.6m (2')	• Hardy perennial requiring full shade, partial shade or full sun.
Typha angustifolia	Small reed mace	3m (10')	3m (10')	• Hardy perennial that needs sun. • The roots are tasty when roasted or boiled like potatoes. The roots can also be dried, ground to a powder and used as a sweet flour substitute.

Black-water treatment for your home

Black water is the term for sewage and waste water from your toilets. The relatively recent practice of pumping human waste into our rivers and seas along with bleach and other noxious chemicals simply *must* stop. Human waste is an invaluable source of fertilizer, which should always find its way back to the land, not into our precious waterways and oceans.

Surely there is a better way than to defecate into clean, treated water and then 'clean' it again using chemicals and vast quantities of energy? If we had to clean our own drinking water at home, I'm certain we wouldn't flush our toilets into it! There is readily available information on how to set up sustainable and ecologically sound methods of managing human waste from our homes so we can safely reuse it. The land is fully capable of accepting this management strategy; our streams, rivers, seas and underground water reserves are not. Perhaps the biggest barrier is that society is not ready to do away with the charade of 'politeness' when it comes to dealing with our own waste, but until we get over this outdated attitude, our environment will continue to suffer.

If you have the space, I recommend creating a specific area for directing and cleaning your own waste, including toilet outflows. This will usually require planning permission, but such systems are increasingly being approved.

A composting toilet is a great option for human waste, and there's a wealth of online information about commercially manufactured products as well as plans for building one yourself. Certainly in Ireland it is currently difficult to find your way through the planning process to get approval for a composting toilet, but it's worth it! I am sure this varies from country to country.

In urban areas, local government councils will eventually have to face the challenge of managing waste in more creative and sustainable ways. Using wetland reed beds for processing waste water on a large scale has been shown to be much more effective than traditional chemical-based treatment plants. Also, reedbed treatment areas become more efficient as the plants mature, whereas present mechanical treatment facilities degrade over time, leading to expensive upkeep. The best part is that reed-bed systems create beautiful, ecologically diverse habitats *along with* the clean water they produce, and they do it at a fraction of the cost. That's what I call a win-win situation.

YEAR 1, STEP 4: SHELTERBELTS

There is no point in planting your garden if the land is on an exposed site, so the first thing you need to do is create protection in the form of a shelterbelt. Once again, patience is required.

Hedgerows are the traditional shelterbelts, but these can be combined with trees and tall shrubs on larger tracts of land. Diverse hedgerows surround your garden with a network of biodiversity that provides a safe habitat for songbirds, pollinating insects, and all manner of wildlife. Mixing hardy native shrubs and trees with fruit trees and nitrogen-fixing shrubs (see page 175) is always a good idea.

Where to place your shelterbelt

Find the direction of prevailing winds. In Ireland, these are usually from the south-west, but we also get very strong winds from the north and east. The wind drives the rain sideways, seemingly from all angles, changing with the seasons and sometimes by the hour. I recently overheard my kids chatting with some pals who had just returned from a holiday in France and were enthusiastically reporting how different it was. One of them excitedly remarked, "Even the rain in France is different. It falls straight down!"

If you are living in an urban situation surrounded by houses, there will be gaps between buildings — alleyways and breaks in walls — that may funnel the wind, creating a 'wind tunnel'. If one of these runs through your garden, you will need to create shelter, or the garden's vigour and productivity will suffer.

Spend some time in your garden getting to know it thoroughly in all seasons. Besides finding wind tunnels, you may also notice frost pockets, large stones or driveways that collect and radiate heat, or buildings that reflect heat and glare. Later, you can design with these things in mind or take measures to modify them.

If your garden is an open field, you should create shelterbelts on all sides if possible. If your land is large, additional windbreaks within the boundaries may also be necessary. This is particularly important in a place such as Ireland, because the strong and changeable winds leave you with nowhere to hide. Depending on your location, the southern boundary may not need as much protection, which is useful as it allows you to grow more sun-loving plants there.

Choosing plants for your shelterbelt

For temperate climates, the table below should provide you with a good starting point. My expertise is in Ireland and England. In other parts of the world you will have different plants of course. Woodland-edge plants tend to be pioneer species that can handle difficult conditions. Species selection for your own land depends on the nature and direction of prevailing winds, soil, climate, elevation, and how close you are to the coast, among other factors. Explore your local area and see which plants can handle winds against all odds. These are the ones to choose. Plants that are fussy will take extra care and may not succeed. As long as the plants are not invasive, a non-native hedge is fine if it allows you to establish a strong defence against the wind and therefore a gentler microclimate.

Some native edible hedgerow plants, such as hawthorn, have been hybridized to create greater production and larger fruits. Do some research to find hybrid varieties that are best at producing food. Even if you don't use the fruits, birds and other wildlife gratefully will. An excellent source of information about plant species for temperate woodland / forest gardens is Plants for a Future (see Resources). They have an amazing database consisting of more than 7,000 plants.

I will indicate which plants are nitrogen fixers. At least 20 per cent of the plant life in your forest garden needs to be able to fix nitrogen, and fruit crops in particular are nitrogen hungry creatures. Nitrogen fixing plants have a symbiotic relationship with certain bacteria on their roots that allow them to absorb Nitrogen gas from the atmosphere and change it into a form that plants can use in the soil. This becomes available to the other plants near them through leaf and root dieback and by making use of these plants as mulching materials.

Shelterbelt options

Botanical name	Common name	Max. height	Notes
Acer campestre	Field maple	10-20m (33-66')	• Clay/loamy/sandy soils. Exposed sites. Wind-tunnel breaks. • Field maple leaves were traditionally used to preserve fruit.
Alnus cordata	Italian alder	15m (49')	• Clay/loamy/wet soils. Exposed sites. • Nitrogen fixer (see page 175).
Alnus glutinosa	Common alder	15m (49')	• Clay/loamy/wet soils. Exposed sites. • Nitrogen fixer (see page 175).
Alnus rubra	Red alder	20m (66')	• Clay/loamy/wet soils. Exposed sites. • Nitrogen fixer (see page 175).
Alnus viridis	Green alder	5m (16')	• Clay/wet soils. Exposed sites. • Nitrogen fixer (see page 175).
Arundo donax	Giant reed	6m (20')	• Wet soils. • Useful for biomass and mulching material, basket making and erosion control. • Edible rhizomes.
Atriplex halimus	Tree purslane	2m (6'6")	• Sandy soil. Exposed coastal sites.
Berberis species	Barberry	1.5-2 m (5'-6'6")	• Loamy/poor soils. Exposed/urban sites. Wind-tunnel breaks.
Corylus avellana	Hazel	4-5m (13-16')	• Loamy/poor soils. Exposed sites.
Crataegus monogyna	Common hawthorn	8m (26')	• Sandy/clay/loamy/poor soils. Exposed coastal sites / urban sites. Wind-tunnel breaks.
Elaeagnus multiflora	Goumi	2-3m (6'6"-10')	• Sandy/poor soils. Exposed coastal / urban sites. Wind-tunnel breaks. • Nitrogen fixer (see page 175).

Botanical name	Common name	Max. height	Notes
Elaeagnus umbellata	Autumn olive	6m (20')	• Clay/loamy/poor soils. Exposed/urban sites. Wind-tunnel breaks. • Nitrogen fixer (see page 175). • Edible fruit and seed. • Invasive in North America.
Euonymus euoropaeus	Spindle tree	3-6m (10-20')	• Clay/loamy soil/sandy soils. Exposed sites.
Garrya elliptica	Feverbush	4m (13')	• Clay/loamy soils. Exposed sites.
Hippophae rhamnoides	Sea buckthorn	1-6m (3-20')	• Sandy soil. Exposed coastal sites.
Ilex aquifolium	Holly	15m (49')	• Clay/loamy soils. Exposed sites.
Ligustrum vulgare	Wild privet	3m (10')	• Clay/loamy/sandy soils. Exposed sites.
Mahonia aquifolium	Oregon grape	1m (3')	• Loamy soil. Exposed sites. • Edible fruits and used for dye making.
Malus sylvestris	Crab apple	10m (33')	• Clay/loamy soils. Exposed sites.
Pinus nigra subsp. maritima	Corsican pine	25m (82')	• Sandy/loamy soils. Exposed coastal sites.
Pinus radiata	Monterey pine	20m (66')	• Sandy/loamy soils. Exposed coastal sites.
Pittosporum tenuifolium	New Zealand pittosporum	10m (33')	• Clay/loamy/sandy soils. Exposed sites.
Prunus avium	Bird cherry Wild cherry	10-15m (33-49')	• Clay/loamy soils. Exposed sites.
Prunus cerasifera	Cherry plum	9m (29'5")	• Clay/loamy soils. Exposed sites. Edible fruits.
Prunus spinosa	Blackthorn / sloe	3m (10')	• Clay soil/loamy/sandy soils. Exposed sites including coastal sites.
Rhamnus frangula	Alder buckthorn	5m (16')	• Clay/wet soils. Exposed sites.
Rosa rugosa	Japanese rose	2m (6'6")	• Sandy/loamy/poor soils. Exposed coastal / urban sites. Wind-tunnel breaks. • Edible hips, jellies, teas, oils.
Rubus tricolor	Chinese bramble (also known as ground-cover raspberry)	2m (6'6") when supported by other plants	• Ground cover under hedges with edible fruit and no thorns. • Blackberries are great too – worth keeping a patch if you have room. However, rampant thorn growth makes them hard to manage in a small garden.
Salix 'Bowles's Hybrid'	Willow hybrid	5m (16')	• Clay/loamy/wet soils. Exposed sites. • Fast-growing straight willow that can be used for living willow structures and basket making..
Salix caprea	Pussy willow	10m (33')	• Sandy/clay/wet soils. Exposed sites, including coastal sites. • Used for basket making,

Botanical name	Common name	Max. height	Notes
Sambucus nigra	Elder	6m (20')	• Clay/loamy/poor soils. Exposed/urban sites. • Wind-tunnel breaks. • Edible fruit, flowers, teas, cordials.
Senecio greyi / *Brachyglottis greyi*	Daisy bush	2.5m (8')	• Clay soil/loamy/sandy soils. Exposed coastal sites.
Ulex europaeus	Common gorse / whin	1.5m (5')	• Sandy/clay soils. Exposed sites, including coastal sites. • Nitrogen fixer (see page 175). • Provides soil stabilization, dyes, and tea from flowers.
Viburnum opulus	Guelder rose	5m (16')	• Loamy/clay/wet/poor soils. Exposed/urban sites. • Wind-tunnel breaks.

Shelterbelt planting and distances

If space allows, I try to plant shelterbelts in a double staggered row. In a small- or medium-sized garden, you may only have room for a single row. If you do have the space and budget for a double row, place the hardier plants in the front line against the wind and the more productive plants on the inside. The shelterbelt plants should not be allowed to grow so tall that they interfere with the amount of light reaching the rest of the garden. In a large garden, plant the trees or shrubs approximately 1-1.5m (3-5') apart to allow them to knit together. You can thin them out later or just let them to do their own thing. In smaller gardens, the plants should be spaced at about 45-60cm (1'2"-2') apart.

A shelterbelt may take a few years to become established, but it will reward you handsomely after that. Remember to keep mulching your shelterbelt plants! It will speed their growth exponentially.

YEAR 1, STEP 5: HÜGELKULTUR RAISED BEDS

I love to change the level of a flat space by sculpting the earth. My favourite pieces of wild land are naturally lumpy and bumpy, and I believe a three-dimensional design always creates a stronger atmosphere. One way of doing that sustainably and within the flow of the land's intentions is by creating Hügelkultur raised beds. This system has been used for centuries in Germany, Eastern Europe and many other places around the world. The word *Hügel* means 'hill' or 'mound' in German, so Hügelkultur means cultivation using raised areas. My friend Claire affectionately refers to them as 'huggels'.

These mounds are the ultimate in raised beds and are quite easy to create. The basic structures are simply piles of woody branches, twigs and tree trunks piled up densely and covered with soil. Over time they provide all the fertility, warmth and water the plants growing in them require, even where the soil is poor. The raised mounds work well on the lower sides of swales in place of berms, but they also work well on their own. The Austrian permaculturist Josef 'Sepp' Holzer has used Hügelkultur beds very effectively on his land in the Alps and has written about them extensively.

The Hügelkultur system is beneficial in several ways. As the wood slowly decomposes, heat is released, giving an extra degree of protection from the cold and effectively lengthening the growing season. The logs become spongy and airy as they decompose, creating the perfect environment for bacteria, fungi and small animals that live in the soil. The logs absorb water during their first winter and spring, activating a sustained release of nutrients. Depending on the size of the wood and type of trees and shrubs used, the flow of nutrients can continue for 20 years or more. Using the vertical space as well as the horizontal is helpful, especially in small gardens, because it creates more surface area to produce food and fodder.

To build a Hügelkultur bed, start by collecting leaves, twigs, branches and logs from your garden. If you don't have enough on site, look for reclaimable wood, fallen fences (untreated), your neighbour's unwanted prunings, and so forth. Pile this material tightly in the shape of the mound you have designed. Make sure you fill the gaps with twiggy material, otherwise it will be difficult to cover with soil. You don't want any four-legged creatures moving into the mounds as a ready-made hotel either, so fill in all of the gaps! Give the pile a good soaking and cover it with at least 10cm (4") of soil. I make these beds in many different shapes, depending on the design and whatever patterns or symbols the land and its guardian needs to express. Hügelkultur beds are especially good for growing annual vegetables on the sunnier sides of the mounds.

In my experience, Hügelkultur beds are too dry in the first year to grow much more than a ground cover successfully, and even that may struggle. They need a full year to settle in and allow the logs to become saturated with water. Once that happens, the leaves and woody tissue begin to decompose, releasing nutrients in a steady stream for years to come, and the logs also act like a slow-release water source for the plant roots. During that first year, you can protect the soil by covering the beds with mulch, straw, compost or another source of organic nitrogen fertilizer, such as seaweed. This will keep the moisture in the wood and stop it drying out which kick-starts the sponge slow-release system after year 1.

Instead of just waiting for the bed to become ready, you can sow seeds of fast-growing green manure crop such as buckwheat, then cover them with a thin layer of compost, organic straw, or strappy leaves such as sedges. This will allow the seeds to germinate through them and grow into a living mulch. Use long, thin branches – hazel twigs bent into U-shaped staples are ideal – to pin the mulch on to the slopes of the bed. Using mulch prevents the soil from washing away until the ground cover spreads over the soil.

In the second year you can install the plants you want to grow, sowing the seeds of ground-cover plants between them. These could be low-growing vegetables, green manure plants, flowers or anything else you feel like growing, just be sure to broadcast them evenly by hand over the entire bed.

One way of distributing the seeds is to encase them in small clay pellets, or seed balls, as advocated by the Japanese farmer and philosopher Masanobu Fukuoka. He mixed the seeds of many kinds of plants together – vegetables, herbs, clover, grains, flowers or whatever he happened to have around – and tossed them into the spaces between his orchard trees. The clay, which was often mixed with humus or compost, protected the seeds from birds and slugs until they were activated by the rain. You really do get a much higher germination rate using this method. Fukuoka used what he called a 'natural design method', which is to say, he simply sowed the seeds and let nature create the design. He never knew exactly which plants would come up where, but the forest garden he created that way was truly miraculous. Fukuoka said that each of those seed balls, some of which contained 40 seeds or more, held within it an entire natural farm: its own universe. It's not exactly what we are doing with our forest garden design, but I find his 'methodless method' to be both ingenious and inspiring.

Hügelkultur beds can also be placed on the lower sides of swales by covering the logs with the soil that was removed from the swale. The logs at the plant roots act as sponges for water, and again become the source of slow-release fertilizer. These raised beds allow you to get through a dry summer without irrigation. You can also bury some of the logs in the ground to make flatter beds. It is very important not to put Hügelkultur beds on contour with swales behind them, on anything other than a gentle slope. Wet wood weighs a lot and it can dangerously collapse downhill after a heavy shower. It would not be structurally sound. So, on anything other than a gentle slope, the Hügelkultur beds must always be perpendicular to the contour lines, or thereabouts.

If you use wood from cedar, walnut or redwood trees, it is a good idea to let them season for a few years before using them, because they contain compounds that inhibit the growth of most plants when they are fresh. Hardwoods break down more slowly than softwoods or coniferous trees, so it is better to have a mixture of the two.

I don't think you should *ever* have to irrigate a plant, especially if you have designed swales into your system. Plant into damp soil and then mulch heavily. Plants need to be encouraged to develop deep roots. If you spoil them by making them dependent on artificial irrigation, they will always be weak and unable to get along on their own. The key to a successful forest garden is *continuous mulching*.

YEAR 1, STEP 6: NURSE CROPS

The most effective long-term strategy for establishing a forest garden on a bare-field site is to imitate the process nature uses to repair itself. Since the land wants to become woodland, we should investigate the stages the land would use to achieve that end.

Bare soil is like an open wound and weeds are like nature's bandage for healing that wound. If left to its own devices, the land would first cover itself with a low-growing ground cover of short-lived annuals, nitrogen-fixing herbaceous plants and shrubs, and deep-rooted pioneer species that remineralize the soil. These hardy, fast-growing plants awaken the soil, preparing the way for the slower-growing and longer-lived varieties to follow. Pioneer species are often referred to as 'nurse crops'.

After the design and build phase of your garden, there will be some areas of bare soil. We will mimic nature's method of covering exposed ground by growing a nurse crop, using species similar to the ones nature would use. These plants protect against erosion, add nutrients, accumulate minerals, retain moisture and add structure to the soil.

It is also helpful to plant deep-rooted species, such as docks, dandelion, Chinese radish (also known as daikon) and burdock. These soften the soil by growing deeply into the subsoil, creating channels for air and water to circulate. They are quite handy for loosening compacted soil, but are sometimes difficult to control in a vegetable garden.

Sow a mixture of nutrient-accumulator plants inside your shelterbelt and around the canopy layer. These plants produce an extensive system of fibrous roots that reach the lower layers of the soil, where they accumulate nutrients and deposit them on to the surface. I find the mixtures that use white clover as the foundation 'carpet' to be the most resilient. A brief list of nutrient-accumulator plants and the minerals they gather in their leaves are given in the table below. These minerals are deposited on the surface when the plants drop their leaves or die back in the autumn. You may find some of the plant suggestions objectionable, such as nettles, but please try to understand that these plants exist for a reason. Plants we regard as weeds are all part of nature's plan and have an important role to play. In any case, this phase is merely one of several steps towards rebuilding a balanced ecosystem. Many of these plants will fade away as the garden becomes shadier.

Nutrient-accumulator plants and minerals they bring into the topsoil

Botanical name	Common name	N	Ca	Cu	Fe	P	K	Na	S	Mg	Co	Si
Nutrient Key: N = Nitrogen fixers (see page 175); Ca = Calcium; Cu = Copper; Fe = Iron; P = Phosphorus; K = Potassium; Na = Sodium; S = Sulphur; Mg = Magnesium; Co = Cobalt ; Si = Silicon												
Lotus corniculatus	Bird's foot trefoil	*				*	*					
Borago officinalis	Borage		*				*					
Stellaria media	Chickweed		*		*		*	*	*	*	*	*
Cichorium intybus	Chicory		*				*	*		*		*
Allium schoenoprasum	Chives		*		*	*	*	*		*		
Galium aparine	Cleavers		*	*				*				
Trifolium spp.	Clover	*			*	*						
Tussilago farfara	Coltsfoot (inedible)		*		*				*	*	*	
Symphytum officinalis	Common comfrey (debatably inedible but very handy external medicinal plant and fabulous mulching plant)	*	*		*		*			*		
Thymus vulgaris	Common thyme		*		*					*		*
Echinaceae	Coneflower		*		*	*	*			*	*	*
Taraxacum officinale	Common dandelion		*	*	*	*	*	*	*	*		
Rumex spp.	Sorrel / sorrel dock		*		*	*	*	*				
Oenothera biennis	Common evening primrose		*							*		
Foeniculum vulgare	Fennel	*				*		*				
Chrysanthemum parthenium	Feverfew		*				*	*		*		*
Cornus florida	Flowering dogwood		*			*	*					
Equisetum arvense	Field horsetail	*	*		*	*	*	*		*		*
Chenopodium album	Lamb's quarters / fat hen		*		*	*	*	*				
Lupinus spp.	Lupin	*					*					
Malva sylvestris	Mallow	*	*		*	*	*	*				
Filipendula ulmaria	Meadowsweet		*			*	*	*	*	*		
Verbascum	Mullein				*		*			*		
Mentha x piperita	Peppermint						*			*		
Plantago spp.	Plantain		*		*				*	*		*
Rheum rhabarbarum	Rhubarb		*		*							
Poterium sanguisorba	Salad burnet		*		*				*	*		

Botanical name	Common name	N	Ca	Cu	Fe	P	K	Na	S	Mg	Co	Si
Nutrient Key: N = Nitrogen fixers (see page 175); Ca = Calcium; Cu = Copper; Fe = Iron; P = Phosphorus; K = Potassium; Na = Sodium; S = Sulphur; Mg = Magnesium; Co = Cobalt; Si = Silicon												
Rumex acetosella	Sheep's sorrel		*		*	*			*			*
Capsella bursa-pastoris	Shepherd's purse							*	*	*		
Potentilla anserina	Silverweed		*	*			*					
Sonchus arvensis	Corn sowthistle / winethistle / hogweed				*		*			*		
Urtica dioica	Common stinging nettle	*	*	*	*	*	*	*	*	*	*	*
Fragaria spp.	Strawberry				*							
Nasturtium officinale	Common watercress		*		*	*	*	*	*	*		
Achillea millefolium	Yarrow		*	*			*	*		*		*

Many tree and shrub species are also considered nutrient accumulators – for example, apple, walnut, birch, dogwood, hickory, pecan and maple. However, trees don't work as well during this initial phase because they are slow-growing. We need a fast-growing ground cover of soil-building plants to protect the earth while the trees are growing. I also toss some vegetables and wild flowers into the mix, just for variety. Clay seed balls, described in detail in *One-Straw Revolutionary* are the best way to get the vegetable seeds into the base layer.

Sowing nurse crops

Some nutrient-accumulator plants must be planted as small plants but many can be grown from seed. Seeds are a much more economical choice for larger areas and require a fraction of the work to establish. I think the seed balls described on page 152 are the best method for establishing a good solid nurse crop. Use a wide diversity of species in your mix.

Seeds are available from garden and farm supply centres as well as online (see Resources). Many species are edible, some have medicinal uses, and a few are toxic. My list is mostly edible. The seed balls should be broadcast by hand as soon as possible after soil has been exposed, as long as it is within the April–August growing season.

Normally, nurse crops are dug into the soil before they set seed. We won't be digging them in here, though. For our purposes, if they set seed, all the better. Many of them are annuals that die back at the end of the growing season. They may self-seed, or you may need to reseed them yourself. Many plants will become naturalized, appearing on their own year after year. It invigorates the ground cover to cut it back from time to time. Just leave the cuttings on the ground where they fall, or gather some up to mulch favoured trees or shrubs.

Once the soil is covered with a living carpet, keep mulching the plants you installed earlier. Soon you will see life begin to flourish on the floor of your fledgling woodland. The ground cover will not compete with your trees, especially if you have mulched carefully around them.

YEARS 2-3: DEVELOPING YOUR LAYERS

These days we are lucky to have access to a wide variety of productive plants from all over the world. If carefully chosen, these plants can speed the natural movement of the land towards maturity (forest succession), and make our gardens more productive than ever before. However, it is important to determine which plants are invasive in your region, and which ones will work happily within an ecosystem based on native plants. An online search will help you learn the plants to avoid and those that may be illegal to bring into your area. In Ireland, for example, Japanese knotweed (*Fallopia japonica*), which is edible in the spring and has other practical uses, has become a disaster by limiting hedgerow diversity. In fact, it is so successful that it overwhelms everything else and ends up as a monoculture. Originally a fashionable ornamental plant, it 'escaped' from gardens to invade natural areas and has developed into a major pest.

There are so many plants that can be a boon to you and your woodland ecosystem. More than two thousand edible plants will thrive in a moderately shady, temperate woodland environment, so you have plenty to choose from. The plant lists I offer in this book merely scratch the surface, so I suggest you create your own list based on availability and personal preference. Discovering new plants and new foods is one of the real joys of gardening!

Remember that young plants are like young children. The longer they are raised in a nursery, spoon-fed and mollycoddled, the harder it will be for them to adapt to 'the real world'. The younger you acquire plants, the better chance they have of adapting successfully to their new home. If you put each plant in the best position to succeed, give them love and attention, mulch them consistently, and encourage them to fend for themselves, they will grow to be strong and healthy. They will send their roots deep and wide and stretch themselves tall to establish their own place in the world.

That's why growing plants from seed is so important; they come to know their home from the very beginning. Just make sure those seeds are organic! Many common seeds are now soaked in neonicotinoid insecticides (neonics), a new class of pesticide that, among other things, kills bees and other pollinators, as the pesticide persists throughout the plant's lifetime, including their flowering phase. Choosing organic also avoids those crazy GMO seeds. In fact, on nature's behalf, I insist you do.

GMOs

Don't believe the hype about genetically modified seeds. To my mind, GMOs are so insidious that they can only be classified a crime against nature. There is emerging scientific evidence concerning the damaging effects of GMOs on our personal health and the well-being of the Earth's delicately balanced web of life. It scares the living daylights out of me. By all means research into this yourself, but be aware that there's a lot of misinformation out there, which is funded by the seed and chemical companies that make huge profits by getting these crops into the mainstream.

In March 2015, the World Health Organization's cancer agency said glyphosate is 'probably carcinogenic to humans'. Most GMO plants have been created so they can survive glyphosate-based herbicides. That means wherever they are grown, the fields are heavily dowsed with chemicals. These herbicides eventually find their way into our water and into the food chain. GMOs heavily increase the application rates of chemicals onto the land.

Another problem is that wind-blown pollen from these engineered plants cross-pollinates with the plants of organic farmers and gardeners who are growing them for seed. Once the plants have been contaminated with GMO pollen, they can no longer be sold as organic. If this is allowed to continue, we may lose *all* organic and heirloom seeds. Often GMOs are engineered to be sterile so they won't reproduce seeds the following year, forcing farmers and gardeners, to buy a new supply of seeds every year. Patenting seeds is just plain wrong! How dare profit-driven companies claim to own something as intrinsic to life as a seed! If we continue down this road of modifying crops and trees, we will either come to a dead end or fall off a cliff.

Unlike chemical or even nuclear contamination, genetic pollution can *never* be cleaned up or reversed. All future generations will have to cope with the mistakes we are making right now. Please support your local seed-saving organizations. It is difficult for these small groups to hold out against giant multinationals, which are specifically trying to destroy the option of non–patented seeds and GMO-free seed banks.

Semi-mature trees and shrubs

I have found that there is no point in wasting money on buying semi-mature trees. It takes them a long time to settle in, and trees that were planted from smaller sizes catch up with them in a few years anyway, especially if they are mulched regularly. Most trees grown in a commercial nursery are quite straight and uninteresting, strapped to their stakes like robotic soldiers standing to attention. They are usually grown so close together that they seem to have been manufactured, with little character or uniqueness of their own. If they stay in the nursery for too long, the roots fill the pots completely, making it hard for them to grow into native soil after they are transplanted. I always try to use small whips or trees from hedgerow mixes so they quickly become part of the landscape and develop their own personalities from an early age.

YEARS 3-10: YEAR 1 ONWARDS

The Seven Layers of a Forest Garden

1 Upper-canopy trees

2 Sub-canopy trees, or canopy trees for smaller gardens

3 Shrubs

4 Herbaceous plants

5 Ground cover

6 Underground plants

7 Climbers or vines

Edible forest gardens imitate the tiered structure of natural woodlands, but have a higher proportion of edible species. There are seven primary layers. The tallest tier, or overstorey, is typically composed of nut trees, standard (full-sized) fruit trees and trees that fix nitrogen. Below them are mid-sized trees, including most familiar fruit trees. Next is the shrub layer, with berries and plants that attract pollinators and offer habitat for birds and other wildlife. Below this a variety of herbaceous plants, including herbs and medicinal plants, form the perennial layer. The ground cover has a mixture of low-growing, edible and often nitrogen-fixing plants, which enrich the soil and help control weeds. The underground or soil layer is composed of edible roots and tubers, and the indispensable community of microorganisms, including fruiting fungi (mushrooms). The final layer consists of vines that trail along the ground, over branches and up into the trees and shrubs.

Designing your layers

As soon as there is enough shelter on your land, you can begin planting the first layers of your garden without worrying about wind damage. You may be able to accomplish this step during the first year if you are lucky enough to have existing shelter on the site.

It's best to design your layers on paper first. A sheet of greaseproof paper placed over your overall garden base map works well and is easy to use. The most common mistake people make when designing their forest garden is to place the overstorey trees too close together. Sketch their positions on paper and draw in their final canopy spreads. It is important that enough light reaches the lower layers of the garden to ensure healthy plants and maximum yields. Mistakes are to be expected, but they can be minimized with careful planning. It's easy to shift a shrub that is causing too much shade, but not easy, or wise, to try and move a tree that has already settled in.

A forest garden needs light to filter through to the forest floor. Classic shade trees such as maple, beech and sycamore are not as suitable for the upper canopy as other species, such as locust and black walnut, which let flickering light through even at maturity. If you decide to include trees that cast dense shade, you will have to thin their branches eventually. If you have existing trees, you can work around them, but again, they may need some branch reduction if they are causing too much shade and you have limited space.

The canopy-layer trees can be large- or medium-sized, depending on the extent of your garden. Select tree species that are suited to your conditions and that you would like to have close to you and be part of your family. The largest over-storey trees should generally be planted in the northern part of your garden to avoid casting too much shade.

HIGHEST CANOPY LAYERS – THE ESSENTIAL PARENT TREES

The largest tree species are too big and cast too much shade for most forest gardens unless they are coppiced. You *can* plant them, as long as you realize that they take more work to maintain later. For those who do have the space, however, below is a list of extremely large, dense trees that are absolutely magnificent at maturity. These are priceless old souls.

Essential parent trees

Botanical name	Common name	Benefits
Castanea sativa	Sweet chestnut	With the climate changing and becoming warmer, sweet chestnut is a tree that will flourish in temperate areas. Sweet chestnuts will grow to at least 10x10m (33x33') over 20 years, and they cast a heavy shade so are not particularly suitable for forest gardening. But if you have enough land, they would work well as an orchard crop, as the nuts are surprisingly low in protein but loaded with carbohydrates. This can be a valuable crop if you are trying to live entirely off your own land. Sweet chestnuts need free-draining soil and a warm climate or microclimate to fruit well. In a smaller forest garden system, they really should be coppiced.
Juglans regia (source modern varieties, as described)	English / Persian walnut	Walnuts are a fantastic food source and beautiful trees, but they will need full sun, a larger garden and lots of shelter. They are prone to frost damage and take up a lot of space as mature trees. If you have room, though, this is definitely a tree I would include. A mature tree can yield 45-68kg (100-150lb) of nuts every year. The older varieties are not worth the wait, as after a decade or so of growth, they will bear very little fruit. Modern varieties are fruitful much more quickly. They include J. regia, 'Buccaneer', J. regia 'Broadview' and J.regia 'Franquette'. Be aware that walnuts secrete chemicals into the soil that inhibit the growth of neighbouring plants. This is known as allelopathy. However, the effect is more noticeable from black walnut (J. nigra). While these are an important food source, they will need a lot of space out on their own. Still they are worth it if you have lots of land at your disposal.
Fagus sylvatica	Common beech	Young, tender beech leaves make a tasty and nutritious addition to salads. Beech nuts are difficult to harvest and the trees rest for quite a few years between the 'mast years'. (Mast years are years in which woodland trees produce an exceptional crop of mast/fruit eg nuts and acorns.) However, the oil extracted from them is extremely high quality. Richard Mabey, author of Food for Free, estimates that you get about 85ml (3fl oz) for every 450g (1lb) of beech nuts. I've yet to try myself.
Quercus spp.	Oak	Once acorns are dried, they are easy enough to dehusk and grind into a lovely nutty flour, which is a wonderful source of carbohydrate. Oaks yield heavily during mast years and rest in between. They provide an invaluable habitat for wildlife.

Layer 1. Canopy trees for temperate climates

The list below contains both tall canopy and sub-canopy trees, but it is merely intended as a starter guide – you will find abundant options once you do some research. Martin Crawford's books about creating a forest garden are my favourites on the topic (see Resources). If you have a large area of land, you will be able to create two layers from this first list. If your garden is a more modest size, you may want to use relatively large fruit trees for the upper canopy and skip the taller trees altogether. In that case, your canopy trees will come from the list of sub-canopy trees on page 167.

Recommended large canopy trees for layer 1

Botanical name	Common name	Height	Spread
Acer saccharinum	Soft / sugar maple	30m (98'43")	12m (40')

- Sugar maple is magic. If you have the space and climate, I recommend you have as many as possible.
- Hardy to US zone 3, sugar maple is slow-growing, can handle semi-shade and even tolerate very acid soils.
- In late winter and early spring, you can tap mature trees for maple syrup, obtaining 40-100 litres (70-176 pints) of syrup in a season. Hot summers and cold winters are needed for them to produce well.
- Insect-pollinated hermaphrodite flowers.
- Leaves are packed around apples and root crops to help preserve them. Field maple leaves will work well too.

Araucaria araucana	Monkey puzzle tree	20m (66')	5m (16')

- Male and female plants are needed to produce nut-like seeds.
- Takes 20 years to be fruitful. Big pods containing lots of edible seeds are produced in late autumn in sporadic harvests, ie some years are better than others. These are best collected by stringing fine nets around the base. Roast or boil for approximately 25 minutes, then slice the shells open with a knife.
- Large parent tree.

Carya laciniosa 'Henry'	Shellbark hickory 'Henry'	15m (49')	10m (33')

- Shade-intolerant.
- Male and female plants are needed to produce sweet and edible nuts (bigger than walnuts), which are best collected by stringing fine nets around the base.
- Nuts dry and keep well, and require a heavy-duty nutcracker to open.
- Nut milks and oils were important traditional staples in the United States.

Carya ovata	Shagbark hickory	25m (82')	9m (29'5")

- Hardy to zone 4 in the UK, this tree is slow-growing and will not tolerate shade, but if you have space and a suitable climate, it is an essential plant.
- Self-fertile.
- Produces nuts (bigger than walnuts), which are best collected by stringing fine nets around the base.
- Nuts dry and keep well, and require a heavy-duty nutcracker to open.
- Nut milks and oils were important traditional staples in the United States.

Ceratonia siliqua	Carob	15m (49')	10m (33')

- Nitrogen-fixing species.
- Male plants produce pollen, female plants produce seed pods.
- Ripe, dried seed pod can be ground to carob powder – a protein-rich chocolate substitute. Seeds can be roasted and ground as a coffee substitute.

Botanical name	Common name	Height	Spread
Gleditsia triacanthos f. *inermis*	Honey locust	20m (66')	15m (49')

- Young seeds can be eaten raw in salads, and taste like garden peas, or can be cooked.
- Large parent tree that needs lots of room to grow.
- Self-fertile.

Botanical name	Common name	Height	Spread
Juglans ailanthifolia var. *cordiformis*	*Japanese walnut*	15-20m (49-66')	10-15m (33-49')

- Happy in most soil types. It prefers deep loamy soil but will grow in most soils. Acid, neutral and alkaline soils are ok. Shade-intolerant.
- Self-fertile.
- Faster-growing than walnuts and producing a similar quality of nut that dries and stores well.
- Husks contain up to 20 nuts and must be removed, ideally by stringing fine nets around base.

Botanical name	Common name	Height	Spread
Juglans regia (good cultivars are available)	English walnut / Persian walnut / Common walnut	20m (66')	20m (66')

- Needs lots of land to grow, as little grows around base.
- Happy in most soil types. It prefers well-drained soil but will grow in most soils. Acid, neutral and alkaline soils are ok. Shade-intolerant.
- Self-fertile.
- Fantastic source of food and wood.
- Invaluable parent tree.

Botanical name	Common name	Height	Spread
Malus domestica	Apple	9m (29'5") on own roots. Size of grafted specimens depends on choice of rootstock (see Chapter 4).	9m (29'5") on own roots. Size of grafted specimens depends on choice of rootstock (see Chapter 4).

- Needs cross-pollination.
- Happy in most soil types. Acid, neutral and alkaline soils are ok. Semi-shade or no shade is tolerated.
- Avoid growing or storing near potatoes. They don't support each other well, damaging respective flavours.
- Nasturtiums grown near trees repel woolly aphids, and onions or chives planted around the tree base can prevent the development of scab – a fungal disease that attacks the skin of edibles.
- Wrap maple leaves around apples to prolong storage life. Blossoms need shelter from winds during flowering times.
- Plants need at least half a day in sunlight.
- Apples can be used in so many ways – fresh fruit, juices, cordials, chutneys, jellies, relishes, baked, purées, cider, etc.

Botanical name	Common name	Height	Spread
Pinus koraiensis	Korean pine	20m (66')	10m (33')

- Requires full sun. Will tolerate wind but not maritime exposure. Prefers acidic soil.
- Not self-fertile (they need to be fertilized from another tree), and most are monoecious. Pines typically have male and female flowers on the same tree. Pollinated by the wind. Needs pollination partner.
- Korean pine produces cones much earlier than stone pine (see below).
- Seeds (pine nuts) are rich in oil. Great source of protein and very tasty roasted.
- Blueberries will partner well with conifers around the tree base.

Botanical name	Common name	Height	Spread
Pinus pinea	Stone pine (also known as Italian stone pine)	20m (66')	10m (33')

- Requires full sun. Will tolerate wind but not maritime exposure. Prefers acidic soil.
- Not self-fertile (they need to be fertilized from another tree), and most are monoecious. Pines typically have male and female flowers on the same tree. Pollinated by the wind. Needs pollination partner.
- Can take a number of years before the tree produces cones.
- Seeds (pine nuts) are rich in oil. Great source of protein and tasty roasted.
- Blueberries will partner well with conifers around the tree base.

Botanical name	Common name	Height	Spread
Prunus avium	Wild cherry	10-15m (33-49')	6-7m (20-23')

- Only suitable for large gardens.
- Happy in most soil types. Acid, neutral and alkaline soils are ok. Semi-shade or no shade is tolerated.
- Requires cross-pollination from another compatible variety/cultivar.
- Most cherries will yield nothing unless netted from the birds, which devour them in the blink of an eye. If you are keen to harvest cherry fruit, I recommend you grow trees on dwarfing rootstocks. Unless you have lots of land and can plant many trees – then the birds may leave some for you!
- Fruits can be eaten raw or cooked, but fruit needs to be ripe, otherwise may be slightly toxic.
- The hard, reddish-brown wood is valued for woodturning, and has often been used for instrument making in Ireland.

Botanical name	Common name	Height	Spread
Prunus domestica	Plum	12m (40') on own roots. Size of grafted specimens depends on choice of rootstock (see Chapter 4).	10m (33') on own roots. Size of grafted specimens depends on choice of rootstock (see Chapter 4).

- Tolerates semi-shade. Needs sheltered, well-drained position but is happy in most soils.
- Some varieties are self-fertile. Some will require a different variety, flowering at the same time. Check with the grower. However, even those that are self-fertile will often produce more if cross-pollinated.
- Grows well fanned against a sunny wall, although the branches may need supporting under the weight of a heavy crop (unless they were never grafted – trees on their own roots tend to bend and the heavy fruit lies on the ground without damaging the trees).

Botanical name	Common name	Height	Spread
Pyrus communis (F) (There are many excellent varieties of pear trees. Those that will produce viable fruit within a few years.)	Pear	10-12m (33-40') on own roots. Size of grafted specimens depends on choice of rootstock (see Chapter 4).	8m (26') on own roots. Size of grafted specimens depends on choice of rootstock (see Chapter 4).

- Tolerates partial shade. Happy in most soil types. Needs lots of mulch to keep moist.
- Pears are one of my favourite fruits to eat, when they are lovely and ripe.
- Some varieties are self-fertile. Some will require a different variety, flowering at the same time. Check with the grower. However, even those that are self-fertile will often produce more if cross-pollinated.

Layer 2. Sub-canopy trees, or canopy trees for smaller gardens

The table below recommends plants that are suitable for the second layer of a large forest garden. If your land is not large enough to support tall overstorey trees, these mid-sized specimens with narrower canopies will form the highest layer of your garden. The list includes some fruit and nut species, shade-tolerant trees, and trees that fix nitrogen. You still may have to prune them eventually to allow light to reach the lower layers.

Recommended canopy trees for layer 2

Botanical name	Common name	Height	Spread
Asimina triloba	Pawpaw	6m (20')	6m (20')
• Requires good light but is a natural understorey tree in North America. Prefers acid to neutral soil. Needs well-drained loamy soil. Will not tolerate shade. • Slow-growing. • Needs two different varieties flowering at same time to pollinate. • Large, tasty fruits commonly eaten raw. Seeds are not edible.			
Arbutus unedo	Strawberry tree	6-8m (20-26')	6m (20')
• Tolerates partial shade. Requires acidic soil. Happy in most soil types but prefers well-drained soil. • As canopy trees, these may need pruning to thin out branches initially, as they are quite bushy and dense. • Self-fertile. • Delicious fresh fruits that make good wines. • Bark traditionally used in the leather tanning process.			
Carya illinoinensis 'Lucas' C. illinoinensis 'Carlson No. 3'	Pecan nut	6m (20')	4m (13')
• Needs full sun. Tolerates highly acidic or alkaline soils. • Self-fertile plant and wind-pollinated, but benefits from being planted in pairs. • Edible nuts are best harvested by stringing nets around the tree base. • Nuts dry and keep well, and require a heavy-duty nutcracker to break them open.			
Cornus species C. capitata C. kousa var. chinensis C. mas 'Elegant'	Dogwoods Chinese dogwood Cornelian cherry	4-6m (13-20') high	3-4m (10-13') wide
• Happy in most soil types. Acid, neutral and alkaline. • Requires semi-shade or no shade. • Self-fertile. However, most will benefit from cross-pollination. • Edible fruits need time to ripen after picking. Delicious raw or cooked. Cornelian cherry is good for jam or wine-making.			

Botanical name	Common name	Height	Spread
Corylus avellana cultivars	Hazel or filbert	5-6m (16-20') – or coppice for smaller spaces.	4-5m (13-16') – or coppice them to allow inclusion in smaller spaces.

- Happy in most soil types. Acid, neutral and alkaline. Requires semi-shade or sun.
- Wind-pollinated and benefits from two or more trees near each other. Occasionally shaking the branches when hazels are in flower in spring helps pollination.
- Edible nuts are best harvested by stringing fine nets around the tree base.
- Nuts can be eaten raw or roasted. Use ground nuts to make oil and milk.
- Invaluable for smaller gardens. Good for coppicing too. They won't fruit for a few years after coppicing, so ideally grow a number of them and coppice a different tree every year to keep a regular hazelnut crop.

Botanical name	Common name	Height	Spread
Crataegus pedicellata	American scarlet hawthorn	7m (23')	7m (23')

- Happy in most soil types. Acid, neutral and alkaline. Requires dappled shade or sun
- Hermaphrodite flowers pollinated by insects. Benefits from cross-pollination.
- In autumn, bears plentiful large, sweet fruit about 10cm (4") in diameter. An excellent dessert fruit.

Botanical name	Common name	Height	Spread
Crataegus arnoldiana	Arnold thorn	2-6m (6'6"-20')	2-3m (6'6"-10')

- Happy in most soil types. Acid, neutral and alkaline. Requires dappled shade or sun
- Hermaphrodite flowers pollinated by insects. Benefits from cross-pollination.
- In autumn, bears plentiful large, sweet fruit about 2cm (0.8") in diameter. A good dessert fruit. Can also be cooked in preserves and pies.

Botanical name	Common name	Height	Spread
Crataegus schraderiana	Blue hawthorn	6m (20')	4-5m (13-16')

- Requires dappled shade or sun. Happy in most soil types. Acid, neutral and alkaline.
- Hermaphrodite flowers pollinated by insects. Benefits from cross-pollination.
- Large, very tasty fruits that can be eaten raw, cooked or dried.

Botanical name	Common name	Height	Spread
Crataegus ellwangeriana	Scarlet hawthorn	6m (20')	4m (13')

- Requires dappled shade or sun. Happy in most soil types. Acid, neutral and alkaline.
- Hermaphrodite flowers pollinated by insects. Benefits from cross-pollination.
- Large, tasty haws with apple-flavoured flesh.

Botanical name	Common name	Height	Spread
Cratageus monogyna	Common hawthorn	4-10m (13-33'), depending on microclimate	2-6m (6'6"-20'), depending on microclimate

- Dappled shade or sun. Happy in most soil types. Acid, neutral and alkaline.
- Hermaphrodite flowers pollinated by insects. Benefits from cross-pollination.
- Early season leaves are traditionally used as salad leaves in Ireland, but leaves of other hawthorn varieties are not usually palatable.
- Haws are small but can be made into a jelly. Discard pips.

Botanical name	Common name	Height	Spread
Crataegus tanacetifolia	Tansy-leaved thorn	4m (13')	3m (10')

- Good variety for smaller gardens.
- Happy in most soil types. Acid, neutral and alkaline. Dappled shade or sun.
- Hermaphrodite flowers pollinated by insects. Benefits from cross-pollination.
- Large, tasty haws with apple-flavoured flesh. Discard pips.

Botanical name	Common name	Height	Spread
Cydonia oblonga	Quince	1.5-7m (5-23')	1.5-5m (5-16')

- Requires full shade, semi-shade or full sun. Happy in poorly drained soils.
- Self-fertile so they will fruit on their own, but the harvest will benefit from cross-pollination.
- Fruit benefits from bletting.
- Bletting is the process of allowing fruit to become soft and semi-rotten during storage.
- Fruits usually need cooking. Make excellent jams and jellies, and add a delicious flavour to apple pies.

Botanical name	Common name	Height	Spread
Diospyros kaki Cultivars are usually better, including 'Fuyu' and 'Mazelli'	Persimmon	4-6m (13-20')	4-6m (13-20')

- Male and female plants are required for pollination.
- Grows in semi shade or no shade. Happy in most soil types. Acid, neutral and alkaline.
- Fruits are like plums, but should be eaten only when fully ripe. Needs a harvest temperature of below 7°C to ripen. Benefit from bletting.
- Bletting is the process of allowing fruit to become soft and semi-rotten during storage.
- Fruits can be dried and used in baking. Seeds can be roasted and ground to make a caffeine-free coffee substitute.

Botanical name	Common name	Height	Spread
Diospyros lotus	Date plum	9m (29'5")	6m (20')

- Male and female plants are required for pollination.
- Happy in most soil types. Acid, neutral and alkaline. It prefers moist soil but will grow in other soil types, in sun or semi-shade.
- Fruits are like plums, but should be eaten only when fully ripe, (may require blettting). Fruits can be dried and used in baking. Roasted and ground seeds make a coffee substitute.

Botanical name	Common name	Height	Spread
Diospyros virginiana	American date plum	15m (49')	8m (26')

- Happy in most soil types. Acid, neutral and alkaline. It prefers well-drained soil but will grow in most soil types, in sun or semi-shade.
- Male and female plants required for pollination.
- Fruit are like plums, but should be eaten when fully ripe, which can be after the leaves have dropped in November. Benefit from bletting.
- Bletting is the process of allowing fruit to become soft and semi-rotten during storage.
- Fruits can be dried like raisins and used in baking. Roasted and ground seeds make a coffee substitute.

Botanical name	Common name	Height	Spread
Elaeagnus umbellata	Autumn oleaster	3-4m (10-13')	3-4m (10-13')

- Needs two different varieties flowering at the same time for pollination.
- Happy in most soil types. Acid, neutral and alkaline. It prefers well-drained soil but will grow in most soils, even very poor soils. Tolerates partial shade but happiest in the sun.
- Fruits are ripe and ready in September/October.
- Nitrogen fixer (see page 175).

Botanical name	Common name	Height	Spread
Elaeagnus x ebbingei	Ebbinge's silverberry	3-4m (10-13')	3-4 m (10-13')

- Needs two different varieties flowering at same time for pollination.
- Happy in most soil types. It prefers well-drained soil but will grow in most soils, even very poor soils. Acid, neutral and alkaline soils are ok. Tolerates sun, partial shade and full shade.
- Early spring fruit, which can be used raw or cooked for jams.
- Nitrogen fixer (see page 175).

Botanical name	Common name	Height	Spread
Ficus carica	Fig	6m (20')	6m (20')

- Self-fertile. However, will benefit from cross-pollination.
- Happy in most soil types. Acid, neutral and alkaline. It prefers well-drained soil but will grow in most soils, even very poor soils. Requires sun.
- Vulnerable to the cold in winter, as the fruits start to grow in autumn and only reach maturity the following year. May need hessian or straw protection throughout winter. In temperate regions, grow against south- or west-facing walls. Also it's best to restrict the tree's roots with an underground barrier system, or it may not fruit plentifully.
- Delicious fresh fruits.

Halesia carolina	Silverbell tree	2-4m (6'6"-13')	2-4m (6'6"-13')

- Self-fertile.
- Slow-growing. Needs acid or neutral soil. Prefers moist soil and tolerates partial shade but will thrive in full sun.
- Edible flowers can be used in salads. Distinctive winged green fruits are ready for picking around the start of July. Crunchy like peas, they can be eaten fresh, steamed or pickled.

Malus domestica	Apple	9m (29'5") on own roots. Size of grafted specimens depends on choice of rootstock	9m (29'5") on own roots. Size of grafted specimens depends on choice of rootstock

- Needs cross-pollination with another apple tree variety, flowering at the same time.
- Happy in most soil types, sandy, clay or loam. Acid, neutral and alkaline. It will grow in sun or semi-shade.
- Avoid growing or storing near potatoes. They don't support each other well, damaging respective flavours.
- Nasturtiums grown near trees repel woolly aphids, and onions or chives planted around the tree base can prevent the development of scab – a fungal disease that attacks the skin of edibles.
- Wrap maple leaves around apples to prolong storage life. Blossoms need shelter from winds during flowering times.
- Plants need at least half a day in sunlight.
- Apples can be used in so many ways – fresh fruit, juices, cordials, chutneys, jellies, relishes, baked, purées, cider, etc.

Malus sylvestris	Crab apple	3-5m (10-16')	3m (10')

- Happy in most soil types, sandy, clay or loam. Acid, neutral and alkaline. It will grow in sun or semi-shade. Needs cross-pollination with another apple tree variety, flowering at the same time.
- Crab apple trees make good pollinators for other apple varieties and make the best rootstock for your own apple grafting efforts. May need some branch thinning to open up their habitat for plants below, as they are quite bushy.
- 'John Downie' is the only good eater that I know. The fruits are usually cooked and made into jams and jellies, as they are high in pectin, which helps preserves to set. My mum's crab apple jelly was always a family favourite.

Mespilus germanica – Pyrus germanica	Common medlar	4-6m (13-20'). Size of grafted specimens depends on choice of rootstock	5m (16') Size of grafted specimens depends on choice of rootstock

- Will grow in most soils and tolerate strong winds but not maritime winds.
- Self-fertile so they will fruit on their own, but the harvest will benefit from cross-pollination.
- Medlars are best left on the tree as long as possible. When they are picked they are inedible due to their astringency. The fruits need to be bletted before they can be eaten.
- Bletting is the process of allowing fruit to become soft and semi-rotten during storage.
- When bletting is complete, the fruit tastes like smoky apple sauce.
- The simplest way to eat medlars is raw, but they can be roasted or baked then served as a dessert. But most medlars are used for making sweet preserves – jams and jellies.

Botanical name	Common name	Height	Spread
Morus alba / M. rubra	White mulberry / Red mulberry	5-10m (16-33')	5-10 m (16-33')

- Happy in most soil types, sandy, clay or loam. Acid, neutral and alkaline. It will grow in sun or semi-shade.
- Tolerates wind but not maritime exposure.
- Can be pruned in early summer to keep small for tight spaces.
- Self-fertile. Hybrids produce better fruit.
- Fruits can be eaten fresh when fully ripened. Or they can be used in cooking, in much the same way as blackberries and raspberries. They can also be dried and ground into flour. Fresh leaves can be steamed to make tea.

Botanical name	Common name	Height	Spread
Prunus cerasus 'Kentish Red'	Sour cherry, morello or amarelle	3.5-4.5m (11'6"-14'6")	3.5-4m (11'6"-14'6")

- A smaller cherry tree that is better for more compact gardens.
- Happy in most soil types, sandy, clay or loam. Acid, neutral and alkaline. It will grow in sun or semi-shade. But it is happy enough in sheltered places without direct sunlight so can be invaluable where other things may not grow so well! Can be trained on a north-facing wall. Self-fertile.
- Fruits can be eaten raw or cooked.

Botanical name	Common name	Height	Spread
Prunus dulcis	Sweet almond	5m (16')	4m (13')

- Happy in most soil types. But it prefers well-drained soil. Acid, neutral and alkaline soils are ok. Tolerates sun, partial shade and full shade.
- Needs a sheltered microclimate for decent cropping in Ireland and the UK. Place rocks around the trunk base to absorb heat from the sun.
- Self-fertile. Don't plant near a peach as they might hybridize making for bitter nuts.
- Wonderful edible nuts that can be eaten raw, blanched or roasted. Can also be used as a source of almond oil or ground to make flour.

Botanical name	Common name	Height	Spread
Prunus insititia	Bullace or Damson	3-6m (10-20') on own roots. Size of grafted specimens depends on choice of rootstock	2-5m (6'6"-16') on own roots. Size of grafted specimens depends on choice of rootstock

- Happy in most soil types, sandy, clay or loam. Acid, neutral and alkaline. It will grow in sun or semi-shade.
- Happy in most positions but will not tolerate salt-laden maritime winds.
- Easy to grow from seed.
- Self-fertile.
- Fruits can be eaten raw but they are particularly sharp so are better cooked with plenty of sugar. Avoid eating seeds. Make good jams.

Botanical name	Common name	Height	Spread
Prunus persica	Peach	6m (20') as a shrub but better trained as a fan against a sunny wall 2m (6'6") high.	6m (20') shrub but happier fan-trained against a sunny wall 2m (6'6") high.

- Happy in most soil types, sandy, clay or loam. Acid, neutral and alkaline. It will require a sunny and sheltered position. Use rocks around the base of the trunk to absorb the sun's heat. Best trained against a sheltered sunny wall. Self-fertile.
- Flowers arrive in spring when few insects are around. To encourage more fruit, pollinate open blooms by hand using a cotton bud or a soft brush. Permaculture teacher and author Patrick Whitefield recommends doing this daily right through the flowering season.
- Fruits. Raw, cooked or dried as 'leather strips' for later use.

Botanical name	Common name	Height	Spread
(*P. pyrifolia* var. *culta*)	Asian pear	Size of grafted specimens depends on choice of rootstock	Size of grafted specimens depends on choice of rootstock
• Happy in most soil types, sandy, clay or loam. Acid, neutral and alkaline. It will grow in sun or semi-shade. • Fruits are very sweet, and can be eaten raw or cooked.			
Sambucus nigra	European elder	3-5m (10-16')	3-5m (10-16')
• Happy in most soil types, sandy, clay or loam. Acid, neutral and alkaline. It will grow in sun or semi-shade. • Self-fertile. • Fragrant, edible flowers can be used to make cordials, wines and 'champagne'. Blossoms picked in May or June are delicious dipped in batter and fried. Fruits are best cooked with other fruits or made into jams, jellies or wine.			
Viburnum trilobum	American highbush Cranberry bush	4m (13')	3-4m (10-13')
• Happy in most soil types, sandy, clay or loam. Prefers moist soil however. Happy in acid, neutral and alkaline soils. It will grow in sun or semi-shade. • Self-fertile. • Fruits are rich in Vitamin C and make a good substitute for cranberries.			

Designing canopy layers

Deciding on a layout for the canopy is actually about designing spaces *between* the trees. You need enough space for light to filter through the canopy while having sufficient trees for the land to feel solid as a multi-tiered woodland. The most common mistake people make at this stage is to plant the trees too close together. Obviously it's better to get it right from the start through careful planning, but sometimes we miscalculate. My rule of thumb is to err on the side of *under*-planting rather than planting too many trees or placing them too close together. If you do that, you'll have the thankless job of thinning the trees in future years, which is a pity and a waste. When designing the canopy layers, I recommend you follow this approach:

1 Draw the canopy layers on your plot survey. These may consist of large trees if you have lots of land, or trees from layer two if you have a smaller garden or an urban yard.

2 Cover the survey map with a sheet of tracing or greaseproof paper to keep the design clean.

3 Draw the outlines of the designed spaces – boundaries, paths, house, and so forth – in one colour. I usually use black for fixed structures. Draw in swales and Hügelkultur beds in another colour – say, green.

4 Choose a third colour to represent the canopy layer (say, blue) and a different colour for the sub-canopy (red).

5 Make a list of the plants you plan to use in the canopy design and note their heights and spreads.

6 Draw blue and red circles to represent the eventual spreads of these plants according to the scale you are working with. If the maximum spread of a canopy tree is 4m (13'), draw a 4m circle around the centre point, which represents the planting position. Be sure to number each circle and make a coded plant list so you'll you remember which trees and shrubs go where.

7 Be sure there will be adequate space between these plants when they reach their projected mature sizes. If you plant them too close together, the plants will become leggy, and unproductive. On the other hand, if the canopy trees are spaced too far apart, you are not maximizing the amount of trees on the land, which is the most important thing.

In temperate climates, a good size for the gap between two trees is about half the average width of the canopy spreads of two neighboring trees. You measure the gap from canopy edge to canopy edge. (In hotter climates, the plants would be spaced closer together to create more shade.)

For example, take two trees, one with a projected mature canopy spread of 2m and the other with a future canopy spread of 5m. Half their spreads are 1m and 2.5m respectively, so the average desired gap between the leaf edges at maturity would be 1.75m (1+2.5 = 3.5 and 3.5 ÷ 2 = 1.75).

To find the planting distance between these two tree trunks, work out the radius of the future canopy of each tree. Then add these two distances to the average radius between them. This is the distance between each tree at planting time.

So in this example, that means the two trees should be planted 5.25m apart (1+2.5+1.75 = 5.25). Remember that it doesn't have to be exact. Just try your hardest.

Let's take another simple example. If the canopy trees in question are projected to have 2m canopy spreads, then half of each of their spreads (the radius) would be 1m. Therefore, the two trees should be planted about 3m apart when you also add the average radius between the canopy spreads which is also 1 m. (1+1+1=3).

If you are designing two layers of trees – the top canopy layer and sub-canopy – things get a bit more complicated. Most upper-canopy trees are taller than the sub-canopy trees, so the gap can be closer on the south-facing side of the taller tree and further apart on the north-facing side, where less light is available.

Use your own reasoning and intuition in making these adjustments. Just remember, the goal is to ensure that enough light filters through the trees to the plants below. You will learn a lot about your land during the first year or two. If you have placed plants too far apart or too close together, you can always move them around while they are still young. This should be done during the dormant season. (The dormant season being November to February in our climate in Ireland.)

Layer 3. Shrubs

Most fruiting bushes, including blueberries, whortleberries, raspberries, nut bushes, flowering shrubs and some medicinal plants, grow in the shrub layer. These plants can be up to 3m (10') tall and generally appreciate as much light as you can give them. If their location is too shady, they will grow well enough, but their production will be minimal. Plant the shade-tolerant species beneath the canopy trees, and the shrubs that need more light in the spaces between the trees and along the edges of the garden.

NITROGEN-FIXING PLANTS

Nitrogen-fixing plants take nitrogen out of the air and put it into the soil through a symbiotic relationship with specific bacteria. They keep the soil supplied with this much-needed nutrient, which is used by plants and microorganisms alike. Try to have 10-20 per cent of your total garden planted with nitrogen-fixing trees and shrubs.

These plants need sunlight to fix nitrogen effectively, so plant them in south- or west-facing positions. Choose thorny nitrogen fixers when grazing animals such as deer or rabbits are present.

Nitrogen-fixing shrubs for layer 3

Botanical name	Common name	Height	Spread
Amorpha fruticosa	False indigo bush	4m (13')	3m (10')
• Not edible. • Good plant for windbreaks and soil erosion prevention. Hermaphrodite, bee-pollinated. • Prefers sandy or loamy soil. Happy in acid, neutral and alkaline soils. It will grow in sun or semi-shade. • Not edible.			
Ceanothus prostratus	Mahala mat	10cm (4")	1.5m (5')
• Evergreen shrub. Tolerates light shade but prefers sun. Prefers sandy or loamy soil. Happy in acid, neutral and alkaline soils. • Hermaphrodite, bee-pollinated. • Not edible but all parts of this plant contain high levels of saponins. If you crush the plant parts (especially the flowers) and mix them with water, they will make a gentle lather which is a good soap substitute – gentle on the skin. Saponins protect the plants from soil-borne pathogens.			
Elaeagnus angustifolia	Oleaster	6-7m (20-23')	5-6m (16-20')
• It prefers well-drained soil but will grow in most soils, even very poor soils. Acid, neutral and alkaline soils are ok. Tolerates sun or light shade. • Great windbreak plant. Tolerates salt-laden winds and heavy pruning. • Seeds ripen from September to October. Both seeds and fruits are edible. The fruit must be fully ripe. The wood is an excellent fuel and is much used for carving.			
Elaeagnus multiflora	Goumi	3m (10')	2m (7')
• It prefers well-drained soil but will grow in most soils, even very poor soils. Acid, neutral and alkaline soils are ok. Tolerates sun or partial shade. • Fixes nitrogen. • A great windbreak and a good hedging plant, traditionally used as a rootstock for plants that were hard to grow from cuttings. • Hermaphrodite, bee-pollinated. Needs two plant selections to ensure cross-pollination and decent crop yields. • Tolerates salt winds and heavy pruning. • Edible fruits that can be eaten raw or cooked. Best as dried fruit.			

Botanical name	Common name	Height	Spread
Hippophae rhamnoides	Sea buckthorn	6-7m (20-23')	6-7m (20-23')

- It prefers well-drained soil but will grow in most soils, even very poor soils. Acid, neutral and alkaline soils are ok.
- Male and female plants are required for pollination. Wind-pollinated. Needs full sun and can tolerate maritime conditions.
- Very good as a hedge/windbreak species.
- Extremely large thorns so works well around fruit trees as a deer/rabbit deterrent.
- Fruits are juicy and acid, and high in vitamin C. The berries are very tart and benefit from lots of sugar but they can be mixed with sweeter fruit juices and they make delicious jam. The fruits get much sweeter if you blet them a little.
- Fruits last on the bushes way into winter and hence are a valuable late source of vitamin C.

Botanical name	Common name	Height	Spread
Myrica cerifera	Wax myrtle (also known as bayberry)	9m (29'5")	3m (10')

- It prefers well-drained soil but will grow in most soils. Acid or neutral soils only.
- Tolerates partial shade and wind but not maritime conditions.
- The flowers are monoecious (that means individual flowers are either male or female, but both sexes can be found on the same plant) and are pollinated by wind.
- Leaves and berries can be used to flavour food. Dried leaves can used to make a tea.
- When the fruit of any *Myrica* variety is boiled, a wax floats on the surface of the water that can be skimmed off. This can be used as a sealing wax in the tree stump / mushroom inoculation process (see page 34).
- Not edible.

Botanical name	Common name	Height	Spread
Robinia hispida	Bristly locust	2m (6'6")	2m (6'6")

- It prefers well-drained soil but will grow in most soils. Acid, alkaline or neutral soils are ok.
- Hermaphrodite, bee-pollinated.
- Will not tolerate shade. It will die from lack of sun when shade from the upper canopy becomes too dense.
- Has very large thorns so works well around fruit trees as a deer/rabbit deterrent. Suckers freely and, again, the thorns are deadly! Be careful when pruning.
- Good for keeping predators away from tree bark while plant is young.
- Not edible.

Botanical name	Common name	Height	Spread
Spartium junceum	Spanish broom	3m (10')	3m (10')

- It prefers well-drained soil but will grow in most soils, even very poor soils. Acid, neutral and alkaline soils are ok. Will not tolerate the shade. Needs good light and is tolerant of winds and maritime conditions.
- Hermaphrodite, insect-pollinated.
- Works well around rocks and in dry situations.
- Not edible.

Botanical name	Common name	Height	Spread
Ulex europaeus	Common gorse	1.5m (5')	1.5m (5')

- It prefers well-drained soil but will grow in most soils. Acid or neutral soils only.
- Fantastic hedging plant that is tolerant of wind and maritime conditions. Needs good light. Can spread invasively if not controlled.
- Fast-growing and extremely thorny so works well around fruit trees as a deer/rabbit deterrent.
- Bee-pollinated hermaphrodite flowers.
- Bright yellow flowers are edible raw and can be made into a tea or sprinkled through salads – they have a bitter, rocket-like taste. The closed flower buds can be pickled in vinegar and used like capers.

Other useful and productive shrubs for layer 3

Botanical name	Common name	Height	Spread
Amelanchier alnifolia 'Martin'	Saskatoon or Serviceberry.	2-3m (6'6"-10')	2m (6'6")

- Self-fertile suckering shrub. (A suckering shrub is one which sends up new stems from its stems or roots.) Vegetative reproduction. Basically they spread outwards from the initial plant stem.
- It prefers well-drained soil but will grow in most soils. Acid, alkaline or neutral soils. Needs good light at woodland edges.
- Large edible fruits in July that are very similar to blueberries. They can be eaten raw or cooked – they make delicious jams. They can be dried to prolong their use (like raisins). Other good cultivars are available with large fruits. Birds love the berries so netting may be required.
- Hardiness zone: 4-6

Arbutus unedo 'Elfin King' (small cultivar)	Strawberry tree	2m (6'6")	2m (6'6")

- It prefers well-drained soil but will grow in most soils. Acid, alkaline or neutral soils. Will grow in semi-shade or no shade.
- Self-fertile.
- Fruits are edible and can be made into jam. They also make good wine.

Aronia melanocarpa 'Hugin'	Black chokeberry 'Hugin'	3m (10')	1m (3')

- It prefers well-drained soil but will grow in most soils. Acid, alkaline or neutral soils. Will grow in full sun or semi-shade, though less sun will lead to a reduced harvest.
- Self-fertile.
- Fruits in August / September are edible raw, but ensure they are fully ripe before eating, as they can be tart. They are high in nutrients and rich in pectin so are good for jam making.

Atriplex halimus	Tree purslane	1-1.5m (3-5')	1-1.5m (3-5')

- It prefers well-drained soil but will grow in most soils, even very poor soils. Acid, neutral and alkaline soils are ok. Even very salty soils are tolerated.
- Needs full sun to grow – will not tolerate shade. Tolerates maritime conditions.
- Self-fertile.
- Leaves are delicious raw in salads, stir-fried or steamed, and are available throughout the year.

Phyllostachys spp. Pleioblastus spp. Semiarundinaria spp. Yushania spp.	Bamboo	3-8m (10-26')	Spreading or clumping varieties

- It prefers well-drained soil but will grow in most soils. Acid, alkaline or neutral soils. Will grow in semi-shade or no shade.
- Self-fertile.
- Clumping and suckering species all have edible shoots. However, you should contain the spreading species with root walls (for example, plant them into the ground in a deep pot with the bottom removed to stop them spreading). They are quite invasive.
- When the shoots emerge from the ground in the spring, they are a source of nutritious, tasty food. Only the top 30cm (1') is edible until the plant grows beyond 1m (3') tall. To prepare, remove the tough outer leaves, chop the shoots into pieces and steam. Bamboo shoots provide useful garden canes too.
- Bamboo seeds are also edible, once de-husked. They are valued as a grain, like rice, in China.

Botanical name	Common name	Height	Spread
Castanea pumila	Chinquapin	3m (10')	2m (6'6")

- It prefers well-drained soil but will grow in most soils, even very poor soils. Acid and neutral soils only. Even very acidic soils are tolerated.
- A suckering shrub that requires full sun. It is a good alternative to sweet chestnut trees if you have a small garden.
- The flowers are monoecious (that means individual flowers are either male or female, but both sexes can be found on the same plant) and are pollinated by insects.
- Produces small, sweet chestnuts in September.

Botanical name	Common name	Height	Spread
Ceanothus prostratus	Mahala mat	10cm (4")	1.5m (5')

- Happy in most soil types. It prefers well-drained soil or loamy soil. Acid, neutral and alkaline soils are ok. Tolerates light shade but prefers sun.
- Hermaphrodite, bee-pollinated. Not edible.
- All parts of this plant contain high levels of saponins. Saponins protect the plants from soil-borne pathogens. If you crush the plant parts (especially the flowers) and mix them with water, they will make a gentle lather that is a good soap substitute – gentle on the skin.

Botanical name	Common name	Height	Spread
Cephalotaxus fortunei	Chinese plum yew	3-4m (10-13')	3-4m (10-13')
Cephalotaxus harringtonia	Japanese plum yew		

- Easy understorey plant. Happy in most soil types. Acid, neutral and alkaline soils are ok.
- This is an evergreen plant that tolerates lots of shade and still fruits abundantly.
- Male and female plants need to be placed relatively close together, as they are wind-pollinated.
- Unusual grape-sized fruits with a nutty flavour when fully ripe. They ripen late in the year. The berries have to be fully ripe or they are horrible. If that doesn't work for you, cook with them instead. Their seeds taste like pine nuts and can be dried.

Botanical name	Common name	Height	Spread
Chanomeles speciosa	Japanese quince	3m (10')	4m (13')
Chanomeles x superba 'Crimson and Gold'			

- Happy in most soil types. It prefers well-drained soil, but will even grow in heavy clay. Acid, neutral and alkaline soils are ok.
- Will grow in full shade or sun.
- Self-fertile.
- Citrus-flavoured fruits in September. Not good raw but delicious for jellies and lemonade.

Botanical name	Common name	Height	Spread
Corylus spp.	Hazels or filberts.	As part of the shrub layer, the plants should be coppiced every 7 years to keep them shrub-sized and manageable	

- Happy in most soil types. Acid, neutral and alkaline. Requires semi-shade or sun. Natural understory tree.
- The downside is that after each coppice cut, the plants will need approx. 3-4 years to start producing nuts again. So ideally grow a number of them and coppice a different tree every year to keep a regular hazelnut crop.
- Happy in most soil types. Acid, neutral and alkaline. Requires semi-shade or sun.
- Wind-pollinated and benefits from two or more trees near each other. Occasionally shaking the branches when hazels are in flower in spring helps pollination.
- Edible nuts are best harvested by stringing fine nets around the tree base.
- Nuts can be eaten raw or roasted. Use ground nuts to make oil and milk.

Botanical name	Common name	Height	Spread
Elaeagnus multiflora	Goumi	3m (10')	2m (6'6")

- It prefers well-drained soil but will grow in most soils, even very poor soils. Happy in acid, alkaline and neutral soils.
- Deciduous plant that is good for hedging and tolerates maritime exposure.
- Fixes nitrogen.
- Hermaphrodite, pollinated by bees.
- Good dessert fruit produced in summer. Must be fully ripe for the flavour to emerge. Good for baking with too.

Botanical name	Common name	Height	Spread
Fuchsia varieties	Fuchsia	1-3m (3-10')	1-3 m(3-10')

- Happy in most soil types. It prefers well-drained soil but will grow in most soils, even very poor soils. Happy in acid, alkaline and neutral soils.
- Tolerant of partial shade. May need frost protection in cold winters. Tolerates maritime exposure.
- Self-fertile.
- All fuchsias produce berries. Some are nicer than others. They have to be ripe. The fruit can be up to an inch long.

Botanical name	Common name	Height	Spread
Gaultheria procumbens	Checkerberry	10cm (4")	1m (3')

- Happy in sandy and loamy soil, even very poor soils. Only happy in acid, and neutral soils.
- Tolerates a deep shade and drought. Self-fertile.
- Oil of wintergreen essential oil from the leaves makes a powerful anti-inflammatory oil to be used externally.
- Fresh leaves makes a good tea.

Botanical name	Common name	Height	Spread
Gaultheria shallon	Salal	1.2m (4')	1m (3')

- Happy in sandy and loamy soil, even very poor soils. Only happy in acid, and neutral soils.
- Tolerates a deep shade.
- Evergreen hermaphrodite shrub, which grows well in full shade, even under conifers and in very acid soil, so it can be useful.
- Fruits in late summer. Taste ok fresh or they can be used in jams or baking. Dried, they make a good raisin substitute.

Botanical name	Common name	Height	Spread
Lonicera caerulea	Blue edible honeysuckle or honeyberry	1.5m (5')	1.5m (5')

- It prefers moist soil but will grow in most soils. Happy in acid, alkaline and neutral soils.
- Tolerates some shade but prefers the sun.
- Hermaphrodite and insect-pollinated, but if you can, plant more than one plant as it benefits from cross-pollination with a compatible variety.
- Edible fruit reminiscent of blueberries. Good raw, for jams and for baking with.

Botanical name	Common name	Height	Spread
Lycium barbarum	Goji berry	2m (6'6")	3m (10')

- Hardy deciduous shrub that tolerates semi-shade and maritime exposure.
- It prefers well-drained soil but will grow in most soils, even poor ones. Happy in acid, alkaline and neutral soils.
- Hermaphrodite, pollinated by bees.
- Young shoots and leaves treated as a vegetable can be steamed or stir-fried like spinach. Related to the same family as potatoes and tomatoes, so **do not eat** if you have allergic reactions to these. Dried fruits are high in vitamin C.

Botanical name	Common name	Height	Spread
Mahonia aquifolium	Oregon grape	1.5m (5')	1m (3')
Mahonia repens	Creeping-rooted barberry	1m (3')	1m (3')

• It will grow happily in most soils, even heavy clay. Happy in acid, alkaline and neutral soils.
• Tolerant of deep shade or no shade.
• Self-fertile.
• Edible flowers in winter. The fruit is seedy but nice raw or for jams. Blue dyes can be extracted from the fruit.

Botanical name	Common name	Height	Spread
Morus alba,	White mulberry	As part of the shrub layer, plants must be coppiced every 5-7 years to keep them shrub-sized and manageable.	
M. rubra	Red mulberry		

• Happy in most soil types. Happy in acid, alkaline and neutral soils.
• Tolerates wind but not maritime exposure.
• Self-fertile. Hybrids produce better fruit.
• Fruits can be eaten fresh when fully ripened. Or they can be used in cooking, in much the same way as blackberries and raspberries. They can also be dried and ground into flour. Fresh leaves can be steamed to make tea.

Botanical name	Common name	Height	Spread
Myrica cerifera	Wax myrtle or bayberry	9m (29'5")	3m (10')

• Happy in sandy, clay and loamy soil, though it prefers well-drained soil. Only happy in acid, and neutral soils.
• Tolerates partial shade and wind but not maritime conditions.
• The flowers are monoecious (that means individual flowers are either male or female, but both sexes can be found on the same plant) and are pollinated by wind.
• Edible fruits can be eaten raw or cooked but not much flavour. Leaves can be used to flavour food like a bay leaf, as can the berries. Dried leaves can used to make a tea.

Botanical name	Common name	Height	Spread
Ribes divaricatum	Worcesterberry, coastal black gooseberry	2-3m (6'6"-10')	1m (3')

• Happy in most soil types. But it prefers well-drained soil. Acid, neutral and alkaline soils are ok. Tolerates some shade.
• Large thorns work well as a predator deterrent around young trees or mixed into your hedging planting plans.
• Self-fertile.
• Lots of gooseberry-like fruits in July and August. Very good fruit raw or good for jams and cooking.

Botanical name	Common name	Height	Spread
Rubus fruticosus	Blackberry	2-4m (6'6"-13') scrambling shrubs. The stems propagate by 'tip-layering' – shoot tips root when they touch the ground.	

• Happy in most soil types. But it prefers well-drained soil. Acid, neutral and alkaline soils are ok.
• Self-fertile and can grow in full shade or full sun.
• A pioneer plant that is quite invasive and fast-growing, but worth the effort to allow them a home in your garden. Fresh, ripe blackberries are the most subtle and wonderful flavour ever (in my opinion).
• Advisable to choose the thornless varieties as these provide a more manageable solution. However, large thorns, on the bog standard plants, are useful as a predator deterrent around young trees or mixed into your boundary hedging planting plans. Large and long stems, de-thorned and halved in November are useful in skep making and in basketry.
• Dyes can made from new shoots and fruit.

Botanical name	Common name	Height	Spread
Rubus idaeus – lots of varieties	Raspberry	Raspberries have stems 2m (6'6") high and spread by means of suckers – they send up new stems near the parent stem and spread outwards gradually.	

- Happy in most soil types. But it prefers well-drained soil. Acid, neutral and alkaline soils are ok. An invaluable plant that is. quite shade tolerant. Allow these to run wild as much as your space allows. They spread by suckers.
- Self-fertile, producing wonderful juicy fruits. Fresh raspberries are one of the best flavours in the world. They can also be cooked and made into jellies and jams. They freeze well too. There are lots of great varieties available, – plant a selection of them so that you have fruit from June into November.

Ribes nigrum – many cultivars available	Blackcurrant	1-2 m (3'-6'6")	1m (3')

- Happy in most soil structures. Acid, neutral and alkaline soils are ok. A self-fertile plant that tolerates light shade.
- Abundant fruits from June to September, depending on variety. Eat fresh or store as jams and preserves. Fruits were traditionally used for dyeing clothes purple.

Ribes rubrum	Redcurrant / white currant	2m (6'6")	1m (3')

- Happy in most soil structures. Acid, neutral and alkaline soils are ok.
- Self-fertile plant that is quite shade-tolerant but the more shade, the leggier the plant and the higher the fruit will be on the bush.
- Fruits are available from June to September, depending on the variety. However, the harvest is susceptible to birds, as they love eating redcurrants! The fruits are a little tart but sweet enough to be eaten raw if sweetened. They can also be cooked and used to make jams, syrups and sauces.

Ribes uva-crispa	Gooseberry	1.2m (4')	1m (3')

- Happy in most soil structures. Acid, neutral and alkaline soils are ok.
- Self-fertile plant that is quite shade-tolerant but the more shade, the leggier the plant and the higher the fruit will be on the bush.
- Needs occasional cutting back to keep fruit plentiful.
- Abundant cooking fruits available from June to August, depending on varieties. They can also be lovely raw as a dessert berry if left to get very ripe. Most gooseberries have husks that will need to be removed. Once made into a compote, can be used for cordials, jams, chutneys, sauces and baking.

Ribes x culverwellii	Jostaberry	2-3m (6'6"-10')	1-2m (3'-6'6")

- Happy in most soil structures. Acid, neutral and alkaline soils are ok.
- Frost-tolerant, self-fertile plant that is happy in semi-shade.
- Fruits available in July-August. Similar to gooseberries but a little sweeter. Can be eaten fresh or cooked and used in preserves, sauces, pies, fools, juice or wine.

Rubus x loganobaccus varieties	Loganberry	2-4m (6'6"-13') scrambling shrubs. The stems propagate by 'tip-layering' – shoot tips root when they touch the ground.	

- Happy in most soil structures. Acid, neutral and alkaline soils are ok.
- Self-fertile and quite shade-tolerant. Similar to blackberry in its behaviour. Allow to drape over large shrubs for support. You could also tie the large shoots to a wire fence each spring.
- Loganberries can be eaten in the same way as blackberries and raspberries, but they usually need sweetening. They can be stewed, baked, puréed, and used for sauces, jellies and jams, etc. Loganberry jam was my mum's prized product from our garden when I was growing up. Best jam ever! Good early and mid-season fruiting varieties are available.

Botanical name	Common name	Height	Spread
Rosa rugosa	Japanese rose	1-2m (3'-6'6") high. Spreads by suckering.	

- Happy in most soil types, sandy, clay or loam. Prefers moist soil however. Happy in acid, neutral and alkaline soils. It will grow in sun or semi-shade.
- Self-fertile deciduous or semi-evergreen shrub. One of the best. Plant them wherever you can along hedges or the edges of woodland.
- Both flowers and hips are edible. The hips need plenty of sun to fully ripen. Agroforestry expert Martin Crawford suggests using a steam juice extractor to avoid fiddling with the seeds. There is a layer of hairs inside the hip, around the seeds that you should avoid eating. The juice can be made into cordials, jellies, syrups and desserts. Dry the hips to make teas once de-seeded and de-haired. Packed with vitamin C – one cup of rosehip tea has more vitamin C than 40 oranges.

Rosmarinus officinalis	Rosemary	1.5m (5')	1.2m (4')

- Evergreen shrub that will cope with maritime exposure.
- Happy in most soil types, sandy, clay or loam. Prefers well-drained soil however. Happy in acid, neutral and alkaline soils and tolerates highly alkaline soil. It will grow in sun or semi-shade. Hermaphrodite and bee-pollinated.
- Young stems and leaves can be used raw or cooked as a culinary herb.
- The flowers are edible, and the leaves and/or flowers can be steeped in hot water to make a tea. Essential oil used in perfumes and many other products.

Sambucus racemosa	European red elder	3m (10')	3m (10')

- Happy in most soil types, sandy, clay or loam. Prefers moist soil however. Happy in acid, neutral and alkaline soils. It will grow in sun or semi-shade.
- Self-fertile.
- Fragrant, edible flowers can be used to make cordials, wines and 'champagne'. Blossoms picked in May or June are delicious dipped in batter and fried. Fruits should be cooked before use. They are best cooked with other fruits or made into jams, jellies or wine.

Staphylea trifolia	American and European bladdernuts	4m (13')	4m (13')
S. pinnata		2m (6'6")	2m (6'6")

- Happy in most soil types, sandy, clay or loam. Prefers moist soil however. Happy in acid, neutral and alkaline soils. It will grow in sun or semi-shade. Hermaphrodite and bee-pollinated.
- Around October / November the tasty seeds can be de-husked, dried and stored or used for oil extraction in large quantities.

Vaccinium corymbosum (varieties)	Blueberry	45cm-2m (18"–7')	45cm-2m (18"–7')

- Happy in most soil structures. Will tolerate soil with a pH as high as 6.0 but prefers a more acidic soil.
- Self-fertile. A long-lived evergreen shrub that needs acidic soil (with a pH below 5.5). Requires full sun; will tolerate only partial shade.
- Nutrient-rich, sweet fruits, commonly eaten as dessert fruits but can be baked in pies and used for jams. Purple dyes from fruit and leaves.
- Lots of fantastic cultivars available, such as *V. australe* 'Darrow' for late cropping.

GROWING SHRUBS FROM CUTTINGS

The easiest way to build the diversity and variety of trees and shrubs in your garden is to share cuttings with your neighbours and friends. A lot of these shrubs are easy to propagate from hardwood cuttings in winter, or softwood cuttings in summer. Willow rooting liquid will help these cuttings grow roots quickly. If you don't know how to take cuttings, there are many good books on the subject, as well as online tutorials. It's dead simple.

DESIGNING THE SHRUB LAYER

The best position for most shrubs within a forest garden is outside the drip lines of sub-canopy trees, because they will get more sunlight there. Some shrubs will eventually encroach into the canopy above them. Try to plan it so these shrubs are the more shade-tolerant species. Put the smaller shrubs on the south-facing sides of the woodland and the taller ones to the back. Remember to leave access for harvesting the trees! Lots of little path networks or simple stepping stones to allow you in and around each area.

LAYER 4. HERBACEOUS PLANTS

In order to achieve stability at maturity, you really should incorporate as many of the woodland layers as possible. If your budget doesn't allow you to install the entire design at once, leave existing grassland under the trees and shrubs until you have the resources to gradually expand them. This *does* leave you with the chore of mowing the grass around the new plantings, or you could use grazing animals to do that for you. Although the land is resting while it is fallow, it is not actively building the fertility it needs to support the planned woodland. So it would be best to clear the land initially really. We cleared our land initially with pigs and then, after they had done their grubbing work, we sowed a range of deep rooting nutrient accumulator seeds that immediately set to work on building up the fertility of the topsoil. Eventually, you will need all the layers of the garden to work together for it to reach its potential.

In a smaller garden, the herbaceous plant layer (usually not much higher than 1m / 3') may actually be the third layer of your forest garden, the shrubs and small trees being the upper layers, but the land will be happy to have any layered structure that replicates woodland. Of course it is still preferable to have trees, but that isn't always possible so do the best you can. Even in a tiny garden, though, it's nice if you can fit in at least one tree. It makes the land very happy, rather than just happy enough.

Trees bring a strong presence and a lot of good energy with them. They help you set your own roots down into the land so you grow strong together. Without trees it is harder for the land to feel stable. In Ireland, people have always been concerned about trees blocking the light in their back gardens. While I understand this, it is so much more beautiful to look out of your window and see a living woodland dappled with light rather than a sunny but lifeless space. Light comes to us in more forms than one, after all.

The herbaceous layer is mainly made up of perennial, soft-stemmed (non-woody) plants including culinary and medicinal herbs, vegetables, mulch producers and self-seeding annuals. You can also include some smaller, woody shrubs if you like.

We seed bombed our herbaceous and root layers with a selection of herb and root vegetable seeds. Nature decides what grows best where. I learned this from *The One-Straw Revolution* (see Resources) and it works brilliantly.

DESIGNING PLANTING POSITIONS FOR THE HERBACEOUS LAYER

Herbaceous plants grow best in open areas and around the edges of the shrubs. As you become more familiar with the movement of light through the garden, you will notice that some places are sunnier than others, so you may decide to put more sun-loving species there. Or you may see a plant that is wilting in the afternoon heat and transplant it to a shadier location.

If your newly planted herbaceous plants have too much competition from other low-growing plants, mulch them heavily until they have a chance to get established. Make sure you place them on the outer edges of the shrubs so you don't have to spend time forever pruning the encroaching shrubs. Choose a diversity of plants that appeal to you and plant heavily enough to ensure a decent harvest right away.

Mixing edible herbs, ground covers and deep-rooted plants throughout the woodland creates a healthy balance and prevents damage from insects and diseases. Also try to include areas of native plants to support the local ecology. It may take a few years before you can recognize all these new plants in your garden, so I suggest you label them and note the ones that are edible.

The list below is a sample of herbaceous plants that I have found particularly worthwhile. Not all of them are edible, but they are all useful. Some help build the soil's fertility, others create habitat for wildlife.

Herbs with strongly scented oils, including many common kitchen herbs, are not only edible but offer other benefits too. Sometimes known as 'aromatic pest confusers', these plants contain highly aromatic essential oils that confuse or even deter pests. The oils also have antibacterial, antifungal and antimicrobial properties, which are highly valued in naturopathic medicine and will also be of great support to their neighbouring plants in a stable ecosystem.

Recommended herbaceous plants for layer 4

Botanical name	Common name	Height	Spread
Alliaria petiolata	Jack-by-the-hedge	0.8-1m (2'8"-3')	40cm (1'4")

- Hardy biennial. Happy in most soil types, sandy, clay or loam. Prefers moist soil however. Happy in acid, neutral and alkaline soils. It will grow in sun or deep shade. Self-fertile.
- Stays green all year in mild climates, otherwise it emerges in very early spring.
- The leaves have a lovely garlic/mustard flavour. Chop finely and add to salads or omelettes or cook them as a vegetable. Its white flowers add a spicy decoration to salads.

Botanical name	Common name	Height	Spread
Allium ampeloprasum var. *babingtonii*	Babington's leek (also known as perennial leek)	0.5m (1'8")	30cm (1')

- Hardy perennial leek. Happy in most soil types, sandy, clay or loam. Prefers dry soil however. Happy in acid, neutral and alkaline soils. It will only grow happily in sun.
- May take a few years to be big enough to harvest regularly, but will provide a good harvest of leaves in winter. It's also possible to harvest the bulb in late summer.
- The leaves and bulb can be eaten raw or cooked and have a mild garlic flavour.

Botanical name	Common name	Height	Spread
Allium cepa Aggregatum Group	Shallot	40cm (1'4") leaves, 1.2m (4') flower	40cm (1'4")

- Happy in most soil types. Prefers sandy or loam however. Happy in acid, neutral and alkaline soils. It will only grow happily in sun. Hermaphrodite and bee-pollinated.
- Bulbs and leaves can be eaten raw or cooked.

Botanical name	Common name	Height	Spread
Allium fistulosum	Welsh onion	0.5m (1'8")	20cm (8")

- A perennial alternative to spring onions. Happy in most soil types, sandy, clay or loam. Prefers dry soil however. Happy in acid, neutral and alkaline soils. It will only grow happily in full sun. Hermaphrodite and bee-pollinated.
- A great salad resource to have in a forest garden.

Botanical name	Common name	Height	Spread
Allium schoenoprasum	Chives	30cm (1')	30cm (1')

- Happy in most soil types, sandy, clay or loam. Happy in acid, neutral and alkaline soils. Grows at woodland edges in dappled shade or sun.
- Self-fertile. Spreads well.
- Leaves have a mild onion flavour and can be used raw in salads or as flavouring in soups, etc. Bulbs can be used as spring onions. Flowers can be used in salads.
- Juice from leaves can be used as an insect repellent and fungicide, and in scented oils. Also an aromatic pest confuser.

Botanical name	Common name	Height	Spread
Allium ursinum	Ramsons	30cm (1')	20cm (8")

- Happy in most soil types, sandy, clay or loam. Happy in acid, neutral and alkaline soils. Grows in full shade, dappled shade or sun. Hermaphrodite and bee-pollinated.
- Likes damp, rich soils. Easy to grow anywhere and will spread. Inhibits the growth of legumes so not compatible with them.
- Leaves die back just as flowers emerge.
- Edible flowers, leaves, stems and bulbs. Flowers can be used as salad garnish. Garlicky/grassy-flavoured leaves make great pesto. Stems can be used as spring onions. Bulbs are similar to cultivated garlic.
- Many medicinal benefits – antiseptic, antioxidant, immune-boosting. Will boost immunity of surrounding plants too.
- Aromatic pest confuser (see page 185).

Botanical name	Common name	Height	Spread
Aralia cordata	Udo	1.8m (6')	0.8 m (2'8")

- Happy in most soil types, sandy, clay or loam. Happy in acid, neutral and alkaline soils. Grows in full shade. Semi-shade is preferable, and shelter from morning sun.
- Edible shoots (use like asparagus) and leaves (use in salads and as cooked greens). Common vegetable in Japan.
- Hermaphrodite and bee-pollinated.

Asparagus officinalis	Asparagus	1.5m (1'8")	0.8m (2'8")

- Happy in most soil types, sandy, clay or loam. Will grow in very acid or very alkaline soils.
- Tolerates maritime exposure, semi-shade and sun.
- Perennial plant but not self-fertile so both male and female flowers are needed if seed is required.
- Stems are steamed as a vegetable. Seeds can be roasted and used in place of coffee beans.

Astragalus crassicarpus	Buffalo pea, ground plum.	0.5m (1'8")	0.5m (1'8")

- Perennial. Happy in sandy or loamy soils. Happy in acid, neutral and alkaline soils. It needs full sun.
- Hermaphrodite and bee-pollinated.
- You can eat the fleshy, unripe seed pods raw or cook them. A bit like plums.
- Nitrogen fixer (see page 175).

Beta vulgaris subsp. *maritima*	Sea beet	0.8m (2'8")	40cm (1'4")

- Happy in most soil types, sandy, clay or loam. Happy in acid, neutral and alkaline soils. Will grow in very saline or highly alkaline soils.
- Hardy perennial that tolerates semi-shade or no shade.
- Hermaphrodite, wind-pollinated.
- Leaves can be harvested all year and make delicious cooked greens. Roots are harvested in winter and are a good beetroot substitute.

Beta vulgaris subsp. *flavescens*	Swiss chard	0.9m (3')	30cm (1')

- Hardy biennial that needs sun.
- Happy in most soil types, sandy, clay or loam. Happy in acid, neutral and alkaline soils. Will grow in very acid or highly alkaline soils. Needs full sun.
- Hermaphrodite, wind-pollinated.
- High-yielding plant with very tasty leaves and leaf stems, when cooked. Flowering stems also work well as a broccoli substitute.

Brassica oleracea var. *ramosa*	Daubenton's perennial kale	0.9m (3')	0.8m (2'8")

- Hardy perennial. Happy in most soil types, sandy, clay or loam. Happy in acid, neutral and alkaline soils. Will grow in very acid or highly alkaline soils. Tolerates semi-shade or no shade.
- Hermaphrodite and bee-pollinated.
- All-year harvest of cabbage-flavoured leaves that can be steamed or stir-fried. Young leaves are delicious eaten raw. Flower heads make a tasty broccoli substitute – keep removing flowers to prolong harvesting time.

Bunias orientalis	Hill mustard	0.9m (3')	0.5m (1'8")

- Hardy perennial. Happy in most soil types, sandy, clay or loam. Happy in acid, neutral and alkaline soils. Will grow in very acid or highly alkaline soils. Needs full sun or dappled shade.
- Hermaphrodite and bee-pollinated.
- Leaves are too hairy when raw, but are a nice cooked vegetable. Flowers and flowering stems are tasty raw or cooked like broccoli.

Botanical name	Common name	Height	Spread
Calamintha nepeta	Lesser calamint	0.6m (2')	0.8m (2'8")

- Perennial herb. Happy in sandy or loamy soil. Needs neutral or alkaline soils. Will grow in highly alkaline soils. Needs full sun or dappled shade.
- Hermaphrodite and bee-pollinated but will benefit from pollination partner nearby so plant more than one plant.
- A sweet and aromatic tea can be made from the leaves. Its essential oil has a potent odour and is used in aromatherapy. Aromatic pest confuser.

Botanical name	Common name	Height	Spread
Calendula officinalis	Common marigold	0.6m (2')	0.5m (1'8")

- Hardy annual that tolerates all soils. Prefers semi-shade or no shade. Good addition to annual seed bombs.
- The flowers are monoecious (that means individual flowers are either male or female, but both sexes can be found on the same plant) and are pollinated by bees.
- Edible petals and leaves. Fresh petals can be sprinkled on soups, stews and salads. Dried petals make excellent seasoning. Common marigold is mainly used as a remedy for skin problems, applied externally to bites and stings, etc.
- Acts as an insect deterrent so it is often used as a companion plant. Attracts beneficial wasps to eat aphids.

Botanical name	Common name	Height	Spread
Chenopodium bonus-henricus	Good King Henry	0.8m (2'8")	30cm (1')

- Hardy perennial. Happy in most soil types, sandy, clay or loam. Will grow in very acid or very alkaline soils. Needs full sun or partial shade.
- Self-fertile, bee-pollinated.
- Leaves, raw or blanched, make a good winter salad addition. The roots are an invaluable food source as they contain inulin, which supports healthy gut bacteria. Cook in the same way as parsnips. They can also be roasted and ground and used as a coffee substitute.

Botanical name	Common name	Height	Spread
Cichorium intybus	Chicory	1.5m (5')	0.5m (1'8")

- Hardy perennial. Happy in most soil types, sandy, clay or loam. Will grow in very acid or very alkaline soils. Needs full sun or partial shade. Hermaphrodite and wind-pollinated.
- From April until June, flowering shoots can be cooked in the same way as asparagus. Cut them at the base and peel. From midsummer, the spinach-like leaves are delicious stir-fried. Roast the seeds and use like poppy seeds.

Botanical name	Common name	Height	Spread
Crambe maritima	Sea kale	0.6m (2')	0.6m (2')

- Hardy perennial. Happy in most soil types, sandy, clay or loam. Acid, neutral and alkaline soils. Will grow in very saline soils. Needs full sun or partial shade.
- Self-fertile, bee-pollinated.
- Young spinach-like leaves are edible raw or cooked. Older leaves are less palatable. Flowering shoots are like sprouting broccoli when steamed.

Botanical name	Common name	Height	Spread
Cymbopogon citratus	Lemongrass	1.5m (5')	0.6m (2')

- Lemongrass is cold sensitive and will not survive a harsh winter. Best to grow it under glass or in a polytunnel if you have one.
- Needs full sun, prefers moist soil.
- Use fresh or dried. Lightly crushed stalks add a citrus flavour to Asian dishes. Leaves can be brewed into tea. Its main component is citral, or lemonal, which has antibacterial, antifungal and antimicrobial properties. The oil is used in aromatherapy and as an insect repellent.
- Aromatic pest confuser.

Botanical name	Common name	Height	Spread
Cynara scolymus	Chards (also known as globe artichoke)	1.5m (5')	1m (3')

- Hardy perennial for a sunny woodland edge. Grows in most soil types, sandy, clay or loam. Acid, neutral and alkaline soils. Tolerates strong winds but not maritime exposure.
- The flowers are hermaphrodite and are bee-pollinated.
- Harvest flower buds in August/September and boil or steam until tender. The edible fleshy lower portion of each flower bract, has a lovely nutty flavour. Dried flowers can be used as rennet for curdling milk. Young leaf stems make a good celery substitute.

Echinacea purpurea	Cone flower	1.2m (4')	0.5m (1'8")

- Grows in most soil types, sandy, clay or loam. Acid, neutral and alkaline soils. Hardy perennial that needs a sunny position.
- Hermaphrodite, insect-pollinated.
- The whole plant has numerous medicinal properties. It is most commonly used to fight infection and boost the immune system. Roots can be dried for storage. I recommend it as an ingredient for all plant tonics.

Fagopyrum esculentum	Buckwheat	1.5m (5')	30cm (1')

- Annual plant that needs sun. Grows in most soil types, sandy, clay or loam. Acid, neutral and alkaline soils.
- Leaves, used like spinach, are edible raw or cooked, but better cooked. Seeds can be harvested 3-4 months after sowing. They can be soaked in water, sprouted and eaten raw. Alternatively, eat the seeds as a flour. Dried and ground into a powder, they make an excellent gluten-free flour alternative. Grain makes a good gluten-free beer.
- Excellent green manure and nutrient-accumulator crop, as it tends to smother all other emerging 'weeds'.

Foeniculum vulgare	Fennel	1.5m (5')	1m (3')

- Perennial plant, evergreen in more sheltered spots. Tolerates wind but not maritime exposure. Grows in most soil types, sandy, clay or loam. Acid, neutral and alkaline soils. Needs a sunny position.
- Self-fertile plant which is insect-pollinated.
- Good productivity all year round in sheltered positions.
- All parts are edible and have a distinctive aniseed flavour. Bulb and stalk can be eaten raw or cooked. Feathery leaves can be added to sauces or used as a garnish. Seeds ripen near September. Dried seeds have a warm, sweet aroma often used in baking breads and cakes. Fennel essential oil is used in aromatherapy.

Matteuccia struthiopteris	Ostrich fern, fiddle head fern	1.2m (4')	0.6m (2')

- Perennial fern that will grow in those wet dark corners of your forest garden that are hard to fill with much else. Grows in most soil types, but prefers moist places. Happy in acid or neutral soils, even very acidic soils. Spreads by rhizomes. Will tolerate deep shade and even full sun if their roots are kept moist.
- The young curled-up shoots (only available for a short spring period), make a good alternative to asparagus, but must be well-cooked. Be sure to cook for at least 15 minutes, or they may upset your stomach.

Melissa officinalis	Lemon balm	0.7m (2'4")	40cm (1'4")

- Hardy perennial that is happy in sun or partial shade. Grows in sandy or loam soil. Happy in acid, neutral and alkaline soils.
- The flowers are hermaphrodite and are bee-pollinated.
- Use fresh leaves in salads and butters. Add to cooked dishes, sauces and marinades. Leaves make a soothing tea, either on their own or combined with china tea. The essential oil is popularly used in aromatherapy. Aromatic pest confuser.

Botanical name	Common name	Height	Spread
Mentha spicata	Spearmint	0.8-1m (2'8"-3')	Spreads into a carpet

- Deciduous perennial that is happiest in heavy and wet soils. Will grow well in semi-shade or sun.
- Mint spreads by runners and can be invasive, but can be kept in check by a mown path. Alternatively, sage plants will stop mint plants spreading – they seem to have a policing effect on them.
- Leaves can be used to make herbal tea or as flavouring in many dishes. Mint sauce is usually made from these leaves. Mint oils sprayed around window edges will keep spiders and ants out of your house. Spearmint essential oil has many health benefits.
- Aromatic pest confuser (see page 185).

Mentha x piperita	Peppermint	0.5m (1'8")	1m (3')

- Deciduous perennial that is happiest in heavy and wet soils. Grows in neutral, acid or alkaline soils. Will grow well in semi-shade or sun.
- Spreads aggressively using underground runners. Can be held in check by a mown path or a border of sage plants.
- Leaves can be used to make herbal tea or as flavouring in many dishes. Mint oils sprayed around window edges will keep spiders and ants out of your house. Essential oil has antiseptic and antiviral properties.
- Aromatic pest confuser (see page 185).

Monarda didyma	Bergamot	0.9m (3')	0.5m (1'8")

- Hardy perennial. Happy in most soil types, sandy, clay or loam. Grows in acid, neutral and alkaline soils. Tolerates semi-shade or no shade.
- Hermaphrodite and bee-pollinated.
- Young leaves and shoots are tasty additions to salads. Flowers add colour and flavour too. An aromatic tea can be made from the leaves. Bergamot essential oil has many medicinal benefits and is frequently used in skincare products and perfumes.
- Aromatic pest confuser (see page 185).

Origanum vulgare	Oregano	0.6m (2')	0.8m (2'8")

- Hardy perennial. Happy in most soil types, sandy, clay or loam. Grows in acid, neutral and alkaline soils. Tolerates full sun to partial shade.
- Hermaphrodite and bee-pollinated.
- Leaves may be used fresh or dried to flavour culinary dishes (dried form is more pungent). Edible flowers can be added to salads or used as a garnish. Essential oil has antibacterial properties and high amounts of antioxidants.
- Aromatic pest confuser (see page 185).

Petroselinum crispum	Parsley	0.5m (1'8")	40cm (1'4")

- Hardy biennial that is happy in sun or partial shade. Grows well in most soil types, sandy, clay or loam. Grows in acid, neutral and alkaline soils.
- Self-fertile.
- Culinary herb that adds a mild flavour to many dishes, or use as a garnish. Leaves are highly nutritious and should be harvested regularly to ensure fresh growth, but it is advised to eat them in moderation.
- Juice from the leaves seems to be a good midge/mosquito repellent.

Botanical name	Common name	Height	Spread
Plantago major or *P. lanceolata*	Greater plantain or Ribwort plantain	10cm (4")	10cm (4")

- Hardy perennial that needs a sunny position. Happy in most soil types, sandy, clay or loam. Grows in acid, neutral and alkaline soils. Tolerates maritime exposure.
- Hermaphrodite and wind-pollinated.
- Seeds can be boiled and used like sago to thicken sauces, or ground into a powder to added to other flours.
- Leaves have antibacterial, antiseptic and anti-inflammatory properties that have many medicinal benefits. Can also be applied externally to treat cuts, wounds and inflamed skin. Chew the leaves into a pulp and apply to fresh cuts to cause the blood to clot.

Botanical name	Common name	Height	Spread
Rheum rhaponticum	Common rhubarb	1.2m (4')	Spreading

- Hardy perennial that prefers sun or partial shade. Happiest when the soil is moist soil. Will grow in acid, neutral or alkaline soil. Can be used as a spreading ground cover.
- Flowers are hermaphrodite and wind-pollinated.
- Thick, fleshy stalks are not to be eaten raw and should be cooked with plenty of sugar. Stew, poach or roast and use in crumbles, pies and preserves. The leaves should never be eaten as they contain oxalic acid.

Botanical name	Common name	Height	Spread
Rosmarinus officinalis	Rosemary	1.5m (5')	1.2m (4')

- Evergreen shrub that needs full sun and excellent drainage. Happy in most soil types, sandy, clay or loam. Grows in acid, neutral and alkaline soils.
- Hermaphrodite and bee-pollinated.
- Aromatic culinary herb containing beneficial nutrients. Leaves can be used fresh or dried (more pungent) to flavour salads, soups and cooked savoury dishes. Essential oil has an array of health benefits.
- Aromatic pest confuser (see page 185).

Botanical name	Common name	Height	Spread
Rumex acetosa	Common sorrel	0.6m (2')	30cm (1')

- Hardy perennial noted for attracting wildlife. Needs partial to full shade. Happy in most soil types, sandy, clay or loam. Grows in acid, neutral and alkaline soils.
- Both male and female plants are needed for pollination, which is dependent on wind. Leaves are usually available all year round.
- Eat leaves fresh or cooked, but they have a bitter, lemony flavour so are best in a mixed salad if raw. Note: the leaves contain high levels of oxalic acid so should be eaten in moderation. Leaf juice can be used as a curdling agent for milk. Seeds can be ground and used as a flour. Roots are also edible when dried and cooked. Flowers can be eaten too.

Botanical name	Common name	Height	Spread
Solidago odora	Blue mountain tea (also known as goldenrod)	1.2m (4')	0.6m (2')

- Hardy perennial that attracts wildlife. Full sun to partial shade. Grows well in sandy, loam and clay soils. Acid, neutral and alkaline soils.
- Hermaphrodite and insect-pollinated.
- This is an herb has antiseptic, antifungal and anti-inflammatory properties with many health benefits. Preparations include tea and tinctures from the dried leaves. Flowers can be infused with oil or used as a poultice.
- Aromatic pest confuser (see page 185).

Botanical name	Common name	Height	Spread
Symphytum officinale	Common comfrey	1.2m (4')	0.5m (1'8")

- Hardy perennial that tolerates sun or partial shade. Happy in most soil types, sandy, clay or loam. Grows in acid, neutral and alkaline soils. Hermaphrodite and bee-pollinated.
- Grows quickly and is tolerant of being cut back several times in a year, creating a lot of biomass, so is a good source of mulch material. Also beneficial as a nutrient accumulator (see page 155) and makes a great plant tonic.
- Poultices are often made from the leaves and roots. Leaves can be used externally to heal wounds, skin complaints and help mend broken bones (sometimes known as 'knitbone'). Harvest before it flowers and dry for later use.

Trifolium pratense	Red clover	0.6m (2')	0.6m (2')

- Hardy perennial that attracts wildlife and fixes nitrogen. Happy in most soil types, sandy, clay or loam. Grows in acid, neutral and alkaline soils. Hermaphrodite and bee-pollinated. Needs a sunny spot and can handle winds but not maritime exposure.
- Young leaves are delicious cooked like spinach. Sweet young flowers can be eaten raw in salads, as can the seeds when sprouted.

Urtica dioica	Stinging nettle	1.2m (4')	1m (3')

- Hardy perennial that will grow in sun or partial shade (woodland edge). A valuable wildlife plant that makes an effective plant tonic. Happy in most soil types, sandy, clay or loam. Grows in acid, neutral and alkaline soils. Needs a sunny spot and can handle winds but not maritime exposure.
- Both male and female plants are needed for pollination, which is dependent on wind.
- Nettles are an extremely nutritious food. Use gloves to harvest the young leaves, then cook or dry them to neutralise the sting before consuming. They make great soup, and nettle tea acts as a cleansing tonic. Remember, only young leaves should be used because older leaves develop gritty particles called cystoliths which act as an irritant to the kidneys.
- The stems provide a flax-like fibre for making string, clothes and paper. A bunch of nettle stems repels flies, so can be used in food storage areas.

Vaccinium deliciosum	Cascade bilberry	30cm (1')	30cm (1')

- Low-growing deciduous shrub that requires acid soils and will even grow under conifers. Likes sandy or loamy soil. Will tolerate sun or semi-shade. Good wildlife plant.
- Flowers are hermaphrodite and are insect-pollinated.
- Fruit is sweet and flavourful when ripe and best eaten fresh, but can be dried or frozen.

Vaccinium myrtillus	Common bilberry (also known as whortleberry)	20cm (8")	30cm (1')

- Same as cascade bilberry – see above.

Layer 5. Ground cover

The herbaceous and the ground-cover layers overlap somewhat, but while some herbaceous plants can tolerate full sun or partial shade, most ground-cover plants are shade-loving. I have tried to include a selection of plants that are also happy in a sunny spot. This layer of plants grow close to the soil, snuggling into gaps between trees, shrubs and perennials. They also tolerate foot traffic.

It's always a good idea to including native ground-cover plants along with exotic species, because it supports the local ecology. As with the native plants you included in other layers, be sure to label the plants until you can remember them all by sight, and note whether they are edible or not. Native plants form complex relationships within local ecosystems. We need to support them as much as possible, even within our own fast-track succession designs.

Recommended ground-cover plants for layer 5

Botanical name	Common name	Height	Spread
Campanula poscharskyana C. porten-schlagiana.	Trailing bellflower, Wall bellflower	20cm (8")	Spreading

- Pretty evergreen perennial that tolerates sun or shade.
- Happy in most soil types, sandy, clay or loam. Grows in neutral and alkaline soils. Self-fertile and bee-pollinated.
- Provides sweet salad leaves all year round. Edible flowers make an attractive blue splash in summer salads.

Chamaemelum nobile	Chamomile	20cm (8")	30cm (1')

- Evergreen hardy perennial. Happy in most soil types, sandy, clay or loam. Grows in acid, neutral and alkaline soils. Self-fertile and bee-pollinated.
- Fresh or dried flowers are used to make herb tea. Useful as a remedy to treat digestive problems and serves as a mild sedative. Essential oil is used as a flavouring and in perfumes.
- Aromatic pest confuser (see page 185).

Claytonia sibirica	Pink purslane	20cm (8")	Spreading

- Evergreen in mild climates. Will grow in all soil types, though it prefers acid or neutral soils. Will grow in the shade of a beech tree and under conifers where few other plants will. Self-fertile and bee-pollinated.
- Leaves can be harvested all year round and used as a salad or as a cooked vegetable, lightly steamed.

Cornus canadensis	Creeping dogwood	20cm (8")	Spreads widely

- Hardy perennial, suitable for acidic and neutral soils. Happy in most soil types, sandy, clay or loam and will grow in very heavy clay. Self-fertile and insect-pollinated. Happy in full sun to partial shade.
- Late-summer fruit tends to be bland, but is high in pectin so can be combined with other fruits to make jams and jellies.

Fragaria vesca	Wild strawberry	15cm (6")	Spreads freely by runners.

- Hardy perennial that will tolerate full shade. Flowers are hermaphrodite and insect pollinated. Grows well in sandy, loamy or clay soil. Happy in acid, neutral or alkaline soil.
- Leaves can be used in salads or to make herbal teas. Delicious small berries in summer and autumn are among my favourite fruits. You can never have enough of these babies finding their way into those shady nooks and crannies.

Fragaria viridis	Green strawberry	30cm (1')	Spreads freely by runners.

- Hardy perennial tolerant of full sun to partial shade. Provides good ground cover between shrubs. Grows well in sandy, loamy or clay soil. Happy in acid, neutral or alkaline soil.
- Male and female plants needed to pollinate flowers and produce fruit.
- Berries produced in June and July are very tasty with a pineapple-like flavour.

Galium odoratum	Sweet woodruff (also known as hay plant or bedstraw)	20cm (8")	0.5m (1'8")

- Hardy perennial providing good ground cover and supporting wildlife. Spreads freely beneath other plants. Grows well in sandy, loamy or clay soil. Happy in acid, neutral or alkaline soil. Self-fertile and insect-pollinated.
- Grow in full to partial shade.
- Traditionally used dried to stuff bedding. Leaves are used to flavour drinks and in perfumery.

Botanical name	Common name	Height	Spread
Gaultheria procumbens	Checkerberry (also known as wintergreen)	30-50cm (1'-1'8")	Spreads slowly

- Self-fertile creeping evergreen shrub that tolerates good amounts of shade. Grows well in sandy or loamy soil. Happy in acid or neutral soil and will grow in very acidic soil. Known to accumulate magnesium from the soil.
- Fruit has a strong medicinal taste and can be eaten raw or cooked. Its dried leaves make a mild herbal tea. Checkerberry has numerous health benefits, but was traditionally used to flavour gums, sweets, drinks and soaps.

Botanical name	Common name	Height	Spread
Ipomoea batatas	Sweet potato	3m (10')	

- Fast-growing perennial climber that doubles as ground cover. Grows well in sandy or loamy soil. Happy in acid or neutral soil. Self-sterile (most sweet potatoes are grown from slips, cuttings, tubers, or tissue culture). Sweet potatoes need cross-pollination from another variety in order to set seed. Allow the plant to clamber over piles of twigs and branches. Needs full sun to be at its best. Many varieties available. Note: sweet potatoes are sometimes confused with yams, but are completely different plants.
- The fleshy roots are delicious and highly nutritious – cook like potatoes. The young leaves and top 5-10cm (2-4") of the growing tips are often eaten as a leafy vegetable, cooked like spinach.
- If you want to store the roots over winter, harvest them in autumn and leave to dry in hot temperatures for a week before storing

Botanical name	Common name	Height	Spread
Mentha requienii	Corsican mint	10cm (4")	Spreads thickly but slowly

- Evergreen ground-cover mint, ideal for planting between stepping stones. Tolerant of full shade. Grows well in sandy, loamy or clay soil and will grow in very heavy clay. Happy in acid, neutral or alkaline soil. Self-fertile and insect-pollinated.
- Leaves have a strong peppermint aroma. Can be used raw or cooked, as flavouring as well as an herb tea. Essential oil sprayed around window-sills will act as a spider or ant deterrent. Rodents also hate the scent of mint and so it was often strewn on drying grain to keep the rodents away.
- Scented oils. Aromatic pest confuser (see page 185).

Botanical name	Common name	Height	Spread
Rubus 'Betty Ashburner'	Groundcover raspberry	0.5m (1'8")	Spreads up to 80cm (2'8") each year

- Prostrate evergreen shrub that tolerates sun or full shade. Grows well in sandy, loamy or clay soil. Happy in acid, neutral or alkaline soil.
- Stems tend to be prickly.
- Produces good raspberry-like fruits in the late summer and autumn. Good for fresh eating or making jam. Stop it from spreading too much by cutting it back or mowing a path around its home. Good plant to pair with mint.

Botanical name	Common name	Height	Spread
Rubus nepalensis	Nepalese raspberry	30cm (1')	Spreads up to 1m (3') every year

- Prostrate evergreen shrub that tolerates sun or full shade, making it a useful forest-garden plant. Grows well in sandy, loamy or clay soil. Happy in acid, neutral or alkaline soil.
- Susceptible to frost damage but recover well. Non-prickly plant that produces raspberry-like fruits in the autumn. Stop it from spreading too much by cutting back or mowing a path around its home. Good plant to pair with mint.
- Good for fresh eating or making jam.

Botanical name	Common name	Height	Spread
Stellaria media	Chickweed	10cm (4")	40cm (1'4")

- Hardy annual. Grows well in sandy, loamy or clay soil. Happy in acid, neutral or alkaline soil.
- Self-fertile and insect-pollinated.
- In leaf in January and can be harvested all year round. Leaves can be used raw or cooked like spinach. Note: they contain soapy substances called saponins so should be eaten in moderation. Seeds can be used as a grain. When ground, they make a good flour alternative.

Botanical name	Common name	Height	Spread
Tetragonia tetragonoides	New Zealand spinach (also known as warrigal)	20cm (8")	1m (3')

- Fast-growing evergreen perennial that provides excellent ground cover. Grows well in sandy or loamy soil and will grow in saline soils. Happy in acid, neutral or alkaline soil. Self-fertile and insect-pollinated. Needs full sun and is frost-tender but will tolerate maritime conditions.
- Young leaves, raw or cooked, make an excellent spinach substitute.

Botanical name	Common name	Height	Spread
Thymus serpyllum	Breckland thyme (also known as creeping thyme)	10cm (4")	30cm (4")

- Evergreen shrub. Prefers sandy or loamy soil. Will grow happily in acid, alkaline or neutral soil but it cannot tolerate shade. Hermaphrodite and bee-pollinated.
- Leaves can be used raw in salads or to add flavour to savoury dishes. Best harvested before the plant flowers if they are to be dried. Makes an excellant tea. Medicinal benefits. Essential oil used medicinally and in perfumery.
- Aromatic pest confuser (see page 185).

Botanical name	Common name	Height	Spread
Thymus x citriodorus	Lemon thyme	10cm (4")	30cm (4")

- Prostrate evergreen shrub that spreads well and can densely cover steep banks. Grows well in sandy, loamy or clay soil. Happy in acid, neutral or alkaline soil. Self-fertile and bee pollinated. Tolerates full sun to deep shade. Good bee plant that flowers sporadically nearly all year.
- Medicinal uses including a homeopathic remedy made from the fresh leaves. Stems are very good for basket weaving.

Botanical name	Common name	Height	Spread
Vinca major	Greater periwinkle	0.6m (2')	0.5m (1'8")
V. minor	Lesser periwinkle	30cm (1')	

- Evergreen shrub. Attracts wildlife. Prefers sandy or loamy soil. Will grow happily in acid, alkaline or neutral soil but it cannot tolerate shade. Hermaphrodite and bee-pollinated.
- Lemon-flavoured leaves are delicious fresh in salads or used as a seasoning. Best harvested before the plant flowers if they are to be dried. They make a refreshing aromatic tea. Medicinal benefits Essential oil used in aromatherapy to treat respiratory complaints, and in perfumery.
- Aromatic pest confuser (see page 185).

Botanical name	Common name	Height	Spread
Viola odorata	Sweet violet	10cm (4")	0.5m (1'8")

- Evergreen hardy perennial that tolerates full sun to partial shade. Grows well in sandy, loamy or clay soil. Happy in acid, neutral or alkaline soil. Self-fertile and bee pollinated.
- Leaves can be harvested all year round. Mild-flavoured young leaves and flowers can be added to salads. Leaves are also used to thicken soups. A tea can be made from the leaves and flowers. Several medicinal uses. Essential oil from the flowers is used in aromatherapy and perfumery.

Layer 6. Underground plants

Most conventional root-layer vegetables – carrots, daikon, onions, parsnips and pota-toes, etc. – like full sun so they are best placed with the other sun-loving plants along the edges of the garden or on the sunny sides of Hügelkultur beds (see page 150). Many naturally growing woodland vegetables, such as wild onion and wild garlic, grow in partial or full shade. The following list of root-layer plants includes many familiar vegetables as well as some lesser-known but very tasty members of this group.

Again, this is a layer that you can develop very well through seed bombing and trusting in nature to put the right plants in the right places (see page 152).

Recommended plants for layer 6

Botanical name	Common name	Height	Spread
Allium ampeloprasum var. *babingtonii*	Babington's leek	0.5m (1'8")	30cm (1')
• Hardy perennial. Grows well in sandy, loamy and clay soil. Can tolerate heavy clay. Happy in acid, neutral and alkaline soils. Tolerates strong winds but not maritime conditions. Needs a sunny position. Hermaphrodite and bee-pollinated. Benefits from more than one plant in the area. • May take a few years to be big enough to harvest regularly, but will provide a good harvest of leaves in winter. It's also possible to harvest the bulb in late summer. • The leaves and bulb can be eaten raw or cooked and have a mild garlic flavour.			
Allium cepa Aggregatum Group	Shallot	40cm (1'4") leaves, 1.2m (4') flower	40cm (1'4")
• Grows well in sandy and loamy soil. Happy in acid, neutral and alkaline soils. Tolerates strong winds but not maritime conditions. Hermaphrodite and bee-pollinated. Benefits from more than one plant in the area. Will grow in sun or dappled shade. • Bulbs and leaves can be eaten raw or cooked.			
Allium sativum	Garlic	0.6m (2')	20cm (8")
• Bulb. Happy in sandy, loamy and clay soils. Grows in acid, neutral and alkaline soils. Likes full sun to partial shade. Hermaphrodite and bee-pollinated. • Bulb is extremely nutritious and can be used raw or cooked in a wide range of foods. Leaves can be used raw, chopped finely in salads, or cooked. • Medicinal and other uses.			

Botanical name	Common name	Height	Spread
Apios americana	Groundnut	1.2m (4')	30cm (1')

- Hardy perennial.
- Needs sun to partial shade. Happy in sandy and loamy soils. Grows in acid, neutral and alkaline soils. Hermaphrodite and bee-pollinated.
- Tubers are a valuable crop. Harvest after 1 year but ideally they need 2-3 years of maturity to become a worthwhile harvest. Can be eaten raw or roasted and have a flavour similar to sweet potato. Seeds are delicious, cooked like peas or beans.
- Nitrogen fixer.

Armoracia rusticana	Horseradish	0.7m (2'4")	0.8m (2'8")

- Perennial. Happy in sandy, loamy and clay soils. Grows in acid, neutral and alkaline soils. Likes full sun to partial shade. Self-fertile, insect-pollinated.
- Young roots can be eaten raw or cooked. Grate to make horseradish sauce. **Avoid during pregnancy**. Many medicinal uses, Also used as a fungicide and repellent.
- Aromatic pest confuser (see page 185).

Beta vulgaris subsp. *maritima*	Sea beet	0.8m (2'8")	40cm (1'4")

- Hardy perennial that requires sun or partial shade. Happy in sandy, loamy and clay soils. Grows in acid, neutral and alkaline soils. Needs full sun to partial shade.
- Young leaves, raw or cooked, provide a delicious spinach substitute. Not as good when leaves mature. Roots are harvested in winter and are a good beetroot substitute. Traditionally this plant was used for treating tumours.

Bunium bulbocastanum	Pig nut	.40cm (1'4")	0.5m (1'8")

- Hardy perennial that requires full sun to partial shade. Happy in sandy, loamy and clay soils. Grows in acid, neutral and alkaline soils.
- Tubers harvested in winter taste like sweet chestnuts when cooked. Leaves, finely chopped, can be used as a salad garnish. Seeds are a cumin substitute.

Camassia quamash	Quamash	30cm (1')	20cm (8")

- Bulb that requires full sun to partial shade. Happy in sandy, loamy and clay soils. Grows in acid, neutral and alkaline soils. Hermaphrodite and bee-pollinated.
- Harvest any time of year. Bulbs release nutty flavour when slowly baked or roasted for a long time. North Americans used this as a staple food, slowly cooking them in a pit over a couple of days.

Glycyrrhiza glabra	Licorice	1.2m (4')	1m (3')

- Semi-hardy perennial that will grow in sun or semi-shade. Happy in sandy or loamy soils. Grows in acid, neutral and alkaline soils. Can tolerate strong winds but not maritime exposure. Hermaphrodite and bee-pollinated.
- Roots can be used raw or as a flavouring. Contain glycyrrhizin, which is 50 times sweeter than sucrose. Dried roots benefit teeth when chewed and help balance hormones if you are trying to wean your body off sucrose. Powdered roots can be used as a sweetener. Several medicinal uses.
- Nitrogen fixer.

Botanical name	Common name	Height	Spread
Helianthus tuberosus	Jerusalem artichoke	2.2m (7'2")	0.5m (1'8")

- Hardy perennial that needs full sun or dappled shade in woodland edge. Happy in sandy, clay or loamy soils. Will grow in nutritionally poor soils. Grows in acid, neutral and alkaline soils. Can tolerate strong winds but not maritime exposure. Hermaphrodite and insect-pollinated.
- Tubers are treated like potatoes, but do not store well, so leave in the ground and harvest when needed. They develop a sweet taste and are best cooked like potatoes. Roasted tubers are a good coffee substitute.

Oxalis tuberosa	Oca	0.5m (1'8")	30cm (1')

- Hardy perennial that needs full sun. Happy in sandy or loamy soils. Grows in acid, neutral and alkaline soils. Hermaphrodite and insect-pollinated.
- Tubers are edible raw if left to dry in the sun. Roots are delicious cooked like potatoes.

Sium sisarum	Skirret	1m (3')	40cm (1'4")

- Hardy perennial. Happy in sandy or loamy soils. Grows in acid, neutral and alkaline soils. Hermaphrodite and insect-pollinated.
- Roots can be used raw (nutty carrot/parsnip flavour), boiled or baked. Roasted root is a good coffee substitute.

Tragopogon porrifolius	Salsify	0.6m (2')	30cm (1')

- Biennial that needs sun. Happy in sandy, clay or loamy soils. Grows in acid, neutral and alkaline soils. Can tolerate strong winds but not maritime exposure. Hermaphrodite and insect-pollinated.
- Young roots, raw or cooked, are a valuable crop from late October to early spring. They store well after harvesting in late autumn. Young shoots are a tasty cooked vegetable, sweeter than asparagus.

Zingiber officinale	Common ginger	1.5m (5')	40cm (1'4")

- Perennial that needs full sun and protection from frost, so best grown in a polytunnel or under a cloche. Happy in sandy, clay or loamy soils. Grows in acid, neutral and alkaline soils.
- Ginger root can be consumed fresh, dried and ground, or as a juice or oil. Used as a spice in Asian cuisine and a flavouring agent in beverages. Commonly used in herbal medicine to treat stomach ailments.

MUSHROOMS

In Ireland, mushrooms have long been considered the food of the gods. They are easy and fun to grow, and provide lots of protein and other nutrients. If you have dark corners in your garden where nothing else will grow, mushrooms are the answer.

In Chapter 1 we discussed ways of introducing mycelia to your garden to increase the number and diversity of microorganisms in the soil, and benefit from a fine crop of edible mushrooms (mycelium fruits). This was done using mushroom spawn – a material that has been inoculated with a specific strain of mushroom mycelium (actively growing mushroom culture). The spawn holds that strain until the cultivator is ready to transfer it to another growing medium, such as logs, tree stumps, tree roots, straw or compost. Depending on the conditions and type of spawn, it may take a few months to a year before edible mushrooms start to appear, but it's well worth the wait. Most of these mushrooms are perennial and are not damaged by harvesting, so they continue to provide a protein-rich crop year after year.

Mushroom spawn is available from a number of online sources, including Paul Stamets' Fungi Perfecti (see Resources). There are some restrictions on shipping spawn internationally, so be sure to check before ordering from an overseas source. You should be able to find a local supplier for most common varieties. The spawn arrives in a sawdust block, mixed with grain, or on wooden plugs or pegs. Some, such as wine-cap stropharia, grow in straw, so you can inoculate the mulch of your Hügelkultur beds and have a crop of tasty mushrooms coming up among the peas and carrots. Others, like shiitake, sprout from inoculated tree stumps or logs, allowing you to create your own mushroom farms in the shadiest corners of your garden. In the tables below, I have listed edible mycelium species for inoculating tree roots as well as logs and tree stumps. A wealth of information about growing mushrooms in your garden and even indoors can be found in the books listed in Resources.

You may also discover wild mushrooms popping up on their own at various times of year, but you have to be absolutely sure you know which ones are safe to eat. Although only 5 per cent of mushroom species in Europe are outright deadly, 25 per cent are considered inedible or slightly toxic. Still, that leaves a whopping 70 per cent that are safe to eat! Many edible species look similar to the deadly or inedible ones, so you need to be completely confident in your ability to tell them apart. There are plenty of good field guides for identifying wild mushrooms (see Resources), but there's no substitute for walking through the countryside and woodlands with a mycologist, knowledgeable naturalist or experienced local mushroom hunter.

Layer 7. Climbers and vines

Climbers can be used in many ways. If you intend to use your larger trees as supports for the climbers and vines, then you will have to wait until the forest garden is at least heading towards maturity. Once the trees grow large, they are able to stand having another plant scrambling up through their branches without causing too much stress, providing another dimension, extra habitat in the overhead layers and more food for us below.

Many perennial vines climb so high that you need a ladder to harvest their fruit. The permaculturist Sepp Holzer uses the ingenious strategy of planting fast-growing willow trees to form supporting trellises for his grape vines in the uplands of Austria. It's unusual to find grapes growing successfully in that region, yet Holzer achieves this by using the heat reflected from his ponds to create warm microclimates. So if you want to experiment with more tender climbers, you could make use of Holzer's methods.

Certain annual climbers, such as peas, cucumbers and squash, are a wonderful addition to the garden and should also be included every year if you like them! You can train them to climb a trellis in front of a south- or west-facing building or grow them on Hügelkultur beds. You can also pile branches here and there, and let the vines clamber all over them to form beautiful ground cover over seriously good wildlife habitats.

Recommended plants for layer 7

Botanical name	Common name	Height	
Actinidia arguta	Bower actinidia, hardy kiwi	9m (29'5")	

- Hardy perennial climber. Happy in sandy, clay or loamy soils. Grows in acid, neutral and alkaline soils. Both male and female plants must be grown for pollination. Happy in full sun or partial shade.
- Fruit, raw or cooked, tastes delicious. It is ripe in November and stores well.

Botanical name	Common name	Height	
Amphicarpaea bracteata	Hog peanut	1.5m (5')	

- Perennial climber that likes partial, but not deep shade. Happy in sandy, clay or loamy soils. Grows in acid, neutral and alkaline soils. Self-fertile, insect-pollinated.
- Seed pods produced on lower part of plant bury themselves under the soil and grow to be quite large. They are used as a peanut substitute, raw or cooked. An invaluable winter harvest.
- Seeds on higher part of plant are smaller and should be cooked like lentils before eating, but they are a bit fiddly and a low-harvest crop.
- Nitrogen fixer.

Botanical name	Common name	Height	
Cucumis melo	Melon	1.5m (5')	

- Annual self-fertile climber that needs sun and a warm microclimate. Happy in sandy, clay or loamy soils. Grows in acid, neutral and alkaline soils.
- Self-fertile, insect-pollinated.
- Refreshing watery fruit in autumn.

Botanical name	Common name	Height	
Cucumis sativus	Cucumber	2m (6'6")	

- Self-fertile annual climber that needs full sun. Happy in sandy, clay or loamy soils. Grows in acid, neutral and alkaline soils. Self-fertile, insect-pollinated.
- Best harvested young and tender. Can be eaten raw in salads or used for juicing.

Botanical name	Common name	Height	
Cucurbita maxima	Autumn squash	0.6m (2') high, up to 5m (16') wide	

- Annual climber that grows in semi-shade or sun. Happy in sandy, clay or loamy soils. Grows in acid, neutral and alkaline soils.
- Self-fertile, insect-pollinated.
- Autumn fruits are delicious when baked, with a similar taste to sweet potato. Store well in cool, dry conditions for up to 9 months. Flowers are often dipped in batter and fried.

Botanical name	Common name	Height	
Humulus lupulus	Hop	6m (20')	

- Hardy perennial climber that grows in full sun or partial shade. Can also be trellissed against a north- or east-facing wall. Happy in sandy, clay or loamy soils. Grows in acid, neutral and alkaline soils. Young leaves and asparagus-like shoots are tasty when cooked.

Botanical name	Common name	Height
Ipomoea batatas	Sweet potato	3m (10')

- Fast-growing perennial climber that doubles as a ground cover. Happy in sandy and loamy soil. Grows well in acid, neutral or slightly alkaline soil. Needs full sun to be at its best. Flowers are hermaphrodite.
- Allow the plant to clamber over piles of twigs and branches. Many varieties available. Note: sweet potatoes are sometimes confused with yams, but are completely different plants.
- The fleshy roots are delicious and highly nutritious – cook like potatoes. The young leaves and top 5-10cm (2-4") of the growing tips are often eaten as a leafy vegetable, cooked like spinach.
- If you want to store the roots over winter, harvest them in autumn and leave to dry in hot temperatures for a week before storing.

Botanical name	Common name	Height
Lathyrus tuberosus	Earth chestnut	1.2m (4') – scrambles through other plants

- Hardy perennial herbaceous climber that requires sun or partial shade. Good bee plant. Happy in sandy, clay or loamy soils. Grows in acid, neutral and alkaline soils. Self-fertile, bee-pollinated.
- Roots are fabulous when baked, tasting like sweet potato, but yields are not terribly high.
- Nitrogen fixer.

Botanical name	Common name	Height
Passiflora incarnata	Apricot vine (also known as maypop)	6m (20')

- Hardy evergreen climber that is happy in sun or dappled shade. Suitable for growing with support on west- or south-facing walls. Happy in sandy, clay or loamy soils. Grows in acid, neutral and alkaline soils. Self-fertile, bee-pollinated.
- Fruit can be eaten raw or cooked in jams and jellies. Edible leaves, raw or cooked. Several medicinal uses.

Botanical name	Common name	Height
Passiflora mollissima	Banana passion fruit	5m (16')

- Hardy perennial climber suitable for a south- or west-facing wall. Happy in sandy, clay or loamy soils. Grows in acid, neutral and alkaline soils. Self-fertile, bee-pollinated.
- Very tasty fruit in autumn.

Botanical name	Common name	Height
Phaseolus coccineus	Scarlet runner bean	3 x 1m (10 x 3')

- Fast-growing perennial that is frost-tender. May need to be treated like an annual and planted from seed each year. Happy in sandy, clay or loamy soils. Grows in acid, neutral and alkaline soils. Self-fertile, bee-pollinated. Needs full sun.
- Immature seed pods have a mild flavour and can be eaten raw or cooked.
- Nitrogen fixer.

Botanical name	Common name	Height
Pisum sativum	Garden pea	2m (6'6")

- Annual self-fertile climber that needs full sun. Happy in sandy, clay or loamy soils. Grows in acid, neutral and alkaline soils. Happy in sandy or loamy soils. Self fertile, bee pollinated.
- Peas from a pod – the best sweets ever. Tender pea-flavoured young shoots can be added to salads.
- Nitrogen fixer.

Botanical name	Common name	Height
Tropaeolum majus	Nasturtium	3.5 x 1.5m (11'6" x 5')

- Perennial that is frost-tender. May need to be treated like an annual and planted from seed each year. Grows very quickly. Happy in sandy, clay or loamy soils. Grows in acid, neutral and alkaline soils. Self-fertile, bee-pollinated. Needs full sun.
- Leaves and flowers make a spicy and colourful addition to salads from spring to the first frosts late in the year. Young seed pods are especially spicy and can be pickled as a caper substitute. Mature seed can be ground and used as a hot pepper substitute. Used in herbal medicine.

Botanical name	Common name	Height	
Vitis vinifera	Grape vine	15m (49')	

- Hardy hermaphrodite perennial climber that requires sun or partial shade. Happy in sandy, clay or loamy soils. Grows in acid, neutral and alkaline soils. Grows well in poor soil but needs good drainage. Self-fertile. Insect-pollinated.
- Fruit can be eaten raw in autumn or dried for sultanas and raisins. Also used for making wine. Young leaves are delicious when wrapped around other veggies and baked.

Bees for Life

Bees are the most important insect pollinators, pollinating over 90 per cent of the world's 254,000 flowering plant species. Without bees and other pollinators, we wouldn't last very long as a species; in fact, four years is the general estimate. Unfortunately, bees are recently dying out in sudden and terrifyingly massive quantities in a newly termed phenomenon called Colony Collapse Disorder. Since we rely on honeybees for our survival, we should do whatever we can to support them, including providing a secure haven for them in our gardens. It may seem intimidating at first, but beekeeping is easy to learn, fascinating and enjoyable.

Bees have been weakened by what society considers 'harmless' chemicals, as well as by climate change, air pollution, radiation from mobile phones, transformers and wi-fi signals, which interfere with their ability to navigate.

Pesticides called neonicotinoids, a class of neuro-active insecticides are the world's most widely used insecticide. Many of those pretty bee-friendly flowering plants you buy commercially are actually transferring traces of neonicotinoids into the unsuspecting pollinators. The plant began life as a seed coated in the insecticide. Neonicotinoids are persistent and stay in the plant throughout its life cycle, transferring to the bees through the pollen. To give you a well-cited agricultural example, just one kernel of corn, coated with a neonicotinoid seed treatment contains enough active ingredient to kill over 80,000 honeybees. If the traces in flower pollen don't kill them outright, they suppress the bees' immune system and reduce their foraging and homing abilities, leading to eventual Colony Collapse.

Glyphosate herbicides have recently been implicated in colony collapse Disorder too. Glyphosate is a neurotoxin, causing endocrine hormone and immune disruption. It also acts as an antibiotic to the bees' beneficial bacteria such as lactobacillus necessary for the bees' digestion processes. One of the consistent factors for Colony Collapse Disorder is malnutrition.

However, there are sustainable, chemical-free methods of beekeeping that help keep bees strong enough to withstand parasites, fight off diseases and survive the many hazards of living in the modern world. By making our gardens a chemical-free haven for honeybees, using organically sourced seeds and plants, we will be rewarded in so many ways, including companionship – all my beekeeper friends are in love with these little creatures!

Another important supportive step would involve allowing bees to swarm. There are almost no wild bee colonies left because we refuse to let them swarm and create a new queen bee in the process. When worker bees grow another queen and swarm, they leave half the colony behind to find a new home. This is natural redistribution and regeneration. This is a big step towards restoring the bees' health, and it still leaves thousands of productive bees in the original hive. If a wild bee colony turns up somewhere unwelcoming as a result of swarming, it is generally easily sorted out by a beekeeper and it is a small price to pay for maintaining a constant supply of food in the world.

If we want to maintain bee health and retain our main pollinators we must also re-examine the design of their hives, which is currently not conducive to bee health. Conventional square-box hives, usually located close to the ground, have been developed with ease of access to honey in mind, but are not supportive of the bees' well-being. They are all take and no give.

I went back to records of old Irish beekeeping practices to research alternative beekeeping methods. Medieval Irish monks developed the art of beekeeping by weaving beehives, called *skeps*, from barley, wheat and oat straw. In the autumn they made rope-like braids from whatever straw was available and created ties to strengthen these ropes out of de-thorned blackberry stems that had been sliced in half. The straw was pulled into braids, bound with the split bramble and overlapped in a spiral shape to form a cone, which was then coated with cow dung. The monks chose this shape because they observed that bees in the wild preferred a curved home.

Skeps are beautiful and easy to make, but I suppose they are more suitable for conservation and pollination rather than honey harvesting, because it is impossible to check on the bees and extract honey from them without destroying the hive. There is a growing movement of natural beekeepers that is challenging the emphasis on the role of bees primarily as pollinators and secondarily as honey producers. A key instigator in this movement is the Natural Beekeeping Trust (see Resources), which has been experimenting with more natural hive designs that promote colony health while allowing beekeepers reasonable access. One such design is the Sun Hive, developed by German beekeeper and sculptor Günther Mancke.

Based on a traditional round skep, the Sun Hive is made from wood and rye-straw and covered with cow dung to insulate it. Mancke's Sun Hive is designed to be suspended 2.5m (8ft) above the ground under a shelter to protect it from the weather. The lower part of the hive is constructed to mimic the natural shape of a wild colony's comb, where the bees communicate, store nectar and pollen, and brood their young. The shape allows the bees to design their own brood nests in a way that is akin to wild bees, rather than dictated by the man-made designs of conventional hives.

The Natural Beekeeping Trust has been testing the Sun Hive design and find swarming bees, given a choice of accommodation, prefer it.

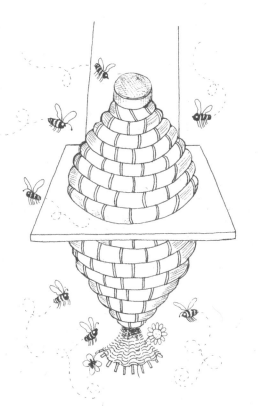

Above: The curved shape of the Sun Hive replicates the natural form of the colony

The final part of our relationship with bees that needs an overhaul is the honey harvest. The Sun Hive is a conservation hive that isn't designed to produce honey, but it is possible to place a small box on top of the hive after the first year. Bees deposit their surplus honey in these boxes so it can be harvested without any sense of greed for the keeper or damage to the colony.

If you are lucky enough to find there is a honey surplus that allows you to harvest, remember to put the bees first. Don't get greedy. In fact during the first year it's better not to take any honey from the bees at all because they need to feed themselves on it to survive the winter, especially when their immunity is already generally compromised by the modern world. Most beekeepers harvest all of the honey and expect the bees to survive on a replacement diet of sugar and water, which is short-sighted and downright thoughtless. Honey is a nutritious whole food, while sugar water has no nourishment whatsoever. Insensitive practices such as these are compromising the bees' immune system and threatening their very survival. We need to become guardians of these little creatures. Not gardeners. A little role swopping is in order.

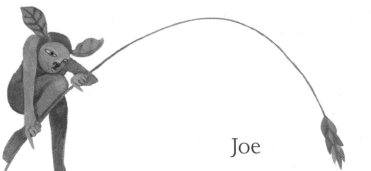

Joe

Joe farmed a few acres of what we call 'marginal land' in Ireland for more than 50 years. I was fortunate to have his friendship for a while and I loved to walk with him through his realm, helping him clear *sceachs* (stunted hawthorn trees), taking cuttings for new hedgerows, mulching his fruit trees, or helping him collect small quantities of honey from his hives.

Every day Joe strolled through his land with his hands clasped behind his back, at peace with the silence and feeling no compulsion to chat. He seemed at ease and I felt wholly accepted in his company. He didn't mind if I came or went. There were no guilt trips or expectations and he lacked the need to express his own opinions or entertain. At times Joe would surprise me with his depth of knowledge on all sorts of subjects and I came to realize that he was very well-read. He accepted whatever life threw at him and was grateful for all that was in his life at that moment. He emanated grace at all times. Joe was simply himself.

He began farming in a natural way many years before and was considered an eccentric within his local farming community. He never had much, but he always seemed happy with his lot in life. I asked him about it one day, but his reply confused me at the time: 'Sur' what else would I need?'

Most of his time was spent observing his land – walking around it, sitting in it, and doing the odd bit of pruning, mulching or harvesting. Walking through his farm was like going on a magical tour through an untamed fruit and vegetable garden. His land was bursting with life; native and exotic plants were growing together with rare heritage varieties of all sizes and shapes. Joe had decided that the best way to farm his land was to copy nature as closely as possible. Now, in hindsight, I recognize it as Joe's version of what we now call forest farming. He was a comforting presence. Joe knew I was interested in nature, so he taught me a few things. Mostly, though, I learned by observing him and the relationship he had nurtured so strongly with his land.

I remember one particular conversation with Joe. It was a lazy summer day and we were sitting on an old stone wall beside a grassy meadow. The wall was capped with a mat of dry, tufty grass that had become a soft cushion over the years. I thought to ask Joe if he believed in God. He smiled to himself and then he talked a little about God and religion.

He believed that if you dug away all the mulch around religions and followed them back to their beginnings, they all had the same root. He spoke about how we had twisted and turned them into righteous sets of rules for reasons that served nobody well. Suddenly he blurted out several sentences, which was unusual for a man of few words, and then paused for a while.

Eventually Joe leaned over, plucked a stalk of flowering grass and held it up for me to examine. I will never forget what he said because it struck me like a hammer with its clear and simple truth. "Mary," he said while contemplating the flower for a moment.

"This is God."

Alternative Management Practices

Is iomaí slí muc a mharú seachas í a thachtadh le h-im.
There are many ways of killing a pig other than by choking it with butter.

The only way to make a sustainable garden system work is to collaborate with nature. Fighting against nature is just plain silly. If you are to treat the land as a living body, you must think in those terms. In order for this land body to be truly healthy and self-sufficient, what nourishment does it need? It needs food, of course, but not petroleum-based chemical food. I mean living food, full of life force, energy and nourishment. Can you imagine trying to bring up a healthy child on a diet consisting purely of vitamin and mineral supplements?

We need to allow the land to grow strong on its own, and that means ending our dependence on chemical fertilizers and pesticides. If you are changing over from the chemical system, you must steadfastly support the land until it is able to provide for itself.

In this chapter, I describe ways to help make your land independent and strong as quickly as possible using mulch, innovative methods of clearing the land, and growing beautiful and low-maintenance alternatives to conventional lawns. I also provide strategies and techniques for maintaining your gardens and protecting them from insect infestations and plant diseases without resorting to toxic chemicals. Finally, we'll take an in-depth look at tree cultivation and care to help you get the most from your woodland or forest garden.

Mulching

Mulching is the key to managing and maintaining the entire system. It protects the land and keeps it healthy from the time the garden is planted until it reaches maturity. It provides the best conditions for small animals and microorganisms in the soil, keeps the ground cool and moist in summer and warm in winter, and helps suppress weeds. Young trees that have been mulched grow twice as fast in the first years as those that have to compete with weeds. All plantings should be mulched immediately, especially on bare-field sites, and as the mulch decomposes it should be replenished faithfully. Herein lies the long-term solution to sustainable soil fertility.

Mulching retains moisture in the soil as well as improving fertility, aeration, drainage and the physical structure of the soil. It also suppresses competition from neighbouring plants, even if those plants are the soil-building ground cover you have introduced yourself. Mulch allows nutrients to become available on the surface and then wash through the topsoil just as it does in a natural woodland.

Once the ground cover grows out, it should be cut back every so often with the cuttings either left where they fall or gathered and placed around the base of selected plants. This is sometimes referred to as the 'chop and drop' method. Eventually the garden comes to have two types of mulch at the same time: the decomposing litter on the surface of the soil and a living mulch of green manure plants growing above it.

Ideally the mulch should be at least 15cm (6") deep. For smaller areas, start with overlapping sheets of plain cardboard and soak them before adding the mulch. For larger areas, just mulch is fine. As the mulch layer decomposes and becomes thinner, add more mulch. In fact, 'add more mulch' is the solution for just about anything in the garden.

There are many types of mulch, but it is best to use a mixture of materials with various sizes and textures. This allows air to circulate freely and provides the plants with a range of fast- and slow-release fertilizers. Use leaf mould, garden cuttings (after first removing unwanted seed heads), household compost, cocoa shells, coffee grounds, hops residues from a brewery, well-rotted manure, bark chippings, or anything else that will naturally decompose. Avoid using bark alone, as it is so high in carbon that it takes too much nitrogen from the soil to break it down.

In my opinion, seaweed makes an outstanding fertilizer, but please, don't go to the seashore and strip it of seaweed for your garden. Better to use what you have on site. Straw is helpful, especially for raised beds, but it must be organic, otherwise it will still be coated with glyphosphate herbicides, hormones and fungicides. Grass cuttings should be returned to the soil, though they need to be mixed with other course-textured mulches to allow enough air circulation for effective decomposition. Branches from trees and shrubs can be shredded and used for mulch. However, leaving them whole on the ground allows you to feed your plants over a long period of time as well as providing food and shelter for wildlife and microorganisms.

There many options, but the main idea is to keep placing cuttings and shreddings around your food plants to reduce competition, retain moisture and increase yields. When you first begin you may have to import some of your mulch material, but before long your garden will provide all it needs by itself.

Ways to Clear the Land

Pigs

Turning the soil over mechanically sets the soil ecosystem back years and should be avoided unless absolutely necessary. So, how do you clear land without disturbing the microbes and damaging the structure of the soil? It's easy if you can get your hands on some pigs! They are far superior to any tiller or cultivator, as well as being adorable and extremely intelligent. They fertilize the land as they work and keep pest control by snuffling around above and below the soil looking for tasty worms and grubs to eat.

Pigs are social creatures so it's best to have more than one. You could buy 8-to-10-week-old piglets and raise them yourself, or borrow some from a local farmer or animal cooperative that shares animals for such purposes. Loaning pigs avoids the need to slaughter animals you have raised yourself, unless that is part of your plan. Some pig species have shorter snouts so they don't root as deeply as other breeds. The Middle White and the Kune Kune breeds, for example, are shallow grazers and are gentler on the land, while breeds such as the Tamworth dig as deeply as a Rotavator.

Pen the pigs in the area that needs to be cleared using a movable solar- or battery-powered electric fence. Pigs are omnivores so they'll root around looking for grubs and worms as well as eating any greens in sight. Roots, briars, bracken, weeds and grassland will all be turned into a grubbed-up seedbed in a surprisingly short time.

Get the pigs to clear a small section of land at a time. If there is a tall, thick sward of meadow there already, consider trimming it back first because it's easier for pigs to plough through shorter grass. They are also great at dealing with problem areas of perennial weeds by unearthing them from the roots. When the pigs have done their job, remove them, gently rake the area to even out the surface and then you're all set to plant your garden. Pigs are also effective for clearing woodlands, but they will damage young trees; so if you have any, they will need protection. If your pigs are already trained to avoid the shock of an electric fence, they will be wary of the wire or tape whenever they see it. A 'pretend' strip of white electric fence tape around each tree will ably keep the pigs at bay.

Avoid leaving the pigs on the same piece of land any longer than is necessary. As soon as they have rooted it up, move them on. By that time they'll probably be plotting an escape to get at the new growth on the other side of the fence anyway.

Pigs have the ability to seal the soil by wallowing in it. To avoid this happening everywhere in the garden, designate one area as the wallowing hole. Dig out a small, shallow pond and fill it with water or allow the rain to fill it. The pigs will be thrilled. You can always refill it with soil after they are gone. If your soil is clay, the pigs' rolling and wallowing seals the bottom and sides of the pond, so you won't need a plastic pond liner.

Pigs also need shelter to protect them from the elements and provide shade. They are natural forest dwellers so they sunburn easily. Another thing they really enjoy is an outdoor shower, which you can rig up fairly easily from rainwater harvested from the roof of their shelter or a nearby shed. Seeing their joy as the water pours over them and hearing their squeals of delight brings a smile to the face of even the most hardened farmer.

Goats

Goats are ideal for clearing land, especially in rocky or steep terrain that is difficult to clear by machine, but they need to be firmly tethered or fenced and monitored regularly. Goats will clear docks, brambles, bracken, thistles, blackberries and just about everything else. They are perfect for clearing weedy shrubs and small trees from woodlands, as they devour anything they can reach. If you want your land grazed down to short stubble, however, sheep are a better bet. While goats are nature's trimmers, sheep are the mowers.

If you have access to an animal cooperative, you can rent a goat or two for a few days if you are in a position to accommodate and care for them. You will need about three goats per acre of heavy brush. Although most breeds will work for this purpose, it is best to chose breeds suitable to your local area. In northern California they mainly use Angora goats because their thick mohair coats keep them warm during the chilly winters before they are sheared in the spring. Pygmy goats will do a good job too, but it takes a little longer to get the job done. A mixture of breeds and sizes would be your best bet for a very dense area of wild land. Like pigs, goats can be contained using a solar- or battery-powered net-style electric fence. If you have young trees, the goats will eat them, so take proper precautions.

Goats are invaluable for reclaiming woodlands that have been overrun with weedy trees, and they do it without a chemical in sight. They will only eat the foliage they can reach but even that puts stress on weed trees. To fast-track the process, it is best to coppice the trees (see page 258 [coppicing section]). When the trees have re-sprouted, bring the goats back to strip them, then move the goats to another area. Repeat this cycle and before long the trees will die. Then it is time to clear the dead wood and replant a proper sustainable ecosystem.

Goats need shelter at night and when it rains. They also need a clean supply of water and they appreciate being treated with respect. That respect will be returned if you give it, but beware because the reverse is also true. Please don't think the poor goats were disrespectful if they ate your young fruit trees; they simply preferred the taste of those particular leaves over others. This is why proper supervision is extremely important when it comes to goats.

Chickens

Chickens are much easier to handle than pigs or goats. They also make wonderful companions and stock your kitchen with a steady supply of eggs. They are extremely useful for helping to prepare the ground for seeding, but you will need at least five or six in the brood to have suitable impact. The birds will scratch away until the ground is nearly bare, at which point they should be moved to the next patch to prepare it for seeding. I think of it as a 'patchwork quilt' method, and it's easy to implement if you use a moveable coop.

I think every sustainable forest garden should have a flock of chickens. The best way to develop a healthy flock is to hatch your own eggs. These days most of the available breeds were developed with prolific egg production in mind, but they have an extremely short lifespan. By hatching your own, you can develop a healthier, more diverse and more sustainable community of hens. There is so much to learn about raising chickens for someone starting out that I can only scratch the surface here, but I have added references in the Resources section in the back of the book to help get you started.

For urban gardens, silkies are a good breed because they are small and quiet and lay about five smallish but tasty eggs per week. Silkies do not damage garden plants, keep caterpillars under control and deposit rich fertilizer as they scratch and peck around. Bantams (and their miniature counterparts) are a fine choice for roaming through a more developed forest garden because they don't dig and scratch very much and have more of a taste for natural vegetation than cultivated varieties.

Chickens are very intelligent creatures that deserve our respect, and one way to offer that is to be sure they have lots of room to roam. Perhaps you can find a large run so they can run around on the days they're not earning their keep by clearing the ground, scratching for bugs, and depositing their rich fertiliser in the future garden beds. It is also good to provide them with a pit containing sand or wood ash because they love to give themselves a dust bath once in a while.

They will need fresh water, an enclosed run and a coop to keep them warm and safe at night. Electrified chicken fencing works quite well, but if it you have an ordinary chicken-wire fence, be sure to bury the wire several inches into the ground to keep predators from digging underneath it. Foxes are notoriously clever, of course, and can jump over 2m (6') fences to satisfy their hunger. You should let the chickens out to wander the garden during the day and return them to the coop at least three hours before sunset. This is the time when the foxes most like to hunt. They also come out early in the morning but we've found them attacking chickens during the day as well. If hungry enough, I suppose they'll overcome their fear of humans.

Chickens need a mixed diet to provide them with protein, minerals and carbohydrates. They are natural forest dwellers and foragers, but until your forest garden is developed you will need to supplement their nutrition. Try to avoid buying supplemental feed, as it is unhealthy and unsustainable. Instead, give them your uncooked vegetable peelings and kitchen scraps, or ask your local vegetable shop for any out-of-date or damaged fruit and vegetables, but try to avoid giving them mouldy or rotten food.

Chickens digest kitchen waste very quickly and process it into a rich, concentrated fertilizer. They love scouring the compost heap for tasty morsels, so keeping it near the chicken run makes a lot of sense. If you are not able to provide enough food from sources such as these, you will have to feed the chickens organic pellets twice a day, especially in the winter when foraging is harder for them.

Chickens don't have teeth so they need to ingest and store grit in their gizzards to grind their food and help them build eggshells. Insoluble grit breaks down the food but is not digested and has no nutritional value. Soluble grit is digestible and contains calcium – which helps build strong eggshells. If they are not going to be free-range chickens, you will need to provide them with both types of grit. Flint grit or fine gravel and snail shells or thin seashells will do the trick.

Sheet mulching

Sheet mulching is a simple way to build the soil and get rid of grassy weeds and herbaceous perennial plants without using herbicides or tilling the soil. First, mow the area and cut back woody growth. Then spread a layer of cardboard, newspapers (but not the glossy pages), cloth, hemp/flax matting, or even wool carpets, and top it with a thick layer of organic mulch, such as leaves, straw or wood chips. Anything will do, as long as it is free of chemicals and will eventually decompose. The mulch deprives the weeds of light, killing them in just a season or two.

I often lay a sheet mulch in the autumn. By spring the mulch has decomposed into rich, crumbly soil so I can plant my garden without tilling or further preparation. Some stubborn weeds that hold a lot of energy in their roots, such as Japanese knotweed and finger grass (or crab grass), may take a bit longer to go away. This mulch method is similar to the method I described in Chapter 1 (see page 34) for restoring fungi to the soil, so it makes perfect sense to combine the two.

Lawns and Lawn Maintenance

Lawns can be used to create calming and simple spaces in your garden design. Acting like woodland glades, these spaces create sunny edge-planting zones in a forest garden. If your lawn is to have a purely aesthetic value, I would recommend creating a low-maintenance, alternative-style lawn, especially if you don't intend to walk on it often. I have found that a well-established stand of white clover or a mixture of hardy, low-growing ground-cover plants wears quite well underfoot. These and other suggestions are described below.

LOW-MAINTENANCE ALTERNATIVES TO HIGH-MAINTENANCE GRASS LAWNS

Moss

If you have a suitable site, moss is a beautiful alternative to lawn grasses – and you don't have to mow it. Moss can't withstand much foot traffic, but in a damp, shady area it will grow well with almost no maintenance. Throw in a few rocks and ferns to create a beautiful dreaming space with almost no effort, and you could add a stepping-stone pathway too. Once established, moss obtains its moisture and nutrition from the air and the surface of the ground because it attaches itself with rhizoids (thin filaments or root hairs) rather than roots.

Making moss

The following preparations will allow you to establish new areas of moss in your garden, which should only be done in late spring and during the summer. There are many different types of moss; some will tolerate dry, sunny places, but most prefer damp, shady conditions. Take little bits of moss from an area with similar growing conditions to the place where you will be installing your moss lawn. Do not strip an area of all its moss!

Moss preparation 1
- Approx. 3 cups of suitable moss species
- 1l (1¾ pints) buttermilk or plain live yogurt
- 1l (1¾ pints) spring water or rainwater

Moss preparation 2
- Approx. 3 cups of suitable moss species
- 2 cans of beer
- 1 tsp sugar or molasses
- 1l spring water or rainwater

1 Remove as much soil as possible from the gathered moss, then chop it finely with a sharp knife, do not blend it, as it damages the structure of the moss and removes its potential to grow.
2 Mix the ingredients together and paint the mixture on to bare soil.
3 The moss should begin growing about six weeks later if you keep it misted. Moss mainly grows in moist areas with partial- to full- shade, so it is essential to mist the area during dry periods until the moss becomes established. You can

also paint the moss mixture on to porous walls and rocks to create your own moss graffiti. Hand-weed any unwanted plants that pop up while the moss is becoming established, but try not to disturb the soil in the process.

Sedges

Short *Carex* species planted en masse form an interesting and very simple lawn. You can let the plants flower for a beautiful effect or, for a more formal look, cut them back from time to time during the growing season using a scythe or a lawnmower with the blades set high. Some sedge varieties can stand full sun, while others like to grow in the shade; there are so many different kinds you are certain to find one that suits your land. You could also interplant flowering bulbs with the sedges if you like. Have fun with this! The sedges should be mowed with the blades set high after the winter to allow them to regenerate. After they flower, let the seeds scatter to fill the gaps between the existing plants and then mow them again.

Wood-rush, wild garlic and bluebells

Wood-rush (*Luzula*) species do very well in temperate climates. They create lovely open spaces in woodland glades and also tolerate light foot traffic. They are stunning mixed with wild garlic, bluebells and other woodland plants. Find the ones that grow well in your area.

Clover

Instead of grass, try sowing a winter-hardy, evergreen white clover as the base for your lawn. Once tightly established, it will handle foot traffic and even activities such as football extremely well. Clover blooms for a very long time, filling the air with a heavenly scent that extends far from the lawn itself, and it is an essential food source for bees and many other insects.

Clover requires a fine soil tilth to germinate initially and the soil temperature must be high enough for the seed to sprout. In Ireland, there is a window from May to September when the soil is warm enough to allow that to happen. Some people also mix clover seed with short timothy-grass seed for added durability.

To encourage a clover lawn to grow in a thick carpet, mow it regularly in the beginning so that it grows sideways rather than tall. After that, it requires very little mowing or other maintenance. Clover needs to be reseeded every few years to keep it full and lush. This is best done using seed balls after a very close mowing and scarifying any time from late spring to early autumn.

UNCONVENTIONAL AND HIGHLY DIVERSE LAWNS

There are many low-growing herbs that make a practical and beautiful lawn substitute: yarrow (*Achillea millefolium*), self-heal (*Prunella vulgaris*), creeping thyme (*Thymus serphyllum*), Corsican mint (*Mentha requienii*) and heath pearlwort (*Sagina subulata*), to name just a few. Taller herbs and greens, such as oregano (or marjoram), thyme, sorrel, plantain and mints, also work well for a lawn with high diversity. Try to select species that can tolerate occasional mowing and light foot traffic. The plants should be cut back now and again to encourage thicker growth. Lawns of this type create a magnificent patchwork-quilt effect, with various textures, scents and colours, while also providing a rich source of food and habitat for other creatures.

Let daisies, plantains, speedwells and scarlet pimpernels find their homes here too. The more the merrier. The less controlled, the more beautiful and varied your lawn will become. If there are thistles, nettles, docks or other species that would make walking on the lawn with bare feet a painful experience, then a few sprays of vinegar, as described on page 241, will keep them under control. However, it's good to allow these prickly species to grow in a few places. Butterflies will be especially happy to find a few flowering thistles in your garden.

Lawn maintenance

How did people ever manage to keep large lawns trim before the advent of lawn-mowers? Large estates in Europe used sheep, but sheep will eat everything else too, if they are simply let loose to graze on their own. Years ago, European estate houses used a landscape design element called a ha-ha to stop livestock from entering the garden. A ha-ha is a deep ditch retained by a wall on its inner side below ground level. This formed a boundary to the garden but was imperceptible from the house, so the lawn seemed to blend perfectly with the fields beyond. As a result, estate gardeners only had to maintain the small section of lawn immediately surrounding the house and the livestock took care of the rest.

Geese are vegetarians that happily graze grass so they are an excellent alternative to a mechanical lawnmower. Like ducks, however, if left to their own devices they would also graze your forest garden plants and damage young trees, so they must be contained within the lawn area. Geese need a pond to swim in, so they are not a sustainable solution unless you have a lot of land or you are sharing them as part of an animal cooperative. Geese create a lot of manure and most people find them hard to handle, but they do make excellent guards against intruders!

I remember when everyone had a push lawnmower that cut the lawn perfectly well if the blades were sharp, though it did take some effort to drive it through grass that had grown more than a few inches tall. People used a sharp scythe for the longer grass. What I particularly like about using a push mower or sheep is that they are quiet – no petrol-gobbling-monster noises to disturb an otherwise peaceful weekend!

Note: Livestock will damage seeded lawns in wet weather. If you have a wide variety of species in the seed mixture, however, the plant roots will create a thick mat that keeps the soil from being damaged easily. Old meadows have a diversity of herb and grass species that allow livestock to graze freely without damaging the land, even during the rainy season. The ability to use old meadows while they were wet also reduced the need for housing livestock and feeding them throughout the winter. So if you are going to use sheep to manage your lawns, you may want to use an 'old meadow' seed mix (see seed suppliers in Resources) to increase the area's viability for grazing in all seasons. A diverse mixture of plants also creates strong and resilient ecosystems and provides habitat for pollinating insects.

Pest Control

Dealing with land that needs rehabilitation often requires initial short-term measures to help bring the ecosystem back into balance, but these tasks will become unnecessary once the land has returned to a healthy condition. The non-toxic measures I recommend for controlling common pests and weeds should only be needed for the first couple of years. Once the soil has improved and diversity is restored, the plants will be strong enough to resist diseases on their own, predators will provide natural insect control, and weeds will largely be held in check by your soil-building ground cover. Harmony and balance will become the norm.

The intention method

Before the advent of industrial agriculture, farmers and gardeners had to deal with the same pests and diseases they face today, but less so because there were more natural predators to provide a balance. They understood that the best solutions for overcoming problems came from working in partnership with the land. At that time, farmers could still communicate directly with the earth.

One of the problems farmers faced was attacks from leatherjackets, the larvae of large crane flies. These fat, creamy grubs would eat through the soft new shoots of cereal crops just as they emerged from the soil, sometimes causing a complete crop failure.

My mum and dad both grew up on farms in south-east Ireland – mum in Kilkenny and dad in Wexford. When they were young they had to cycle many miles to the local Franciscan monastery in the spring. There they purchased a quantity of 'traens' water and took it back home to the fields of emerging crops. This was a common practice in Ireland. Traditions like this one emerged from pagan customs and got absorbed into the Christian religion over the years. At the entrance to each field, the farmer would draw a circle with a cross on the earth using a sharp stick. Then he would recite the monk's prayer (which came with the water) in each corner of the field and sprinkle the land with the water. This special water had a specific intention: to protect the crops from grubs.

The funny thing is, they remember that this practice always worked. When farmers started using chemical pesticides and fungicides, however, the traens water no longer had an effect because people stopped believing in it. The 'green revolution' had arrived, and with it a loss of faith in the old ways. The new farming methods also promised that hunger and poverty would be eliminated forever.

This promise never came true, of course. Belief was the key to how those practices worked, but now they are looked on with cynicism and contempt.

Biodynamic farming still uses similar methods for placing instructions into the land. In terms of fertility, fire is believed to be the opposite of water, so biodynamic preparations for fertilizing are made using water and preparations for pest control are made using fire. One biodynamic pest control method involves finding one of the offending creatures – a slug, for example – and killing it. The slug's body is then burned using a simple wood flame, and the resulting ash is peppered on to the land. While spreading the ashes, the slugs are asked to leave. If this ceremony is repeated, and if all goes according to plan, the population of slugs will decline in each successive year, and after about four years they will have disappeared altogether.

Never one for pulling legs off spiders or burning slugs, I prefer to simply ask them to leave. I usually allocate a place in the garden for them to eat what they need and request that they keep away from surrounding plants. So far they have always listened. I might lose the odd cauliflower to some hungry caterpillars, but out of apparent respect for my appeal, the neighbouring cauliflowers will be left alone. The success of biodynamics depends on your belief in its methods and your ability to fortify your intentions. If you have a strong enough conviction in your abilities, you won't need to use ceremonies.

To begin with, it is best to try out the intention method on a small area and during good times, when success or failure will not jeopardize your welfare or that of your family. The only way to learn to trust yourself in this is by trying it out. If you are afraid of starving or if your heart is filled with angst and anger, I doubt this simple method would work. I always ask from a place of peace and respect. Being at ease with oneself while respectfully acknowledging the other creatures that share the earth with us somehow opens a direct line of communication with them. Respect is returned in kind.

Until you feel comfortable and confident using the intention method, and until the land is rebalanced, it may be handy to have some non-toxic remedies for controlling pests in your garden.

Slug control

Slugs are the bane of many gardener's lives. If you don't keep them under control they will mow your young seedlings overnight and prevent you from growing any plants from seed. Slugs live in shady, damp areas, so freshly mulched gardens are a perfect place for them to thrive, at least initially. As your garden ecosystem establishes itself, their population will be kept in check because their predator numbers will grow. In nature it's all about balance. Until balance is restored, however, you'll need to have tools that will allow you to handle slugs and other challenges as they arise.

Slugs are nocturnal creatures that spend their days hiding in sheltered, dank places. They have no teeth so make tearing sounds while eating. If you visit your garden at night and are really quiet, you will hear them rasping away.

For slug control, most conventional garden centres only offer the well-known toxic blue pellets. What they do not mention is that those pellets also kill the birds, frogs and other small creatures that eat the slugs' bodies after they have ingested the pellets. In my opinion, using toxic slug bait is entirely irresponsible. I *never* use it, and I beg that you refrain from doing so too.

Until a proper balance between predator and prey is reestablished, it is best to use gentler, yet effective, methods for controlling slugs. I have described some of them below.

BIRDS

Birds are a great source of company, beauty and entertainment … *and* they consider slugs and snails to be an irresistible delicacy. We should do all we can to invite these wise and whimsical creatures into our gardens by creating nesting boxes and other habitats where they will feel at home. Your land will literally be *hopping* with them once it is back to health and flowing with abundance again.

My dad's relationship with nature changed as he aged. Six children, a job and a farm kept him busy – too busy for a gentle awareness. As he grew older, he had a few experiences that changed his attitude. One memorable incident involved a family of crows. Worried that his crop of barley would be eaten by the hungry birds, he decided one day to make a pre-emptive strike. He shot one of the birds to scare the rest off, then hung the poor dead creature from a tall stick in the middle of the field. This was meant to warn the rest of them what would happen if they crossed his invisible line.

That night as he was going to bed, he noticed that there was a dead crow on the flat roof outside his bedroom window. He picked it up and examined it. The bird had been shot. Thinking it was strange, he flung the body from the roof into a copse of woodland beside the house. The next morning the dead crow was back on the roof outside his window. He flung it back again and quietly stood hidden to watch what happened. Soon enough, the crows picked up their dead family member and deposited it on the same roof. Dad buried the bird with care, got rid of the gun, and has had much more respect for other creatures since then.

NEMATODES

Nematodes are microscopic worms that eat slugs from the inside out – pretty unpleasant but very effective. These creatures are always present in healthy soils, but many of them are needed to fight an infestation of slugs in an imbalanced ecosystem. You can order nematodes in powdered form online and then water them on to the soil. A single treatment for an area of 200m² (2,152ft²) costs about £20. The treatment is effective for a month or so. Once the nematodes are in the soil, they go looking for their prey and parasitically invade them. The slugs swell up and die within a few days.

The drawback of this method is that the treatment can be *too* successful. By killing *all* the slugs in the garden, you remove a major source of food from their natural predators, so they have to search elsewhere. When that happens it is difficult to control the slug population without constantly replenishing the population of nematodes. Using nematodes, then, is not a sustainable solution, although it may be handy for a while. Still, it's a better option than using toxic pellets.

HEDGEHOGS

Hedgehogs love a good meal of slugs. Your garden boundaries should contain hedgehog passageways such as pipes set at ground level to allow and encourage free movement of these nocturnal creatures throughout your garden. If your garden is surrounded by walls, you could drill a hole at the base, as long as you don't undermine the wall's stability. An undisturbed log pile in your garden will encourage hedgehogs to take up residence and so help keep the slug population under control.

DUCKS

If your garden is large enough, ducks are wonderful for controlling slugs and snails, and they provide delicious eggs as well. Two or three ducks should be enough to take care of the slugs in all but the largest of gardens, but it's nice to have a family unit consisting of a drake and at least four ducks. This makes for a happy flock, highly social creatures that they are. The best carnivorous ducks to use are Indian Runners and Khaki Campbells, as these breeds are more likely to leave your vegetables alone.

Ducks need a pond or a tub of sorts, which must be cleaned regularly. And unless their pond is large, they will graze on all the plants that grow there, so be aware of this if you are trying to establish a planting scheme using aquatic plants or aquaculture. You might consider creating a second, duck-free pond for growing water plants.

Ducks also need a penned area to contain them when they are not out on slug patrol. If left to their own devices, they will eat your vegetables and flowers, so they should have a run that is separate from the garden. They need to be locked-up safely every evening to protect them from predators and released every morning so they can run around and forage. One possibility for controlling their range is using an electric perimeter fence, though you still have to keep an eye on them to be sure they are focusing on slugs and not your plants. You could also set up a second run that doesn't include your forest garden or other recently planted areas. Even if the ducks are kept out of the garden and only allowed to run around a grassy perimeter path, they will eat enough of the offending munchers to keep them from getting a foothold in your food production areas.

Farming with ducks is a major commitment and responsibility, as it is with any domesticated animal, so plan on being around every day or having a trusted friend or neighbour ready to assist you if you intend to be away.

FROGS

Even if your garden is relatively small, try to find space for a small pond with gently sloping sides to allow access for wildlife. Once you add a source of water to your garden, frogs and other amphibians will naturally find their way there. Although frogs are not as effective at controlling slugs as ducks or some of the other methods I have mentioned, they do help and are delightful to have around. By the way, ducks also eat frogs, so bear that in mind when planning your slug maintenance programme.

BEETLES AND CENTIPEDES

Beetles, such as the common ground beetle and its larvae, and centipedes are night-time predators that have a particular liking for slug eggs. It's a good idea (as well as good fun if you have kids around) to build insect-friendly abodes to encourage them to make their home in your garden. You can do this with reclaimed materials such as wooden pallets, bricks, flowerpots, corrugated cardboard, pine cones, old leaves and sticks. Stack the materials to provide nooks and crevices where the beetles can find shelter.

COPPER

Slugs and snails won't cross a thick copper barrier because it gives them tiny electric shocks, so for small areas you can protect your plants with strips of copper wire or copper-backed tape. The plants need to be completely encircled with the material, or the slugs will find their way through the gaps. You can place seedling trays onto a table and wrap copper strips around the base of each leg to protect them.

HAND-PICKING

Another option involves going out at night with a torch and catching the slimy culprits while they are in the act. Hand-pick the slugs and snails off the plants and place them in a jar until the following morning and then get rid of them as you like. I often let them loose on the roof of my shed in the mornings to feed the crows.

Although I've focused on ways to get rid of slugs, it is important to remember that they have an important role in the ecosystem too. The idea is not to eradicate them but to keep them in balance with other insects as well as birds, mammals and plants that share the same territory. Of all the methods I have described for controlling these creatures, I hope you will at least try my favourite one: ask them firmly yet politely to leave by next year, or make a deal with them that they can live in a certain part of the garden as long as they leave the rest alone. This method has worked extremely well for me for years.

Natural Remedies

All the remedies I have recommended below can be made quite simply from common kitchen and garden ingredients. Most are applied as sprays and will be especially handy for your fruit trees and annual vegetable garden.

Hold the intention for the preparation you are making in the forefront of your mind while you are mixing and applying these sprays. After you have poured the completed mixture into the spray container write the intention of the preparation onto the bottle. This helps hold the intention true.

Colloidal silver – the all-purpose superhero

Colloidal silver water is an excellent all-purpose exterminator of fungi, bacteria and viruses. For years this magical brew has allowed my children and me to stay antibiotic-free, and my potatoes blight-free – which is pretty impressive, considering the cold and rainy Irish climate.

Silver water works by disabling the enzyme that single-celled bacteria, viruses and fungi need for their oxygen metabolism. It also affects the individual cells in strands of fungal mycelia. The pathogen dies from lack of oxygen. However, silver water is completely safe for multi-celled organisms such as plants, animals and human beings.

Soaking seeds in colloidal silver water before planting them will remove the pathogens that cause damping off (a fungal infection) and other diseases associated with germination and early plant growth. When sprayed on plants that are already affected by fungi, bacteria or viruses, the offending organisms are quickly eliminated. Do not soak seeds of nitrogen-fixing plants if they have already been inoculated with bacterial spores.

Distilled water is used when making colloidal silver water for medical purposes, but spring water will work fine for our purposes. If you purchase your own colloidal silver generator, you will be able to make large quantities easily and inexpensively in your own home. It has worked brilliantly for me with no side effects of any kind. There's a great deal of information about how to make colloidal silver online, including a number of instructional videos, so I ardently suggest that you look into it (see Resources).

COLLOIDAL SILVER PREPARATION

Colloidal silver maker – can be ordered online for approx. £75-100 or simple versions can be made from batteries, 14-gauge silver wire and electrodes with crocodile clips:

- Dash of saline solution (to increase the water's conductivity)
- Distilled water, spring water or rainwater
- Make up a 5-20l (1-5 gallon) drum of silver water, depending on your needs

Add a quantity to a spray bottle and write the intention of the spray on the bottle. Spray the upper and under sides of affected leaves, holding the reason for the treatment in your mind as you do so. Repeat daily or weekly as necessary.

Natural fungicides

REMEDIES FOR THE TREATMENT OF:

- Anthracnose
- Early tomato blight
- Leaf blights and spots
- Leaf scab
- Mosaic disease
- Powdery mildews
- Rose black spot

BAKING SODA AND NEEM

- 1 tbsp bicarbonate of soda
- 2 tbsp neem oil
- 1 tbsp Castile soap
- 5l (1 gallon) spring, rain or well water

Lightly mist the upper and under sides of the affected leaves and repeat weekly as necessary. Keep shaking while you spray to prevent the ingredients from separating.

Note: Neem oil, which is extracted from the leaves of the neem tree, is one of the most powerful natural insecticides. It has a fine texture so rarely clogs horticultural sprayers. It is available in most garden supply centres, and also in health-food shops because of its wide-ranging uses in health and beauty products.

APPLE CIDER VINEGAR

- 4 tbsp cider vinegar
- 2 tbsp neem oil
- 1 tbsp Castile soap
- 0.5l (18fl oz) spring, rain or well water

1 Stir the ingredients together while holding the reason for the spray in your mind. Pour into a spray bottle and write the spray's intention on the bottle.
2 Spray the upper and under sides of the leaves and repeat weekly as necessary. Keep shaking while you spray to prevent the ingredients from separating.

ELDERFLOWER LEAF

- 450g (1lb) elderflower leaves
- 1 tbsp Castile soap
- 1l (1¾ pints) spring, rain or well water

1 Put the water and leaves in a saucepan and bring to the boil. Reduce the heat and simmer for 30 minutes.
2 Add the soap and stir thoroughly while holding the reason for the spray in your mind. Strain into a spray bottle and write the spray's intention on the bottle.
3 Soak the upper and under sides of the leaves and repeat weekly as necessary.

GARLIC AND CHILLI

- 1 whole garlic bulb
- 3 hot chilli peppers
- 1 lemon

- 1 tbsp Castile soap
- 1l (1¾ pints) spring, rain or well water

1 Place all the ingredients into a blender and blend until finely chopped. Store overnight in the fridge.
2 Strain the liquid into a clean glass preserve jar, then mix in the soap.
3 Mix 4 tablespoons of this concoction into 0.5l (18fl oz) of water, putting the rest back into the fridge.
4 Soak the upper and under sides of affected leaves, holding the spray's intention in your mind as you do so. Repeat weekly as necessary.

REMEDIES FOR THE TREATMENT OF:

- Apple scab
- Downy mildew on cucumbers and pumpkins

CHIVES

- 3 cups chopped chives
- 1l (1¾ pints) spring, rain or well water (enough to cover the chives in a pan)
- 1 tbsp Castile soap

1 Put the water and chives into a saucepan and bring to the boil.
2 Reduce the heat and simmer for 10 minutes. Allow to cool.
3 Add the soap and stir thoroughly.
4 Spray the upper and under sides of the leaves and affected parts, and repeat three times a week as necessary.

GARLIC

- 1 whole garlic bulb
- 1l (1¾ pints) spring, rain or well water
- 1 tbsp Castile soap

1 Peel and crush the garlic cloves and add this to the soapy water. Allow to soak for 1-2 hours and then pour into a spray bottle. Write the intention for the spray on the bottle.
2 Spray the upper and under sides of the leaves and affected parts and repeat twice a day until the fungus disappears.

Natural insecticides

Hold the intention for the preparation you are making in the forefront of your mind while you are mixing and applying these sprays. After you have poured the completed mixture into the spray container write the intention of the preparation onto the bottle. This helps hold the intention true.

REMEDIES FOR THE TREATMENT OF:

- Aphid attacks
- Insect attacks

CHIVES

- 1 cup (approx. 45 teaspoons) cayenne pepper
- 2 tbsp neem oil

- 5 drops rosemary or clove oil
- 3l (5 pints) spring, rain or well water

1 Stir the ingredients thoroughly while holding the reason for the spray in your mind and then pour into a spray bottle. Write the intention for the spray on the bottle.
2 Lightly mist the upper and under sides of the leaves and affected parts. Repeat twice a day until the insects disappear.

NETTLES

- Generous handful of stinging nettles
- 2 tbsp neem oil
- 3l (5 pints) spring, rain or well water

1 Use heavy gloves to collect the nettles. Chop them up roughly and add to the other ingredients. Stir thoroughly while holding the reason for the spray in your mind. Allow the mix to sit for 24 hours.
2 Pour the mix into a spray bottle and write the intention for the spray on the bottle.
3 Lightly mist the upper and under sides of the leaves and affected parts. Repeat twice a day until the insects disappear.

GARLIC

- 4 garlic cloves, crushed
- 2 onions, chopped
- 2 tbsp neem oil
- 1l (2 pints) spring, rain or well water

1 Add the garlic cloves, onions and neem oil to the water and allow to soak for 1-2 hours.

2 Strain the mixture into a spray bottle and write the intention for the spray on the bottle.

3 Lightly mist the upper and under sides of the leaves and affected parts. Repeat twice a day until the insects disappear. The mixture should keep in the bottle for up to a week.

CHRYSANTHEMUM FLOWER TEA

- 100g (3½oz) dried chrysanthemum flowers
- 1l (2 pints) spring water
- 1 tbsp neem oil

1 Put the dried flowers in the water, bring to the boil and simmer for 20 minutes.

2 Strain and cool the mix, then put into a spray bottle.

3 Lightly mist the upper and under sides of the leaves and affected parts. Repeat twice a day until the insects disappear. The mixture can keep in the bottle for a couple of months.

Note: Chrysanthemum flowers contain a natural insecticide called pyrethrum. Interplanting chrysanthemums with plants susceptible to insects or worms helps to protect them from those pests. Marigolds can also have a repellent effect on insects.

NATURAL HERBICIDES

Is olc an t-éan a shalaíonn a nead féin.
It's a bad bird that soils its own nest.

There is a blind acceptance of using commercial herbicides indiscriminately these days because people have been brainwashed into believing the chemicals they contain are safe. The truth is, these products are lethal to our own health and to the natural cycle of life. There is a wealth of information about the dangers of our most commonly used herbicides, yet somehow this never finds a way into mainstream media and general public awareness. "Ah, but do real alternatives actually exist?" I regularly hear when I try to persuade people to refrain from using chemical herbicides. "They certainly do!" I reply. "But they're not offered as options because the chemical manufacturers and GMO seed companies can't make money on them."

I have spent lots of time researching non-toxic natural herbicides and have successfully used them in my own garden. Here are some of my favourites:

VINEGAR WEED-ELIMINATION PREPARATION

- 1 large orange
- 1l (2 pints) 10% acidity* white vinegar made from grain alcohol
- 1 tbsp sugar
- 1 tbsp Castile soap
- ½ cup of Epsom salts

*This can burn skin and eyes so use with caution. If you can't find 10% acidity vinegar, use common white distilled vinegar, which is normally sold at 5% acidity.

1 Peel the orange and put the peelings in the vinegar. Leave overnight to extract the orange oils.

2 Remove the orange peel, then add the epsom salts, sugar and soap. Sugar increases the absorption rate because the plant thinks it is being fed. The soap and the orange oils act as surfactants (a substance that reduces the surface tension of a liquid in which it is dissolved, increasing its spreading and wetting properties). Mix and pour the ingredients into a spray bottle or backpack sprayer.

3 Spray the plants on a dry, sunny day during the growing seasons. Soak the plants, then, re-spray 3 times within 24 hours.

It's as simple as that. No micro-life, butterfly, frog, bee or bird deaths, and no increased risk of cancer for the gardener or farmer. It even works for invasive weeds such as Japanese knotweed, if exposed stems are cut and injected with a good squirt of the mixture in the spring, as soon as the stems hollow out enough for the job. This can be done with a veterinary syringe without a needle. It is better for the soil micro life if you don't use the Epsom salts, but add them if more strength is needed. It's still heaps better than chemical herbicides!

THE TRADITIONAL, TIME-HONOURED SOLUTION

• Gardening gloves
• Knee pads, an old cushion or an old stuffed hot water bottle
• Hand trowel or weeding fork and maybe a long-handled hoe

Do you ever consider hand-weeding? I find it amazing that most people seem to have forgotten this is an option for smaller areas! Whenever the soil is moist, the roots of the unwanted plants come free with little effort. If you are able and willing, hand-weeding can be relaxing, even meditative, because there is nothing to think about except what is right in front of you.

FILL IN THE GAPS

Nature abhors bare soil and will use whatever is available from the local bank to cover it up. When the soil is disturbed, weed seeds are exposed to oxygen and sunlight and begin to sprout, rather like a scab forms over a wound to heal it.

The most common cause of bare soil is human activity, so we would be wise to avoid disturbing it if we want to get a handle on controlling weeds. Keep the soil clothed with a diverse cover of vegetation at all times. Fill the open spaces with a multi-layered community of trees, shrubs, perennials and groundcover plants. This removes the need for herbicides because there is no place for weeds to gain a foothold. In the absence of plant cover, mulch the area heavily with whatever material is at hand, including garden prunings, grass clippings, organic straw and leaves. A deep mulch protects and nourishes the soil, represses weeds and encourages plants to grow far more quickly than they would have done without the cover.

Tonics, Fertilizers, Potting Mixtures and Tree Protection

This section is devoted to a variety of simple techniques that I have found useful during my years of learning to garden in cooperation with nature. Some might consider them to be 'unconventional', but I see them as simple, common sense, inexpensive and non-toxic.

Tonics and fertilizers

Plants generally suffer from diseases when they are under stress. If they are robust, they will be able to withstand diseases on their own, so the best approach is prevention – by growing vigorous plants in a nourishing environment. Applying the following plant foods will help you do that – it's similar to giving children a herbal multivitamin tonic to boost their immune system.

Most herbaceous wild plants can be used in tonics, but certain species are particularly beneficial. You could also use any soft-leaved nutrient-accumulator plant (see Chapter 3, page 175 for a list of these plants) or seaweed, which makes an excellent fertilizer too. If you harvest wild plants from somewhere other than your own land, make sure they haven't been contaminated by chemical herbicides or pesticides.

PLANT TONIC

- 5 cups (approx. 250g depending on dryness) of one of the following herbaceous plants: comfrey, horsetail or nettle. Other options: seaweed or a nutrient-accumulator plant
- 1 cup (approx. 50g) of coneflowers (*Echinacea*) or a few drops of tincture
- 2l (70fl oz) water, preferably spring water or rainwater

Put the coneflowers or tincture and plants of your choice into the water for one day, stirring occasionally. It is best to use spring water or rainwater rather than tap water, as tap water is dead and laced with chemicals that will attack the plants' immune system, thus defeating the whole purpose. After 24 hours the liquid tonic can be sprayed directly on to the plants.

To make a powerful plant fertilizer, leave the plant material in the water for a few weeks, or until the plants have completely softened and 'melted', stirring the mixture each day. When ready, take a cupful and dilute it with 5l (1 gallon) of spring water or rainwater. It can be applied as a foliar spray or poured around the roots of the plants.

Note: *Echinacea* should be used in all tonic mixtures designed to boost your plants' immune system. Try to find a place to grow coneflowers in your garden and make a store of dried flowers or make a tincture from them. Their presence will also strengthen the immune system of the land they grow in.

Animal Manure

Animal manure	Benefits
Cow manure	Provides potash. Especially effective for root crops.
Rabbit manure	Promotes strong leaves and stems.
Chicken manure	A rich source of nitrogen. Use for heavy feeders such as tomatoes.
Horse manure	Best support for leaf development.
Bat and seabird droppings	Not easy to find, but the most potent manure of all. Rich in nitrogen, phosphorous and potassium.

1 Fill a large bin with fresh spring water or rainwater. Add four shovelfuls of the manure of your choice. Stir it every day for at least a few minutes. As you are stirring, whip the water into a vortex while holding the reason for making this mix in your mind – or better still, say it out loud and also write it on the side of the bin.
2 After two weeks, strain the mix and use the liquid wherever needed – but only on the ground, not as a foliar spray.

COMPOSTS AND POTTING MIXTURES

For many years, peat has been the substrate of choice for gardeners to start their seeds and cuttings. That practice is not sustainable, however, and must stop immediately. Peat is an extremely valuable resource: it contains and sequesters carbon in the same way trees do. Scientists estimate that 25 per cent of the world's carbon is stored in peatlands.

With one sixth of the country classified as bog, Ireland has more peatlands than any country in Europe other than Finland, yet in the last hundred years alone 50 per cent of our original peat bogs have been lost, and extraction for horticulture is a major contributor. Peat takes such a long time to develop that we should consider it a non-renewable resource, and yet we are mining it as if there were no tomorrow.

Since using peat in our gardens and greenhouses is not sustainable, why not substitute other sources of compost, such as worm castings, leaf mould, decomposed nettles or other plants that can be found right outside your door?

Worm castings

Worm composters use two common species of worms, red wigglers (*Eisenia fetida*) and red earthworms (*Lumbricus rubellus*), to transform kitchen waste, food scraps and other organic material into vermicompost (also known as worm castings, worm humus or worm compost). This material is an extremely potent soil amendment, conditioner and fertilizer and is also useful as a peat substitute.

Wormeries are perfect for small spaces, making them ideal for urban situations. They are simple to set up, do not smell, and they make compost more quickly than conventional methods. There are many books and online tutorials that show how to create one of these mini-farms yourself, or you can buy your own vermicompost bin. Composting worms can be bought online or from a reliable local distributor.

Leaf mould

Find a corner in your garden to make a big pile of leaves. The fine-textured material that forms underneath the pile as the leaves decompose is an ideal, all-purpose compost. It is particularly useful as an ingredient in making potting soil for germinating seeds.

Nettle squash

Dig a hole approximately 30cm (1') deep and fill it with a big bundle of nettles, then cover them and leave them there until the following spring. When you dig up the nettles you will find a crumbly, rich compost in its place. You can mix this compost with worm castings, leaf mould and other soil fertilizers in various proportions to produce potting mixes specifically designed for germinating seeds. A practical reminder: mark the location where you buried the nettles so you can find them the following year!

Compost potting mix for germinating seeds

50% leaf or nettle compost and/or worm castings (sieved)
50% aggregates (perlite or pumice dust) or sand

Mix your home-made leaf or nettle compost with ingredients that promote good drainage to strike a balance between moisture retention and drainage. If the soil stays too moist, it leads to damping off disease, which means that the seeds die before they germinate or just after they sprout.

Hormone rooting powder

Willows offer an easy, cost-free alternative to synthetic rooting powders because they contain hormones that naturally encourage root growth. Cut young willow branches of any species into sections an inch or so long. Steep them in a small amount of natural spring water or rainwater for about a week. Dip cuttings of any kind into the resulting liquid to encourage root growth. Cuttings allow you to propagate large quantities of plants for your forest garden without spending a penny.

Methods for protecting tree bark from deer and other grazing animals

Protecting woodland trees from deer, wild goats, rabbits and other grazing animals is often a major problem for a people who are growing trees for their woodland or forest garden. These creatures like to eat the bark off young trees, weakening and sometimes killing them. If the tree is girdled (the bark around the trunk has been removed), it will die straightaway. Here are some non-toxic methods for protecting young trees:

Method 1

Surround each young tree with a thicket of plants that have large thorns, such as blackthorn, wild roses or barberry. In Ireland, gorse (*Ulex europaeus*) is a great choice because it also fixes nitrogen. The grazing animals prefer the soft young shoots of these prickly plants, causing them to grow thick and bushy and forming a protective collar for the trees.

Method 2

Fence your entire garden. However, this can be difficult and quite expensive, especially if you have a large area. A less expensive option is to use a temporary battery- or solar-powered electric fence.

Method 3

Wrap the trunks in a material such as drainage pipe. Slice sections open and wrap them around each tree trunk, keeping the sections as tall as you can without damaging the lower branches of the trees.

Method 4

Use the intention method I described in Chapter 2 (see page 36) by connecting yourself to the earth, grounding yourself, and asking the predators to leave the plants alone. This method has worked reliably for me for many years because I believe in it; if you are sceptical, it won't work. The energetic effect of your thoughts is only successful if you are strong and steadfast in your belief. Either sacrifice an area of the garden for the animals' use or provide them with an alternative source of food as a trade. These grazing animals haven't been sent to torment you but are simply trying to survive, just like we are.

The Cultivation and Care of Trees

Trees are the guardians of the land; its elders. To re-establish a loving and mutually beneficial relationship with the earth we need to treat trees with respect and gratitude, nourishing them and allowing their life force to thrive. After all, the trees' needs go hand in hand with our own.

The first part of this section looks at the needs and cultivation of fruit trees, while the second discusses coppicing, pruning and grafting.

The hungry gap

It is essential to know something about preserving the food you harvest during the overabundance of summer and autumn so you can survive during the cold winter months until the abundance of late spring and summer arrives once more. In Ireland, this period was known as the 'hungry gap'. Forest gardening helps you bridge that gap by allowing you to produce edible crops all year round. If you can afford them, greenhouses and polytunnels also help extend the growing season so you can get through the hungry gap with relative ease.

When choosing your trees and plants, try to include early-, mid- and late-fruiting varieties. Preserving and storing food is very important for developing self-sufficiency, and there's a lot of satisfaction to be gained from doing so. There are a number of helpful books available on the subject, which I have listed in Resources.

Pollination – make sure those flowers turn into fruit!

When choosing which fruit tree varieties to grow, you must find out whether they will grow well in your area and whether or not they will be pollinated successfully by other trees. In order for your trees to produce fruit, the flowers must be pollinated.

Fruit starts off as a female flower, which will only turn into fruit if pollen from a male flower fertilizes it. Fruits are usually pollinated by bees and other flying insects transferring male pollen to the female flower and are rewarded for their efforts with nectar. Some plants, such as hazelnuts, can be pollinated by the wind.

Some plants are self-fertile (self-pollinating) because they have both male and female parts on the same plant, either in the same flower or separate flowers. This means you need only one plant in your garden for them to pollinate successfully. This makes self-fertile trees a good choice for smaller gardens. I have found, however, that even if they say 'self-fertile', it is always a good idea to have more than one pollinator, if you have the space. Plants such as the kiwi fruit or date plums (a type of persimmon) have separate male and female plants so you need to have both growing near each other to get fruit production.

Most fruit trees, however are self-infertile – that is, they cannot be pollinated using pollen from the same tree, so they require a pollination partner. To complicate things further, pollinating partners need to be a *different* variety of the *same* species that is flowering at the same time. Some varieties of the same type of fruit tree flower early and some later, so it is important to choose them carefully. These include apples, most pears, many plum trees, sweet cherry, chestnuts, walnuts and blueberries. There are so many possibilities that I cannot possibly cover them all here, but most tree nurseries give this information in their catalogues (see Resources).

It's really not as confusing as it sounds. Plant two or more varieties of the same type of fruit tree no more than 50m (165') apart and choose varieties that flower at the same time. By keeping your own beehives, you will ensure successful pollination and perhaps reap a crop of delicious honey in the process.

Grafted stock

Almost all commercial fruit trees are *grafted* specimens. Grafting basically involves joining two different parts of living material – the scion (top growth) and root-stock (roots and lower trunk) – to make a single specimen. The practice of grafting a tree on to the rootstock (roots and lower trunk) of a different yet related species has been carried out for thousands of years. Practically every fruit tree in my great-grandfather's garden, for example, was grafted onto *sceachs*, (a traditional Irish term for sturdy hedgerow trees and shrubs of little perceived value) which were usually hawthorn rootstock that acted as an all-purpose graft host for fruit-tree propagation. However, grafting isn't always necessary.

Graft your own trees or grow them from seed

The beauty of grafting your own trees is that you will avoid the need to prune the trees from the start. Better still, you can grow the trees yourself from cuttings or from seeds!

Several forest gardening books and online tutorials give information about how to graft your own tree. Grafting is an easy process. All you need is a clean, sharp knife, a sturdy cutting, or scion, from the specific tree or variety you want to grow, and the right host rootstock. The idea is to join the scion with the rootstock so the two grow together and become one plant.

The rootstock controls the size of the tree and is often resistant to specific pathogens in the soil. The scion grows true to its parent and provides all of its desirable characteristics. Willow-rooting mixture (see page 247) helps the grafts close quickly. Nut trees are harder to graft than most fruit trees, but are worth a try. If you use the intention method as you are grafting, water and mulch the tree with care, and sprinkle in some nurturing, loving thoughts, you will have a greater chance of success.

The main problem with buying grafted fruit trees is that they have already been pruned at the nursery. Once pruned, you have to keep pruning them, or the trees will suffer. In other words, they become dependent children for their entire lives. After years of experiments with unpruned fruit trees versus pruned, grafted varieties, the Japanese natural farmer Masanobu Fukuoka and Austrian permaculturist Sepp Holzer came to the same conclusion: that it was better to allow orchard trees to grow to their natural form from the very beginning. Most commercial growers prune fruit and nut trees low and wide so they can be harvested easily, but it doesn't help the trees in the slightest. You will reap plenty of yield from trees that are allowed to grow to their natural form, and gain satisfaction from knowing that they are growing up wild and free.

A better compromise might be to grow your own trees from seed, graft a scion of the tree you want to grow onto a wild variety of the same species, or grow the trees from cuttings. That way you won't have to prune the trees at all. There is a difference between pruning and thinning. Thinning involves removing the lower branches when the tree is young to allow more sunlight reach to lower levels of your garden. Pruning involves hacking away at the tops of the trees.

Wild, sturdy rootstocks that are useful for grafting include crab apple (*Malus sylvestris*) for apple varieties, hawthorn for medlar, and wild cherry for cherries. By grafting your own trees on to suitable related species and not pruning them, you can still benefit from having smaller trees in a small- or medium-sized garden without having to do any work at all. The branches of most trees grown this way can cope with the weight of a heavy fruit load without breaking.

Unpruned fruit trees don't produce fruit every year, which is one of the reasons they are shunned by our production-obsessed society, but surely they are entitled to a period of rest, don't you think? I remember that some of the very old fruit trees in my parents' garden had bumper crops some years, while in other years they bore almost no fruit at all. There didn't seem to be any rhyme or reason for it; it was just one of those mysteries that no one could explain.

If you have grafted fruit trees that were already pruned by a nursery, think of switching to summer-pruning as a way to lessen the damage and work. Pruning during the summer reduces the number of suckers (shoots growing from the base of the tree) that sprout the following spring. It also increases the tree's ability to heal the pruning cuts, because the sap is still available to heal over the wounds.

I love to grow trees from seed, but it is impossible to know how large the tree will become or what the fruit will be like. The fruit from these trees is rarely of commercial quality but it is usually good enough to eat fresh or be used for jams and preserves. Growing trees from seeds helps maintain the genetic diversity in your garden and in your corner of the world. Sometimes these trees grow up to be magnificent specimens. One way or another, whenever a tree grows from seed, you are in for a surprise

Own-root trees

Fruit trees that are allowed to grow using their own roots are hardier against attacks from pests and diseases. They pollinate more easily, produce more seeds, and live longer than trees that have been grafted. Their fruits may be a little smaller but the taste is incomparably better, and they have a longer storage life.

The only disadvantage of own-root fruit trees is that their growth is not restricted so they will grow to their natural full size. Most will be larger than those grown on MM11 or MM106 rootstocks, which are normally the largest grafted fruit trees. It will make the trees more difficult to harvest, but this isn't an issue if you are not growing them commercially. Besides, what you don't harvest for yourself will be eaten by birds and other wildlife, eventually finding its way back to the soil.

If you don't have enough room for large fruit trees, you may have to persevere with young trees that have been grafted on to a rootstock that restricts their size (see the table below). These smaller trees can wobble, however, so it's a good idea to put two or three heavy rocks around their base to keep them solid in the ground. The stones also help create a warm microclimate, releasing the heat stored during the warm daylight hours slowly during the evening.

DWARF FRUIT TREES

Dwarf fruit trees are forced to remain stunted and immature by being grafted onto severely dwarfing rootstock. Vigorous fruit trees need a certain amount of care while they are young – such as mulching, weeding and perhaps staking – but soon they become relatively independent and self-sufficient. By contrast, dwarf species require care throughout their lives, even though they live for only 15-20 years. I don't use true dwarf fruit trees in my own gardens, but I have included them here because space-wise they *are* practical. However, there are plenty of lesser-known food-producing alternatives to dwarf fruit trees for a small garden, so I urge you to seek these out using the Plants For A Future database (see Resources).

Fruit tree rootstocks

Apples (*Malus* spp.)		
Rootstock	**Dwarfing effect on original variety**	**Size of mature tree**
MM111	25%	6-7m (20-23') high and wide
M25	25%	6-7m (20-23') high and 6m (20') wide
MM106	35%	4-6m (13-30') high and wide
M26	50%	3-4.5m (10'-14'16") high and 2.5-4m (8'-13')wide
M9	65%	3m (10') high and wide
M27	75%	2m (6'6") high and wide

Almond (*Prunus dulcis*)	
Rootstock	**Size of mature tree**
St Julien A	4-5m (13-16') high and 3-4m (10-13')wide
Torinel	4m (13') high and 3-4m (10-13') wide

Apricot (*Prunus armeniaca*)	
Rootstock	**Size of mature tree**
St Julien A	4-5m (13-16') high and 3-4m (10-13') wide
Myran	4m (13') high and 3-4m (10-13') wide

Cherry (sour) (*Prunus cerasus*)	
Rootstock	**Size of mature plant**
Colt	Bush: 4m (13') high and 3.5m (11'6") wide. Fan: 2m (6'6") high and 4-5m (13-16') spread
Gisela 5 (dwarf)	Bush: 2m (6'6") high and 1.5m (5') wide

Medlar (*Mespilus germanica*)	
Rootstock	**Size of mature tree**
Hawthorn root-stock	4-6m (13-20') high and wide
(Quince A)	4m (13-20') high and wide
(Quince C)	3m (10') high and wide

Pear (*Pyrus communis*)	
Rootstock	**Size of mature tree**
Quince MA (Quince A)	3-6m (10-20') high and wide
Quince MC (Quince C)	2-5m (6'6"-16') high and wide

Plum (*Prunus domestica*)		
Rootstock	**Dwarfing effect on original variety**	**Size of mature tree**
Brompton	25%	5.5-7m (18-23') high and wide
St Julien A	40%	4m (13') high and 3m (10') wide

Pixy	50%	2-4m (6'6"-13') high and 2-3m (6'6"-10') wide
VVA-1	60%	2-3m (6'6"-10') high and wide
Peach (*Prunus persica*)		
Rootstock	**Size of mature tree grown on a trellis against a wall.**	
St Julien A	4-5m (13-16') spread trained on a wall on horizontal wires. 2m (6'6") high	
Brompton	5-7m(16-23') spread trained against a wall on horizontal wires	

Plants for coppicing and pollarding

Coppicing is a form of woodland management that has been practised throughout the world for thousands of years. It involves periodically cutting dormant broadleaved trees and shrubs to ground level to stimulate growth. The new shoots that appear from the stump regrow into multi-stemmed shoots. Pollarding involves cutting off the top and branches of a tree to encourage new growth at the top. Stems are cut off at 2m (6'6") or more, usually to prevent livestock from eating the lower limbs.

After coppicing, shoots grow much faster than with single-stemmed trees because the roots are already well established. The new shoots grow with fewer nodes and branches so they are particularly valuable for building. If you have the space, consider allocating an area for coppice trees. This would give you a steady and sustainable supply of wood without having to replant more trees. It would also provide a dependable source of firewood as well as pliable shoots for basketry and fence weaving. If you plant the trees 1.5m (5') apart, you will be able to cut them by hand every 5-10 years.

Many temperate-climate trees can be coppiced and pollarded, but I have listed some of the more useful species in the table below.

Tree species for coppicing and pollarding

Botanical name	Common name	Time between coppicing
Acer campestre	Field maple	4-15 years
Asimina triloba	Pawpaw	5-15 years. Will take at least 4-5 years before fruit is borne again after coppicing.
Castanea sativa There are many good fruiting cultivars available	Sweet chestnut	7-15 years. Needs pollination partners. Large trees, but if you coppice them every 10 years or so, this allows you to keep more of them in a smaller garden. They won't fruit for at least 5 years after coppicing, so have a number of them growing if possible and coppice a different clump every year to keep the chestnut crop coming regularly.
Corylus avellana	Hazel	5-15 years. Will take at least 4 years before nuts are borne again after coppicing.
Cretageus species	Hawthorn hybrid species	Will take at least 4 years before haws are borne after coppicing.
Diospyros kaki	Persimmons	5-7 years. Will take at least 4 years before nuts are borne again after coppicing.
Fagus sylvatica	Beech	7-25 years
Fraxinus excelsior	Ash	7-25 years
Ginkgo biloba	Maidenhair	7-25 years. Will take at least 4-5 years before nuts are borne again after coppicing.
Malus species	Apples	7-15 years. Will take at least 4-5 years before fruit is borne again after coppicing.
Morus alba and M. rubra	Mulberries	Will take at least 4 years before nuts are borne again after coppicing.
Prunus spp.	Cherries / plum	5-15 years. Will take at least 4 years before fruit is borne again after coppicing.
Quercus spp.	Oak	7-50 years
Salix spp.	Willow species	2-25 years. Shoots that are 1-3 years old are brilliant for weaving living willow structures and baskets, so well worth coppicing.
Tilia cordata	Small-leaved lime	1-10 years. Coppiced for the edible leaves, which are a great source of salad greens from spring to autumn.

Éireoidh tonn ar uisce balbh.
A wave will rise on quiet waters.

I love this earth that we live on. In fact I love it so much that I am absolutely sure that my physical heart looks just like a miniature planet earth. However, there were times when I rejected Nature or forgot about her, but I was lucky enough to find my way home again.

This book is a sort of treasure map for finding your way back to the truth of who you are. The directions are simple; the methods are intuitive and draw on the wisdom of our ancestors. We have temporarily forgotten that we are children of the earth. Our mother is worn out and needs us now, so we must grow up, step up, and become the caretakers. Guardians are needed now, not gardeners. If you can just slow down and reintroduce yourself to the earth, a magical gate will open for you. Make a promise that you are committed to your land's guardianship, willing to help it grow strong and healthy, and Nature will carry you with her on the path. One day you will notice that both of you have healed over the cracks in your hearts and become whole again.

It's the journey of a lifetime.

Resources

Artwork

Ruth Evans
www.thehedgerowgallery.com
The wonderfully talented artist who filled this book with a visual feast.

Specific references from the book

Bees and Beekeeping (see page 204)

The Natural Beekeeping Trust, UK
www.naturalbeekeepingtrust.org
This site is filled with information about bee-centred versus conventional beekeeping and information about Sun Hives. There are links to other groups, classes and conferences, as well as articles and a list of recommended reading.

Collecting seeds and growing plants from seed (see page 128)

Buttala, Lee and Siegel, Shanyn. *The Seed Garden: The Art and Practice of Saving Seed*. Iowa, USA: Seed Savers Exchange, 2015.
Written by members of the Seed Savers Exchange and the Organic Seed Alliance.

Bubel, Nancy. *The New Seed-Starters Handbook*. Emmaus, Pennsylvania, USA: Rodale Press, 1988.

Colloidal silver generator (see page 233)

Health Leads, UK
www.healthleadsuk.com/healthcare-devices/miscellaneous
A source for purchasing a Deluxe Colloidal Silver Generator, with AC adapter.

Amazon
Amazon sells several models of colloidal silver generators, search for "colloidal silver generator".

Instructables
www.instructables.com/id/how-to-make-colloidal-silver-easy
Instructions for making your own colloidal silver generator for almost nothing.

Composting human manure (see page 144)

Joseph Jenkins, Inc., USA
www.josephjenkins.com
Online resource about composting human manure. Including products such as the 'loveable loo', an eco-friendly composting toilet.

Jenkins, Joseph. *The Humanure Handbook: A Guide to Composting Human Manure*. 3rd edition. Grove City, Pennsylvania, USA: Joseph Jenkins, Inc., 2005.

Foraging for wild edible plants (see page 129)

Wild plant guide, UK

www.wildplantguide.co.uk
Wild plant foraging online resource.

Edible wild food, USA

www.ediblewildfood.com
Wild plant foraging.

Mabey, Richard. *Food For Free*. London, England: Collins (Gem series), 2012.
A handy guide to have when foraging for wild plants. One hundred edible species are listed and illustrated, along with recipes and details of their uses over the years.

Growing winter vegetables and garden produce preservation (see page 249)

Crawford, Martin and Aitken, Caroline. *Food from Your Forest Garden: How to Harvest, Cook and Preserve Your Forest Garden Produce*. Cambridge, England: Green Books, 2014.

Dowding, Charles. *How to Grow Winter Vegetables*. Cambridge, England: Green Books, 2011.

Katz, Sandor. *Wild Fermentation: The Flavor, Nutrition, and Craft of Live-Culture Foods*. White River Junction, USA: Chelsea Green Publishers, 2003.
This book explains how to prepare and preserve food at home using the transformative powers of bacteria and fungi.

Hupping, Carol. *Stocking Up: How to Preserve the Foods You Grow Naturally*. 3rd edition. Emmaus, Pennsylvania, USA: Rodale Press, 1990.

Indigenous Irish roots (see page 20)

Anam Holistic Healing Center, Ireland

www.anamspirit.com
A retreat centre in Wicklow offering classes and workshops on dowsing, shamanism, yoga and many other healing and self-renewal topics.

Mullally, Joe. *The Healer's Secret*. Kerry, Ireland: Anam. This book explores the indigenous heart of the people living in the rural areas of the Irish countryside. It describes the dramatic awakening that occurs when people reconnect with the land and the healing power of traditional ways.

Jackson, Peter Wyse. *Ireland's Generous Nature: The Past and Present Uses of Wild Plants in Ireland*. St. Louis, Missouri, USA: Missouri Botanical Garden Press, 2014.
An 'epic exploration' of the historic and present-day uses of wild plants in Ireland. Accessibly written with beautiful illustrations.

Mushrooms (see page 199)

Fungi Perfecti, USA

www.fungi.com
Owned by Paul Stamets, renowned American mycologist. The website is filled with practical information and you can order mushroom spawn and other supplies. Check on international regulations before importing spawn.

Ann Miller's Speciality Mushrooms Ltd, Scotland

www.annforfungi.co.uk
A great place to order mushroom spawn and supplies.

The Mushroom Patch, Ohio, USA

www.sporetradingpost.com
Mushroom spawn, kits, DVDs, books and
mushroom growing equipment.

Rogers Mushrooms, UK

www.rogersmushrooms.com
A great online guide for mushroom identification.

Stamets, Paul. *Mycelium Running: How Mushrooms Can Help
Save the World*. Berkeley, California, USA: Ten Speed
Press, 1994.

Stamets, Paul. *Growing Gourmet and Medicinal Mushrooms*.
3rd Edition. Berkeley, California, USA: Ten Speed
Press, 2000.

Microorganisms and compost tea (see page 34)

Gardening With Microbes

www.gardeningwithmicrobes.com
Information about the importance of soil
microorganisms and aerated compost tea.

Keep It Simple, Inc., USA

www.simplici-tea.com
Compost tea brewers and organic bio-amendments.

Mycorrhizal Applications, Inc., USA

www.mycorrhizae.com
Run by Dr Mike Amaranthus, a professor of
microbiology at Oregon State University, they grow
and sell mycorrhizal fungi in liquid, powder and
granular form.

Lowenenfels, Jeff and Lewis, Wayne. *Teeming with
Microbes: The Organic Gardener's Guide to the Soil Food Web*.
Revised edition. Portland, Oregon, USA: Timber
Press, 2010.

Describes the fascinating interaction among
microorganisms, soil and plants.

Amaranthus, Michael. "A Look Beneath the Surface
at Plant Establishment and Growth." Spring, 1999,
Florida Landscape Architecture Quarterly. Also reprinted at
www.mycorrhizalproducts.com

Sacred architecture and mythology (see page 72)

Mann, A.T. *Sacred Architecture*. London, UK: Vega
Books, 2003.

Campbell, Joseph. *The Power of Myth*. New York, USA:
Anchor Books, 1991.

Campbell, Joseph. *The Flight of the Wild Gander*. Novato,
California, USA: New World Library, 2002.

Water intention experiments (see page 53)

Emoto Peace Project, Japan

www.emotoproject.com
Results of Masaru Emoto's water experiments,
including photos of water crystals, after they were
exposed to positive and negative messages.

Emoto, Masaru. *The Hidden Messages in Water*. New York,
USA: Atria Books, 2005.

Radin, Dean; Hayssen, Gail; Emoto, Masaru and
Kizu, Takashige. "Double-Blind Test of the Effects
of Distant Intention on Water Crystal Formation".
2006. *Explore the Journal of Healing*, 2: 408-11

Radin, Dean; Lund, Nancy; Emoto, Masaru and
Kizu, Takashige. "Effects of Distant Intention
on Water Crystal Formation: A Triple-Blind

Replication". 2008. *Journal of Scientific Exploration*, 22(4): 481-93.

Water management (see page 139)

Oasis Design, USA

www.oasisdesign.net
Information, articles and links on collecting your home grey water and reusing it for other purposes, especially in the garden.

Sierra Sustainable, USA

www.sierrasustainablelandscape.com/diy-frame-level-contour-marking
A permaculture community including detailed information on constructing swales.

Ludwig, Art. *The New Create an Oasis With Greywater – Choosing, Building and Using Greywater Systems.* Santa Barbara, USA: Oasis Design, 2006.
A greywater encyclopedia of the design principles and specifics for building your own system.

Lancaster, Brad. *Rainwater Harvesting for Drylands and Beyond* (Vol. 2): *Water-Harvesting Earthworks.* White River Junction, USA: Chelsea Green Publishers, 2007.
How to select, place, size, construct and plant water-harvesting structures on your land; including mulch, grey water, shade trees and check dams.

Worm composting (see page 70)

Working Worms

http://working-worms.com
Information about starting your own worm composting system, including a very low cost DIY system.

Appelhof, Mary. *Worms Eat My Garbage: How to Set Up and Maintain a Worm Composting System*, 2nd Edition.

Kalamazoo, Michigan, USA: Flower Press, 2003.
This is the bible for starting your own worm-composting system. A bit quirky, but contains all the information.

General resources: sources for plants and seeds

Agroforestry Research Trust, UK

www.agroforestry.co.uk
A research organization and plant nursery run by Martin Crawford, a leader in forest gardening. They offer a large variety of forest garden plants and seeds to order directly online. The Trust also gives courses, seminars and tours.

Badgersett Research Corporation, Minnesota, USA

www.badgersett.com
One of the pioneers of what they refer to as "woody agriculture". Hazelnuts, chestnuts and hickory-pecans.

Brown Envelope Seeds, Ireland

www.brownenvelopeseeds.com
A fine Irish company selling "organic vegetable, grain and herb seed grown on the farm in West Cork". All seeds are open-pollinated.

Echo Community, USA

www.echocommunity.org
International non-profit organization with a good selection of seeds and some plants for agriculture and forest gardening in the tropics.

English's Fruit Nursery, Ireland

www.englishsfruitnursery.ie
Great family-run nursery in Wexford, Ireland with a ide range of fruit trees and shrubs.

Food Forest Farm, Massachusetts, USA

www.foodforestfarm.com

A good source for perennial vegetables, tree crops and other permaculture and forest-gardening plants.

Forest Farm Nursery, USA

www.forestfarm.com

Useful, multi-purpose forest garden and permaculture plants. Located in the Applegate Valley, Oregon.

Fruit and Nut, Ireland

www.fruitandnut.ie

This great fruit- and nut-tree nursery specializes in nut trees, such as cobnut (a cultivated form of wild hazel nut), heartnut, almonds, chestnuts and pine nuts, but they also have a good selection of popular and not-so-common fruit trees. Varieties well-suited to Ireland and similar conditions.

Future Forests, Ireland

www.futureforests.net

"The most extensive range of bare-root and potted plants in Ireland." Excellent mail-order service but visiting this whimsical nursery in Cork makes for a fantastic outing.

Jurassicplants Nurseries, Wales.

www.treeonlinenursery.co.uk
Great specialist family-run plant nursery.

Irish Seed Savers Association, Ireland

www.irishseedsavers.ie

"Working together to conserve Irish biodiversity." We all need to support small seed-saving trusts like this one. Buy their seeds and donate if you can. Their huge variety of seeds includes the "bee-loving flower mix".

Nolin River Nut Tree Nursery, Kentucky, USA

www.nolinnursery.com

Nut trees from the deciduous forests of the eastern United States, including shagbark hickory, pecan, chestnut, black walnut, Persian walnut, butternut and pawpaw.

Plants for a Future, UK

www.pfaf.org

A non-profit organization set up to support research on edible and otherwise useful plants suitable for growing outdoors in a temperate climate. Over 1,500 edible species tested, and a plant database, which currently consists of approximately 7,000 species. The database can be searched by a host of criteria and characteristics, then links each plant with suppliers. A truly wonderful way to search for plants!

Raintree Nursery, USA

www.raintreenursery.com

A mail-order nursery on the slopes of Mt Rainier, with a wide variety of cold-climate edible plants, and trees for a forest garden. Their website and catalogue are filled with useful information about rootstocks, pollination and plant care.

Richters Herbs, Toronto, Canada

www.richters.com

An edible plant and seed nursery with a nice online catalogue. Exceptional for herbs and vegetables, especially in small sizes.

Seedaholic, Ireland

www.seedaholic.com

Mail order a wide range of perennials, vegetables, wild edibles, medicinal, culinary, green manure, wildflower and companion plants. The section "get your garden buzzing", which lists plants that attract bees and other insects, has more than 170 entries.

Seed Savers Exchange, USA

www.seedsavers.org
A non-profit co-operative dedicated to saving and sharing heirloom seeds. They have a huge selection of seeds as well as seed-collecting supplies and some tools.

Siskiyou Seeds, USA

www.siskiyouseeds.com
Specializes in heirloom and open-pollinated seeds grown on their farm in southern Oregon or nearby.

University of Minnesota Plant Database, USA

www.plantinfo.umn.edu
Very handy for finding plants and seeds in the USA. Type in the plant and it will tell you which nurseries stock it.

Forest gardening

www.scottishforestgarden.wordpress.com
Blogs on a variety of interesting topics including growing shiitake mushrooms from plugs. In fact, there is a post about almost anything related to forest gardening .

Crawford, Martin. *Creating a Forest Garden: Work with nature to grow edible crops.* Cambridge, England: Green Books, 2010.

Crawford, Martin. *Trees for Garden, Orchard, and Permaculture.* Hampshire, England: Permanent Publications, 2015.

Jacke, Dave, with Toensmeier, Eric. *Edible Forest Gardens.*

Vols. 1 and 2. White River Junction, USA: Chelsea Green Publishing, 2005.

Beresford-Kroeger, Diana. *The Global Forest: Forty Ways Trees Can Save Us.* New York, USA: Penguin Books, 2011.

Whitefield, Patrick. *How to Make a Forest Garden.* 3rd edition. Hampshire, England: Permanent Publications, 2002.

Natural gardening and farming supplies

Grow It Yourself, Ireland

www.giyinternational.org
An Ireland-based worldwide network of people growing their own food. The mail-order business for gardening supplies includes books, seeds, wormeries, nematodes, polytunnels and small greenhouses.

Grazing animals for land clearance and weed control

Grazing Animals Project, UK

www.grazinganimalsproject.org.uk
A partnership of farmers, land managers and conservation organizations, this excellent website has case studies, courses, a newsletter and a forum on grazing to benefit the environment and maintain our cultural heritage.

Goats R Us, California, USA

www.goatsrus.com

Rent a Ruminant, Washington, USA

www.rentaruminant.com

Eco-Goats, Maryland, USA

www.eco-goats.com

Ewe-niversally Green, Georgia, USA

www.eweniversallygreen.com

The Goat Lady, Washington, USA

www.thegoatlady.com

Organic, GMO-free, animal food supplies

Robins Glen Organic Produce, Ireland

www.robinsglen.ie

Organic grain and animal-feed products for farm animals. Delivered in small packs of 1kg to 25kg.

The Organic feed company, UK

www.organicfeed.co.uk

A family-run business providing a range of feeds made from 100% organically grown, agricultural ingredients.

Poultry

Henkeepers' Association, UK

www.henkeepersassociation.co.uk

An information network supporting poultry keepers. "Lobbying for the protection of small garden flocks, and campaigning for improved welfare conditions within the poultry industry."

The Kitchen Garden, UK

www.kitchen-garden-hens.co.uk

This site is maintained by the multitalented Francine Raymond "to encourage you to spend more time in your garden". There are a host of her articles and journals and links and information about home gardens, keeping hens, farmers' markets and much more.

Backyard Poultry: Dedicated to more and better small-flock poultry, USA

www.backyardpoultrymag.com

Bi-monthly magazine and useful website.

Ussery, Harvey. *The Small-Scale Poultry Flock: An All-Natural Approach to Raising Chickens and other Fowl for Home and Market Growers.* White River Junction, USA: Chelsea Green Publishing, 2011.

Natural farming and permaculture

Natural farming

Fukuoka, Masanobu. *The One-Straw Revolution: An Introduction to Natural Farming.* Emmaus, Pennsylvania, USA: Rodale Press, 1978.
An introduction to Mr Fukuoka's natural farming philosophy and techniques.

Fukuoka, Masanobu. *Sowing Seeds in the Desert: Natural Farming, Global Restoration, and Ultimate Food Security.* White River Junction, USA: Chelsea Green Publishing, 2012.
Mr. Fukuoka discusses his travels and his plan for regreening the human-caused deserts using natural farming.

Korn, Larry. *One-Straw Revolutionary: The Philosophy and Work of Masanobu Fukuoka.* White River Junction, Vermont, USA: Chelsea Green Publishers, 2015.
A book about Mr Fukuoka written by one of his students. Korn describes living with other student workers in huts in Mr Fukuoka's orchard and travelling with him on visits to the United States.

Permaculture

Permies

www.permies.com

The most-visited permaculture website in the world. This site mainly hosts forums on all permaculture topics including food forests, farm animals, energy, natural building, homesteading and community. It also has links to other groups and a lot of information about Sepp Holzer.

Temperate Climate Permaculture

www.tcpermaculture.com

A very nice website maintained by John Kitsteiner.

Holzer, Sepp and Sapsford-Francis, Anna. *Sepp Holzer's Permaculture: A Practical Guide to Small-Scale, Interactive Farming and Gardening.* White River Junction, USA: Chelsea Green Publishing, 2011.
Holzer explains his unique approach to permaculture and how he makes Hügelkultur raised beds.

Hemenway, Toby. *Gaia's Garden: A Guide to Home-Scale Permaculture.* 2nd edition. White River Junction, USA: Chelsea Green Publishing, 2009.
The best overall introduction to permaculture. Easy to follow with informative illustrations and plant species lists.

Bloom, Jessi and Boehnlein, David. *Practical Permaculture for Home Landscapes, Your Community, and the Whole Earth.* Portland, Oregon, USA: Timber Press, 2015.

Permaculture Magazine, UK

www.permaculture.co.uk
A fine permaculture magazine with an international scope.

Permaculture Design Magazine, USA

www.PermaCultureDesignMazazine.com
Formerly The Permaculture Activist. Articles about finding practical solutions for self-reliant living. The website has sources for plants and seeds, as well as a worldwide permaculture directory.

Documentary videos

A Farm for a Future

Originally shown as part of the BBC's Natural World series, wildlife film-maker Rebecca Hosking investigates how to transform her family farm in Devon, England. This is episode 14 of 16, 2008-2009. Available free online.

Unnatural Histories

Three-part 2011 BBC documentary exploring humanities impact on three iconic wilderness areas: the Serengeti, Yellowstone National Park and the Amazon rainforest. Available free online.

Index

A

acid soils 137, 138
alder 147
alder buckthorn 148
alkaline soils 137, 138
allelopathy 163
almond 171, 256
American highbush 172
apple 156, 165, 170, 252, 253, 256, 258
apricot 256
apricot vine 203
ash 258
asparagus 187
autumn olive 148

B

Babington's leek 186, 197
bacteria restoration 35-6
bamboo 177
barberry 147, 180
bayberry 176, 180
beauty 42-3, 74
bedstraw 194
beech 162, 163, 258
bees and beekeeping 204-8
beetles 231
bellflower 194
bergamot 190
berms 138, 139, 141
bilberry 192
biodynamic practices 36, 52-3, 226-7
birch 65, 156
birds 228
black chokeberry 177
black-water treatment 144-5
blackberry 148, 180
blackcurrant 181
blackthorn/sloe 148
bladdernut 182
bletting 169, 170
blue mountain tea 191
bluebell 222

blueberry 138, 165, 166, 174, 182, 252
bonding with the land 18, 30, 44, 62, 124-5, 136
boundaries, walking the 24-5, 51, 54
buckwheat 152, 189
buffalo pea 187
bullace 171
burdock 154

C

calamint 188
carob 164
centipedes 231
centring yourself 30-1, 36
chamomile 194
chards 189
checkerberry 179, 195
Chelsea Flower Show 46-9
cherry 148, 166, 171, 252, 253, 256, 258
cherry plum 148
chickens 218-19
chickweed 155, 196
chicory 155, 188
children's spaces 69
Chinese bramble 148
Chinese radish 154
chinquapin 178
chive 155, 170, 186, 237, 238-9
Christianity 15-16, 25, 50, 77, 226
chrysanthemum 240
circles and spheres 74, 76, 77, 78, 101, 106, 108, 116
clay soils 138
clearing land 214-20
climbers and vines 160, 201-4
clothes lines 70
clover 154, 155, 192, 222-3
co-creating with nature 13-14, 16, 22, 39, 45, 99, 126-7, 212
coastal black gooseberry 180

colloidal silver water 233-4
comfrey 155, 192
composting areas 70
composting toilets 144
composts 245-7
coneflower 155, 189, 244
conifers 138
copper barriers 231
coppicing 135, 163, 168, 217, 257-8
crab apple 148, 170, 253
cranberry bush 172
cross symbol 77, 116
crystals 57, 62, 63, 64, 65
cucumber 201, 202
cultivating the soil 31-3
curses 50-2
cuttings 183

D

daisy bush 149
damping off 233, 247
damson 171
dandelion 154, 155
date plum 169, 251
Daubenton's perennial kale 187
design process 42-119
    intention method 46-71
    paper plans 93-119
    sacred geometry 71-9
    special areas 61-71
    symbols and imagery 79-92
dock 154
dogwoods 155, 156, 167, 194
Druids 50
ducks 230

E

earth chestnut 203
Eastern gardens 42
Ebbinge's silverberry 169
ecosystem design 127, 128, 130
    see also forest gardens

elder 149, 172, 182
energized places 14-15, 16, 49, 125
energy fields 25
energy flows 75, 80
equilateral triangles 78-9, 101

F
fairy mounds 64
false indigo bush 175
feeding plants 243-5
feminine energy 65, 76, 129
fennel 155, 189
fertilizers and tonics 243-5
feverbush 148
Fibonacci series of numbers 73
fiddle head fern 189
fig 170
filbert 168, 178
fire pits 68-9, 111, 116
food production 128-30
  see also forest gardens
forest gardens 39, 97, 121-209
  canopy and sub-canopy trees 162-74
  climbers and vines 201-4
  food production 131
  ground cover 193-6
  herbaceous plants 183-92
  Hügelkultur beds 150-3
  information resources 132, 265
  layers 160-204
  maintenance 131
  nurse crops 153-7
  shelterbelts 145-9
  shrubs 174-83
  successional planting 133-4
  timeline 134-60
  underground plants 197-200
  water management 139-45
frogs 231
fruit trees 138, 160, 250-7
  dwarf fruit trees 255
  grafted stock 252-4, 255, 256-7
  growing from seed 253, 254
  own-root trees 254-5

pollination 251-2
pruning 253, 254
  thinning 253
fuchsia 179
fungi 32, 33, 34-5, 160
fungicides 233-8

G
gardener's sulphur 138
garlic 197, 236-7, 238, 239-40
geese 224
ginger 199
globe artichoke 189
glyphosate 158, 205, 213
GMOs 158-9
goats 216-17
goji berry 179
golden mean (golden ratio) 72, 73, 74
goldenrod 191
good King Henry 188
gooseberry 181
gorse 149, 176, 248
goumi 147, 175, 179
grape vine 204
grass cuttings 213-14
green manures 135, 152, 213
grey water 142
ground cover plants 160, 193-6, 213
grounding yourself 30, 31, 249
groundnut 198
guardianship of the land 19, 20, 25, 259
guelder rose 149

H
'hare's corners' 38
hawthorn 64, 146, 147, 168, 253, 258
hazel 147, 168, 178, 258
healing the land 14, 18, 22-39, 126
heart centre and energy 31, 55-6, 64, 66
heath pearlwort 223
hedgehogs 229-30

herbaceous plants 160, 183-92, 193
herbicides 38, 241-2
herbs 185
  aromatic pest confusers 185
  as lawn substitutes 223
hickory 156, 164
hill mustard 187
hog peanut 202
holly 148
'holy' water 25, 54, 226
honey locust 165
honeysuckle 179
hop 202
hormone rooting powder 183, 247, 253
horseradish 198
Hügelkultur beds 135, 138, 139, 150-3, 201
human waste treatment 144-5
hungry gap 249

I
insecticides 238-40
integrated ecosystems 18, 39
  see also forest gardens
intention method 36-7, 46-71, 79, 123, 124, 226-7, 232, 249, 253
  intention of the land itself 124
  intentional spaces 61-71
invasive plants 157
Irish ways of interacting with the land 14, 15-16, 20, 24, 38

J
Jack-by-the-hedge 186
Japanese knotweed 157, 220
Japanese rose 148, 182
Jerusalem artichoke 199
jostaberry 181

K
kiwi 202, 251

L

labyrinths 67, 80
large garden plans 97, 111-19
lawns 128, 220-5
    alternatives to grass 220-4
    maintenance 224-5
leaf mould 246
leatherjackets 225
lemon balm 189
lemongrass 188
licorice 198
lime 138, 258
listening to the land 26, 27,
    30, 44
    see also bonding with the land;
    meditation
livestock
    pens and spaces 70, 230
    see also chickens; ducks; goats;
    pigs; sheep
locust 162, 176
loganberry 181
love 58, 123

M

magic 46, 50, 62, 122-3, 125
mahala mat 175, 178
maidenhair 258
manure 245
maples 147, 156, 162, 164, 258
marigold 188, 240
maypop 203
meditation 27, 29, 30, 55, 56,
    81
medium garden plans 97, 104-
    10
medlar 170, 253, 256
melon 202
microorganisms in the soil 32,
    33, 34
mints 143, 155, 190, 195, 223,
    290
monkey puzzle tree 164
Monterey pine 148
moon and sun 99
moss 220-2
mulberry 171, 180, 258
mulching 153, 212-14, 243
    sheet mulching 219-20

mushrooms 31, 32, 34-5, 199-
    200
music and singing 25, 63
mycelia 32, 33
    restoration 34-5, 199-200

N

nasturtium 165, 170, 203
native plants 131, 132, 185, 193
neem oil 235
nematodes 229
neonicotinoids 158, 204-5
nettles 154, 156, 192, 223, 239
    nettle compost 246
New Zealand spinach 196
night-time places 61-2
nitrogen-fixing plants 131, 143,
    147, 154, 160, 175-82, 248
no-till methods of cultivation
    32-3
nourishment and healing prayers
    57-8
nurse crops 135, 153-7
nut trees and bushes 160, 174,
    253
    see also specific varieties
nutrient-accumulator plants 154-
    6, 184, 244

O

oak 163, 258
oca 199
oleaster 169, 175
oregano 190, 223
Oregon grape 148, 180
ostrich fern 189

P

pagan religions 15, 16, 50, 72,
    226
parsley 190
passion fruit 203
pawpaw 167, 258
pea 201, 203
peach 171, 257
pear 166, 172, 252, 256
peat 245

pecan nut 156, 167
periwinkle 196
persimmon 169, 258
personality of the land 19, 20,
    21, 22, 25, 44, 62, 122-3, 125
pest control 225-32
pH 137-8
pig nut 198
pigs 183-4, 214-16
pine 148, 165, 166
pittosporum 148
plantain 155, 191, 223
platonic solids 75
plum 166, 252, 256-7, 258
plum yew 178
pollarding 257-8
ponds 70, 142, 230, 231
potting mix 247
praying places 66-7
privet 148
protection prayers 29, 57
purslane 194

Q

quamash 198
quince 169, 178

R

ragwort 37-8
rainwater capture and storage
    139-41, 142
ramson 186, 222
raspberry 174, 181, 195
redcurrant 181
reed-bed systems 145
reeds 143, 144, 147
releasing places 68-9, 111
remineralizing the soil 154-6
resonance 75, 80, 116
rhubarb 155, 191
rituals 55, 56, 69
root-layer plants 197-200
rosemary 182, 191
Royal Botanic Gardens, Kew 82,
    83, 84, 87
runner bean 203
rush 143

S

sacred geometry 71-9
sacred places 15, 16, 76
salal 179
salsify 199
sandy soil 137, 139
saskatoon 177
sea beet 187, 198
sea buckthorn 148, 176
sea kale 188
seaweed 144, 213
sedges 143, 222
seed
   GMO seeds 158-9
   organic 158
seed balls 152, 156, 184, 197
self-heal 223
serviceberry 177
shallot 186, 197
sheds 70-1
sheep 224-5
shelterbelts 135, 145-9, 154
   planting 149
   plants for 146-9
shrubs 160, 174-83
   from cuttings 183
silverbell tree 170
six-pointed star (Star of David)
   79
skeps 180, 205-6
skirret 199
slugs 226, 227-32
small garden plans 97, 98-103
soil
   analysis 136-7
   bacteria restoration 35-6
   drainage 138-9
   erosion 32, 141-2
   mycelium restoration 34-5,
   199-200
   pH 137-8
   remineralizing 154-6
   structure 32, 33
   types 137, 138, 139
sorrel 155, 191, 223
Spanish broom 176
speaking to the land 25, 64
spearmint 190
spindle tree 148
spirals 76-7, 80, 101, 108, 111

sprays 35-7, 232-42
square 78, 106
squash 201, 202
star 111
stones 62-3, 64, 65, 81
straw 213
strawberry 156, 194
strawberry tree 167, 177
surveys 94-5
swales 135, 139-41, 142-3,
   152-3
   swale-friendly plants 143-4
sweet chestnut 163, 258
sweet potato 195, 203
sweet woodruff 194
Swiss chard 187
sycamore 162
symbols and imagery 79-92

T

'The Stolen Child' (WB Yeats)
   84-6
thistles 223
thyme 155, 196, 223
tree of life garden 88-92
tree purslane 147, 177
trees 184
   canopy and sub-canopy trees
   162-74
   coppicing and pollarding
   257-8
   cultivation and care of 136,
   249-58
   mast years 163
   moving 174
   mulching 212
   planting distances 173-4
   prayer trees 66
   protecting young trees 247-9
   semi-mature, buying 159
   wishing trees 64, 65, 111
   see also fruit trees
triskele 77, 80, 108, 114

U

udo 187

V

vermicompost (worm compost)
   246
vesica piscis 73, 76, 98-9
violet 196

W

walking the land 24-5, 30, 51,
   54, 209
walnut 156, 162, 163, 165, 252
warrigal 196
water, energized 36-7, 53-4
water management 139-45
wax myrtle 176, 180
weed control 37-8, 241-3
   clearing land 183-4, 214-20
   hand-weeding 242
   natural herbicides 241-2
Welsh onion 186
whitecurrant 181
whortleberry 174, 192
wild garlic 186, 222
wild landscapes 15, 16, 17-18,
   48, 49, 89, 125
willow 65, 148, 201, 258
   willow-rooting mixture 183,
   247, 253
wind tunnels 146
wintergreen 195
wishing places 62-5, 87
wishing wells 64
wood-rush 222
woodland ecosystems 15, 44, 97,
   124, 125, 127, 130-1, 142
   see also forest gardens
Worcesterberry 180
wormeries 246

Y

yarrow 156, 223
yellow flag 143
yellow iris 143
yin yang 78

Also by Green Books

Creating a Forest Garden
Working with nature to grow edible crops
MARTIN CRAWFORD

Creating a Forest Garden tells you everything you need to know to grow edible crops, while letting nature do most of the work. Whether you want to plant a small area in your back garden or develop a larger plot, it includes practical advice on planning, design (using permaculture principles), planting and maintenance. With a detailed directory of over 500 trees, shrubs, herbaceous perennials, annuals, root crops and climbers – almost all of them edible and many very unusual – this is the definitive book on forest gardening.

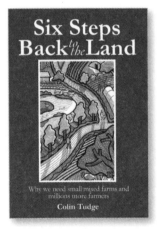

Six Steps Back to the Land
Why we need small mixed farms and millions more farmers
COLIN TUDGE

Colin Tudge coined the expression "Enlightened Agriculture" to describe agriculture that is "expressly designed to provide everyone, everywhere, with food of the highest standard, nutritionally and gastronomically, without wrecking the rest of the world". In *Six Steps Back to the Land*, he explains how we can achieve that, and have truly sustainable, resilient and productive farms.

About Green Books

green books

Environmental Publishers for 25 years
For our full range of titles and to order direct from our website, see
www.greenbooks.co.uk

Join our mailing list for new titles, special offers, reviews, author appearances, events:
www.greenbooks.co.uk/subscribe

For bulk orders (50+ copies) we offer discount terms. Contact **sales@greenbooks.co.uk** for details.

Send us a book proposal on eco-building, science, gardening, etc. –
www.greenbooks.co.uk/for-authors

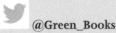 **@Green_Books**    **/GreenBooks**